THE SIGN OF JONAS

BOOKS BY THOMAS MERTON

The Seven Storey Mountain
The Waters of Siloe
The Ascent to Truth
The Sign of Jonas
The Last of the Fathers
No Man Is an Island

THOMAS MERTON

The Sign of Jonas

A HARVEST/HBJ BOOK

HARCOURT BRACE JOVANOVICH

NEW YORK AND LONDON

Printed in the United States of America

Ex Parte Ordinis
Nihil Obstat: Fr. M. Maurice Malloy, O.C.S.O.
Fr. M. Paul Bourne, O.C.S.O.
Fr. M. Albert Derzelles, O.C.S.O.
Imprimi Potest: Fr. M. Gabriel Sortais, O.C.S.O., Abbot General
Nihil Obstat: Thomas W. Smiddy, S.T.L., Censor librorum
Imprimatur: ✠ THOMAS EDMUNDUS MOLLOY, S.T.D.
Archiepiscopus-Episcopus
Brooklyniensis

LIBRARY OF CONGRESS CATALOGING IN PUBLICATION DATA
Merton, Thomas, 1915–1968.
The sign of Jonas.
(A Harvest/HBJ book)
1. Merton, Thomas, 1915–1968.
2. Trappists in the United States—Biography.
I. Title.
BX4705.M542A32   1979   271'.125'024   79-10283
ISBN 0-15-682529-5

First Harvest/HBJ edition 1979

ABCDEFGHIJ

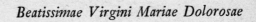

Beatissimae Virgini Mariae Dolorosae

The sign Jesus promised to the generation that did not understand Him was the "sign of Jonas the prophet"—that is, the sign of His own resurrection. The life of every monk, of every priest, of every Christian is signed with the sign of Jonas, because we all live by the power of Christ's resurrection. But I feel that my own life is especially sealed with this great sign, which baptism and monastic profession and priestly ordination have burned into the roots of my being, because like Jonas himself I find myself traveling toward my destiny in the belly of a paradox.

CONTENTS

THE SIGN OF JONAS

Journey to Nineveh

This book, which is a collection of personal notes and meditations set down during about five years of my life in the monastery of Gethsemani, was not written with any thought that it might be read by persons unfamiliar with the monastic life. Therefore in writing it I never bothered to explain the customary events and regular exercises of a Trappist's daily life and never thought it necessary to fill in the background. But some of this *Journal* may be puzzling unless the reader has at least a sketchy outline of the monastery and of community life in his mind.

Two things are important. First, what the Trappist life itself is and second, the special force acquired by that life under the momentum of what is called a "period of fervor." Much of the meaning of this *Journal* lies in the fact that it has been written at a rare and unusual moment in the history of one particular monastery. The book is not about the monastery, nor about its surprising present condition. But it reflects something of the reactions of an individual caught in the throes of that "condition."

The average Trappist monastery is a quiet, out-of-the-way place—usually somewhere in France—occupied by a community of seventy or eighty men who lead a silent energetic life consecrated entirely to God. It is a life of prayer and of penance, of liturgy, study, and manual labor. The monks are supposed to exercise no exterior ministry—no preaching, teaching, or the rest. The only teaching done by the monks is confined to classes of theology and philosophy within the monastery itself—classes attended by the young monks, or "scholastics," preparing for the priesthood.

The life is physically hard, but the compensation for this hardship is interior peace. In any case, one soon becomes used to the hardships and finds that they are not so hard after all. Seven hours of sleep are normally enough. The monks' diet is extremely plain, but is ordinarily enough to keep a man healthy for long years, and monks traditionally die of old age. One soon gets used to sleeping on straw and boards. Most monks would find it difficult to sleep on a soft mattress, after their simple pallets.

The life is usually quiet. There is no conversation. The monks talk to their superiors or spiritual directors when necessary. In the average monastery, Trappist silence is an all-pervading thing that seeps into the very stones of the place and saturates the men who live there.

Farm labor is the monks' support, and the ordinary thing is for all the monks to work outdoors for five or six hours a day. When they are not working, or praying in choir, the monks devote their time to reading, meditation, contemplative prayer. The whole day is supposed eventually to become a prolonged prayer in which the monk remains united with God through all his occupations. This is the real purpose of the monastic life: a more or less habitual state of simple prayer and union with God which varies in intensity at different times of the day, which finds a particular and proper rhythm in the life of each individual, and which brings the soul of the monk at all times under the direct and intimate influence of God's action.

But now, let us suppose that within four or five years, several hundred men decide that they want lives of silence, prayer, labor, penance, and constant union with God in solitude. And suppose they all decide to enter the same monastery. Although they do not all enter exactly at the same moment, they come in great numbers, continually, and the monastery of seventy grows to a hundred and seventy and then to two hundred and seventy.

Thus two hundred and seventy lovers of silence and solitude are all packed into a building that was built for seventy. Priests are needed to give them their formation and spiritual direction. It takes at least eight years to train a man for the priesthood, unless he has been in a seminary before coming to the monastery. Meanwhile, to relieve the pressure, four foundations—that is, new monasteries—are made. But these new monasteries are staffed with the most capable of the priests in the Mother Community. Consequently there are very few priests left at the Mother House to shoulder the burden of governing and caring for a community of two hundred and seventy. Hence they have a lot of extra work to do!

Meanwhile, new buildings have to be put up, and the farm has to be completely reorganized and expanded, so that all these new arrivals may be fed and housed. Since all this work has to be done in a hurry, many machines are needed. When you have a great crowd of postulants, much work, new buildings, and a small mechanized army of builders all working at high pressure, the silence is not always absolutely perfect.

The young monk who makes his vows at Gethsemani in this unusual moment of crisis and transition is therefore exposing himself to something far more than the ordinary vicissitudes of a Trappist monastery. He is walking into a furnace of ambivalence which nobody in the monastery can fully account for and which is designed, I think, to serve as a sign and a portent to modern America.

The phenomenon which has suddenly happened at Gethsemani came about without anybody's foreseeing it and without anyone making any logical attempt to control it. It was apparently beyond foreseeing and beyond control, and there is no one in the monastery who does not sometimes find himself fearful when he considers its possible issue.

The notes set down in this *Journal* must be seen in this context of ambivalence, of questioning, of supreme spiritual risk. I do not know and do not attempt to guess what supernatural issues may hang upon the loyal and successful living out of our special problem in this Gethsemani. But I know that the peculiar situation here has given each one of the monks his own opportunity to share in the mysterious and secret testing of spirit which was Christ's own Gethsemani. Our monastery was not named in vain for the Garden of the Agony, but I promise not to be dramatic about that side of our existence. I have a peculiar horror of one sin: the exaggeration of our trials and of our crosses.

The journal starts with my preparation for solemn and perpetual vows. It covers the remaining years of my scholasticate, my advancement to sacred Orders and especially to the Priesthood. It goes on through my first years as a priest, in which I begin to teach classes and give conferences, and then am appointed to be Spiritual Director of the scholastics.

Where does all this take place? In a valley in Kentucky which is very hot in the summer and sometimes cold in the winter. The monastery was built in the so-called "knob country" about the time of the Civil War. It is a few miles from the place where Abraham Lincoln was born, and my monastic childhood has had, as its background, the same landscape of steep wooded hills, broad fields of corn, and rocky creeks where the boy Lincoln hunted and read and meditated by the fire. Lincoln's first teacher is buried in the cemetery outside the monastery gate.

The monastery is a huge square building around a central court, surrounded by a flock of large and small, old and new barns, shops, garages, and outhouses, with a large vegetable garden and a dairy farm and some seven hundred acres of forest in which I am very much interested and in which I have a small and unimportant job which makes me very happy.

The most important part of Gethsemani is the Monastic Church. In fact, it is not only a church but a basilica. It was decorated with this dignity, much to the surprise of all the monks, in our centenary year, 1949. The church has a long plain nave and a simple nineteenth-century Gothic apse, crowned by a wooden steeple plated over with tin. The central part of the nave is occupied by the choir of the monks where they chant the Canonical Office—consisting mostly of Psalms—during the night vigils and at various times during the day.

Here too the priests say Mass each morning, about four o'clock; here the laybrothers and scholastics go to Communion. Here we spend much of our time in meditation and private prayer. The central event of the daily liturgy is of course the conventual Mass, which is celebrated in the middle of the morning. The celebrant is called the "hebdomadary"—the "weekly" priest—because we take turns at singing the Mass for a week at a time. The priest who sings the Mass is assisted by a deacon, who sings the Gospel of the Mass, and sometimes also by a sub-deacon who sings the Epistle. Meanwhile the common and proper parts of the Mass are chanted by the monastic choir. I explain this in some detail here, because a young priest's turn in the sanctuary is, for the Trappist, much as it seems to have been for the Levitical priesthood of the Old Testament, the hinge on which a whole season of his life will turn.

It must not be imagined that the priesthood is something essential to the monastic state as such. On the contrary, one can be a monk without being a priest and in Saint Benedict's day (that is, in the fifth century, when the monastic life as we now know it was established in the western Church) only one or two monks in each monastery were priests. Nevertheless since our present monastic liturgy centers on the Mass and since the scholastics, novices, and brothers can only be directed by priests in our time, it is the priests of the monastery who normally assist the Abbot in the duty of teacher, director, and administrator of the monastic community, and who officiate in the liturgy.

These tasks which are not in themselves difficult are sometimes arduous under the cumulative effect of extra work, summer heat, poor health, and other factors, and so they sometimes demand an unexpected sacrifice. Greater still of course are the burdens of the Father Abbot who has to govern and guide the whole community, worry about its finances, provide for his monastic family and watch over the development of his "daughter houses"—the new foundations—and then, every other year, travel to France to the General Chapter. This is a gathering of all the Abbots of the Order. The General Chapter is the highest authority in the Order. It is headed by the Abbot General. From time to time the pages of this journal will refer to "Visitations" periodically made by the Abbot General or by a delegate of his, or else by the Abbot of Melleray in France, which is Gethsemani's Mother House. These Visitations are intended to preserve regular discipline, to settle the problems that arise in monastic communities, and to prevent more serious problems from arising in the future. They always leave a big impression in the soul of the monk, and sometimes make great changes in the community's way of life.

These are not very striking or very dramatic things, but they are the big events in a monk's ordinary existence: his taking of vows, his advancement to Orders, his turn as hebdomadary, his work in the monastery, the fasts, the feasts, the seasons, the books he reads, the changes in the face of the monastic community, the bare flight of time. . . . There is not much more that a monk can write about, in his exterior life. It has usually not been thought worth putting down on paper at all.

Much more important are the events that take place in the depth of a monk's soul. These usually keep pace with exterior events of one kind or another. They coincide with the great sacramental moments of life, but at the same time they have a free development of their own that may or may not flow quietly with the calm current of feasts and seasons!

I have treated none of these interior developments in great detail. I have sketched them out in a few lines. I have not attempted to keep what is formally called a "spiritual journal" although I have here and there attempted to write, as best I can, about spiritual things. In doing so, I have of course tried to put down my ideas in my own words, avoiding all technical terminology. I have attempted to convey something of a monk's spiritual life and of his thoughts, not in the language of speculation but in terms of personal experience. This is always a little hazardous, because it means leaving the sure, plain path of an accepted terminology and traveling in byways of poetry and intuition. I found in writing *The Ascent to Truth* that technical language, though it is universal and certain and accepted by theologians, does not reach the average man and does not convey what is most personal and most vital in religious experience. Since my focus is not upon dogmas as such, but only on their repercussions in the life of a soul in which they begin to find a concrete realization, I may be pardoned for using my own words to talk about my own soul.

These brief notes would have been far more interesting if I had been able to write more about the monks I live with. Some of them are the most wonderful people in the world. But they have a right which I, through my own fault, have lost: a right to their own privacy, to anonymity. I have not even given living monks their real names, except in the case of Abbots and of one priest who is a well-known author. I have necessarily had to spare them a recital of their virtues, which would in some way have made up for the disappointment and perhaps the scandal of my own obvious mediocrity.

The Cistercian monks made five vows, at the time of their profession: poverty, chastity, obedience, stability, and conversion of manners (*conversio morum*, or *conversatio morum*).

The whole meaning of the monastic vocation is summed up in these vows, which are given to the monk as a means of consecrating his life to God. They deliver him from the uncertainties and cares and illusions that beset the man of the world. They imply struggle and difficulty. They demand complete self-renunciation. They lead to a life perfectly hidden in Christ. They embrace the whole life of man and all his desires with a singular completeness.

One of the most significant of these vows is the vow of stability which binds a monk to one monastic community. Unless the Superiors decide to send him to a foundation, the monk lives and dies in the monastery of his profession. It takes a special dispensation from Rome for a monk to move to another monastery.

Saint Benedict, like the Desert Fathers on whom he based his Rule, had a very realistic sense of human values. He introduced this vow into his Rule precisely because he knew that the limitations of the monk, and the limitations of the community he lived in, formed a part of God's plan for the sanctification both of individuals and of communities. By making a vow of stability the monk renounces the vain hope of wandering off to find a "perfect monastery." This implies a deep act of faith: the recognition that it does not much matter where we are or whom we live with, provided we can devote ourselves to prayer, enjoy a certain amount of silence, poverty, and solitude, work with our hands, read and study the things of God, and above all love one another as Christ has loved us.

Stability becomes difficult for a man whose monastic ideal contains some note, some element of the extraordinary. All monasteries are more or less ordinary. The monastic life is by its very nature "ordinary." Its ordinariness is one of its greatest blessings. The exterior monotony of regular observance delivers us from useless concern with the details of daily life, absolves us from the tedious necessity of making plans and of coming to many personal decisions. It sets us free to pray all day, and to live alone with God.

But for me, the vow of stability has been the belly of the whale. I have always felt a great attraction to the life of perfect solitude. It is an attraction I shall probably never entirely lose. During my years as a student at Gethsemani, I often wondered if this attraction was not a genuine vocation to some other religious Order. It took me several years to find out that all contemplative Orders have much the same problems. Every man called to contemplation is called to some degree of solitude. God knows well enough how much each one needs. We need faith to let Him decide how much we are to obtain. My own solution of this problem is the main theme of the present book. Like the prophet Jonas, whom God ordered to go to Nineveh, I found myself with an almost uncontrollable desire to go in the opposite direction. God pointed one way and all my "ideals" pointed in the other. It was when Jonas was traveling as fast as he could away from Nineveh, toward Tharsis, that he was thrown over-

board, and swallowed by a whale who took him where God
wanted him to go.

A monk can always legitimately and significantly compare
himself to a prophet, because the monks are the heirs of the
prophets. The prophet is a man whose whole life is a living witness of the providential action of God in the world. Every
prophet is a sign and a witness of Christ. Every monk, in whom
Christ lives, and in whom all the prophecies are therefore fulfilled, is a witness and a sign of the Kingdom of God. Even our
mistakes are eloquent, more than we know.

The sign Jesus promised to the generation that did not understand Him was the "sign of Jonas the prophet"—that is, the sign
of His own resurrection. The life of every monk, of every
priest, of every Christian is signed with the sign of Jonas, because we all live by the power of Christ's resurrection. But I
feel that my own life is especially sealed with this great sign,
which baptism and monastic profession and priestly ordination
have burned into the roots of my being, because like Jonas
himself I find myself traveling toward my destiny in the belly
of a paradox.

PART ONE

Solemn Profession

December, 1946 to December, 1947
This Journal *started when I had been five years in the monas-*
tery. That meant that I was coming to the end of my term of
simple vows and was making up my mind to take solemn vows
and stay in the monastery for good.

When you enter a Cistercian monastery you spend some time
as a postulant. After that you are a novice for two years, during
which you hope to learn the rudiments of the Trappist life and
discover whether or not you belong in the monastery. After that
you make temporary simple vows for three years. These serve
to prolong your probation. If, after these five years of probation,
you want to leave, you are free to do so. If you stay, you make
solemn perpetual vows. By these vows you consecrate your
whole life to God in the monastery. After that you just forget
about going back to the world.

By the grace of God it was easy for me to forget the world as
soon as I left it. I never wanted to go back. However, I often
wondered if I should not go to some other monastery. This was
what is known as a "temptation." But at the time when I began
writing this Journal *I could not be quite sure whether it was a*
temptation or not. And I was a great nuisance to my spiritual
directors on that account.

At that time I thought I was upset by the fact that Dom

Frederic, who was then Abbot, wanted me to write a lot of books. Perhaps I was less upset than I thought. But in any case, I did have to write a lot of books, some of which were terrible.

In December, 1946, I received word from a New York publisher that one of these books had been accepted. The book was called The Seven Storey Mountain *and it was an autobiography. As things turned out, it became quite popular. I thought it would, but I did not like to admit it, because that might possibly be pride. And maybe it was.*

(I remember when I was a novice, before I wrote the book, I went to confession and confessed, as a temptation, that I had thought of writing an autobiography, and the confessor found this extremely funny. He said: "Ha! Ha! Ha! When Chesterton wrote his autobiography he showed it to one of his friends and he was told that it didn't amount to much. Now if that happened to Chesterton, what would happen to you? . . ." And, indeed, I have been told in set terms by some of the readers of the book that it does not amount to much. I do not say that I expected it to be a good book, I just say I expected it to be popular.)

All this time I was studying theology, and I was a cleric in minor Orders. To be exact, I had been ordained exorcist on the Feast of Saint Michael and All Angels in 1946, and it seemed that I would not reach the priesthood for a hundred years.

So on the Feast of Saint Joseph—March 19, 1947—I made my solemn vows.

I did not become a better monk after solemn vows than I had been before them, and I went on worrying about much the same things and striving to write a book called The Waters of Siloe *in which I solemnly declare how monks are supposed to act if they want to be monks. I am beginning to realize how much of an impertinence this was. The reason why I wrote the book was that Dom Frederic wanted a history of the Order and of the monastery to be published when we celebrated the hundredth anniversary of our foundation. But I found myself involved in a discussion of monastic ideals. Perhaps, from my own point of view at least, this was useful. Thinking about monastic ideals is not the same as living up to them, but at any rate such thinking has an important place in a monk's life, because you cannot begin to do anything unless you have some idea what you are trying to do.*

There is nothing to prevent a monk from praying even while he writes a book. This discovery did not come to me until I finally resigned myself to being a writer, and found out that the job had one big compensation: it brought me solitude. In 1946 and 1947 I did not have a room to myself to write in, and so it did not occur to me to pray while I was writing. The room where I worked was shared by another monk with another typewriter—a canonist, working on some involved problem of law. He was, in fact, my professor of theology and later became my confessor. He was also one of the censors whose penance was to read the pages that flowed with such regularity from my typewriter in those innocent days.

Among other things that happened during this year, I had to serve as the secretary of the Abbot General of the Order when he came to Gethsemani to make an official Visitation. Then in July some monks were sent to Utah to make a foundation. During the year I had the job of assistant cantor, which sounds like much more than it is, and during the summer I read books aloud in the dining-room of the guest house to the visitors who came on weekend retreats to the monastery.

December 10 ADVENT [1946]
It is five years since I came to the monastery. It is the same kind
of day, overcast. But now it is raining. I wish I knew how to
begin to be grateful to God and to Our Lady for bringing me
here.

There was a long interval after afternoon work. It was good
to be in the big quiet church. The church is dark, these winter
afternoons.

December 13 SAINT LUCY
The years since I entered Gethsemani have gone by like five
weeks. It was a fine bright day, not very cold, with little clouds
very high up in a clear sky. Yesterday, although it is Advent
and we are not supposed to receive any letters at all, Dom
Frederic* gave me a letter from Naomi Burton of Curtis Brown,
Ltd. I had sent her the manuscript of *The Seven Storey Mountain*. Her letter about it was very good and she is quite sure it
will find a publisher. Anyway, my idea—and hers also—is to turn
it over to Robert Giroux at Harcourt, Brace.

At work—writing—I am doing a little better. I mean, I am less
tied up in it, more peaceful and more detached. Taking one
thing at a time and going over it slowly and patiently (if I can
ever be said to do *anything* slowly and patiently) and forgetting
about the other jobs that have to take their turn. For instance,
Jay Laughlin wants two anthologies for New Directions press.
I wonder if I will ever be able to do them. If God wills. Meanwhile, for myself, I have only one desire and that is the desire

*Dom Frederic Dunne was Abbot of Gethsemani until his death in
August, 1948.

for solitude—to disappear into God, to be submerged in His peace, to be lost in the secret of His Face.

December 14 SATURDAY

This afternoon we were working on the road from the old horse-barn to the lower bottom, filling in a deep gully that had washed out all along the road, down to the bottom of the hill. It was another bright, warm day. The new brick horsebarn, under the water tower, where the vineyard used to be, is almost finished. They are clearing ground already for the new garden house. There were some fat turkeys in the pen. Father Joel has already started to put up the crib, in the church, and that means Christmas is here. The novena begins tomorrow. Tonight at Vespers we sang the *Conditor alme siderum* which has not been heard for a week on account of Our Lady's octave. But what an octave! I keep thinking of the words, *Posuit immaculatam viam meam,* and of the *Alleluia* of the Mass (*Tota pulchra es*). That is what Duns Scotus is singing in heaven.

Lady, Queen of Heaven, pray me into solitude and silence and unity, that all my ways may be immaculate in God. Let me be content with whatever darkness surrounds me, finding Him always by me, in His mercy. Let me keep silence in this world, except in so far as God wills and in the way He wills it. Let me at least disappear into the writing I do. It should mean nothing special to me, nor harm my recollection. The work could be a prayer; its results should not concern me.

December 24 CHRISTMAS EVE

Old Father Alberic preached the sermon in Chapter. He looks very ill. He said it was his last sermon and I wouldn't be at all surprised. It was all about mutual encouragement. I think he must have been very lonely in the infirmary, all these years. He is a kind, and simple and solitary little person. When he appears in the *scriptorium*, he comes slowly along the cloister like a wraith, holding on to the walls, just to be where people are. The other day he showed me a holy picture. I wish I could have done something more for him than just look at the holy picture

and smile, and I was ashamed of the thought that my smile perhaps showed the embarrassment I felt over two facts—first that
artistically it was a frightful picture and second that my looking
at it was against the rule of the house. Dom Frederic interprets
the rule that two monks may not read together out of the same
book, in the strict sense that no monk may show another monk
anything, any writing, any picture, anything one would want
to look at. . . . This time I think charity came first.

One of the things I liked about his sermon was the ingenuous-
ness and simplicity with which Father Alberic talked about
"devotion to our Superiors." That a novice should instinctively
make sacrifices for "his dear Father Master." It was not just
something he got out of a book. It was in him and part of him
and his whole wasted little person proclaimed the meaning of
what he said.

One day when I was in Father Abbot's room complaining that
I was not the contemplative or the solitary that I wanted to be,
that I made no progress in this house and that I ought to be
either a Carthusian or an outright hermit, Dom Frederic casually
remarked that there were some men in the house who could
come to him and tell him their troubles and go out quite satisfied
with whatever answer he gave them. From a certain point of
view the solution sounds utterly horrible. And yet it is also quite
wonderful. It implies a faith and simplicity without which it is
hard to live the contemplative life. We really have to believe in
our Superiors. We cannot simply judge them by human stand-
ards, taking the things they tell us as opinions that are to be
weighed in the balance with our own. I do not know if I shall
ever be able to do it. But I need something of that and I hope
Jesus will give me the grace for it.

December 29 SAINT THOMAS OF CANTERBURY
The four big feast days were wonderful. Plenty of time to pray
and no obligation to do anything else. *Paradiso!*

Yesterday in the confessional, Dom Gildas said a lot of good
things and it would be well not to forget them. So I write them
down.

1. First he said I ought to be very grateful for my attraction to prayer. I ought to cultivate it and seek recollection and remain quiet before the Tabernacle.

2. That I ought to pray to understand writers like Ruysbroeck and go on reading him.

3. To teach contemplation, and especially to let people know, in what I write, that the contemplative life is quite easy and accessible and does not require extraordinary or strange efforts, just the normal generosity required to strive for sanctity.

4. He said I must remember that my desire to become a Carthusian is full of self-love and only some very extraordinary upheaval in my whole life would justify my leaving here for a Charterhouse.

5. To profit by all the crosses Jesus sends me, especially the ones that come in connection with work—delays, accidents to manuscripts, adverse criticism, insults, and so on.

6. To realize what pleasure it gives Jesus when He sees that we recognize the action of His love, doing good to us in all these trials.

7. To read Carthusian writers and make use of anything of value that they say and if they make me want to pack up and run off to the Charterhouse I should treat that desire like any other movement of disordered appetite and not get upset about it.

Then, yesterday at dinner, when the reader in the refectory was reading some spectacular stuff by Bossuet on Saint Thomas of Canterbury, out of the *Liturgical Year* (the martyr dies, with his tongue still forming the word "*l'église*"), Father Prior handed me a telegram. I had been thinking: "If anything comes to me in the mail, I shall take it as a present from Saint Thomas à Becket." But when I saw the telegram my heart sank into my dinner. The first thought that came to my mind was that the manuscript of *The Seven Storey Mountain* had been lost. Naomi Burton gave it to Harcourt, Brace only a week ago. I knew quite well that publishers always make you wait at least two months before saying anything about your manuscripts. . . . I waited until after dinner and opened the telegram. It was from

Bob Giroux. And it said: "Manuscript accepted. Happy New Year."

January 5   VIGIL OF EPIPHANY [1947]
It is gray outside, and snow falls lightly.

This morning Father Abbot announced in Chapter that I had made my petition to be admitted to solemn vows. This was in order that the community might be able to vote on me.

I have been made assistant cantor, which meant moving to the other side of the choir. For some reason that side seems gloomy—perhaps because all the days have been dark days so far.

January 7
Father Abbot is starting off for Utah to look for land for a new foundation. This morning we had the Chapter of Faults and it was extremely peaceful and charitable. The whole monastery is as happy as Christmas morning.

January 12
I am fascinated by Martene and Durand's *Voyage Littéraire de Deux Benédictins.* It is the record of their journey around France in the early eighteenth century, collecting material for the *Gallia Christiana,* in the archives of the old monasteries. And there were hundreds of them. Monastic life was, on the whole, rich and vital even in that dead age. There were many scattered reform movements going on, and they were effective enough, within their limitations. But few of them seem to have extended very far and almost all of them have been completely forgotten. Monasticism was a big tree full of dead wood. It needed to be pruned. It was, in fact, all but cut down. Many rich and beautiful customs were lost with the monasteries that the French revolution swept out of existence. Much art too, I suppose. But when it was all over I think the monasteries that survived came out richer in the love of God.

January 14
God's love takes care of everything I do. He guides me in my work and in my reading, at least until I get greedy and start

rushing from page to page. It is really illogical that I should get temptations to run off to another monastery and to another Order. God has put me in a place where I can spend hour after hour, each day, in occupations that are always on the borderline of prayer. There is always a chance to step over the line and enter into simple and contemplative union with God. I get plenty of time alone before the Blessed Sacrament. I have got in the habit of walking up and down under the trees or along the wall of the cemetery in the presence of God. And yet I am such a fool that I can consent to imagine that in some other situation I would quickly advance to a high degree of prayer. If I went anywhere else I would almost certainly be much worse off than here. And anyway, I did not come here for myself but for God. God is my order and my cell. He is my religious life and my rule. He has disposed everything in my life in order to draw me inward, where I can see Him and rest in Him. He has put me in this place because He wants me in this place, and if He ever wants to put me anywhere else, He will do so in a way that will leave no doubt as to who is doing it.

January 18

On Wednesday Father Abbot came back from Utah without a farm.

He may or may not tell us about it on Sunday.

Today the Last Sacraments were given to Father Odo. Being assistant cantor I was close to his cell. I knelt opposite the doorway but the long line of novices kept passing and passing, between me and the cell, and they were still going by when Reverend Father began the anointing. I did not get more than a glimpse of Father Odo whose face was sunken and drawn and who seemed to be suffering much. His huge body used to shake with an asthmatic cough on the days when he would come down to Chapter in his wheel chair. (On his jubilee he sat with his hand cupped behind his ear during Dom Frederic's speech and when it was all over he made a sign that he had heard not a word.) The cough used to go on and on. But now he is so weak that he cannot even cough. He received the Sacraments very devoutly but I did not hear him say anything. If he tried to speak, his voice was too weak to reach me, out in the hall.

He is ending* a long monastic life—over fifty years, half of which were spent in France. He used to be Cellarer at Acey, in the Jura.

January 27

This week I am serving Father Abbot's Mass. He says Mass in the back sacristy, when the conventual Mass is going on in the church. You can hear the choir, indistinctly, through the two closed doors. On the other side, outside, down the hill at the mill this morning the brothers were filing the teeth of the big buzz-saw. In choir the monks were singing *Justus ut Palma florebit*, in the Mass for the Feast of Saint John Chrysostom. And outside the saw rang under the grating file. The sounds of prayer and of distant work mingle well. There, on the altar, in the midst of these various discrete sounds of homage, in the midst of the order ruled by love for Him, the Lord of all things said nothing, but filled the room with peace.

After dinner the day turned into spring. It was one of those warm winter days which, in Kentucky, suddenly turn into blinding cold. But as long as it was warm, the garden was like Eden and I walked there reading Ruysbroeck.

Later in the afternoon Dom Frederic placed in my hands one of the most beautiful books I have ever seen. It is an album of pictures of one of our ancient Abbeys, in Provence—Sénanque is its name. Both the photographs and the layout are wonderful. I was very happy.

Cistercian architecture explains many things about our rule and our life. A church like Sénanque is born of prayer and is a prayer. Its simplicity and its energy tell us what our prayer should be. It simply says what Saint Benedict already told us: that we must pray to God "with all humility and purity of devotion . . . not in many words but in purity of heart and in

*Father Odo recovered and lived for a year, dying on February 26, 1948.

the compunction of tears."* The churches of our Fathers expressed their humility and their silence. There was nothing superfluous about either the office of our Fathers or their architecture, nothing useless in their private prayer. They did not waste words with God or with men and in their buildings they did not waste anything either. They did not use up stone and time in an appeal to sentimental taste or in reverence to some false, arbitrary criterion of piety in art. They knew a good building would praise God better than a bad one, even if the bad one were covered all over with official symbols of praise. Their churches were built around the psalms. Their cloisters were like the chant in our gradual and in our old antiphoner. Their buildings were a fit setting for the *Consuetudines* of Saint Stephen. A perfection so pure and so vital, springing directly from a religious Rule and way of life, argues a spiritual fruitfulness deeper than we can appreciate today. And I think it is a fruitfulness that belongs to the cenobitic life as such. The simplicity of Sénanque or Fontenay could only house a community of cenobites. A monastery of hermits is necessarily so clumsy that it can only be an architectural monster. However, I agree that one hermitage for one hermit stands a good chance of being beautiful!

February 1

Tomorrow is Septuagesima. Tonight we sang the last *alleluia*. When it is sung again I shall be on the eve of my solemn vows.

Today, at work in the woods, I nearly cut off both my legs. The ax kept glancing off the felled pine tree I was supposed to be trimming. It flew at my knees like a fierce, bright-beaked bird and my guardian angel had a busy afternoon fencing with the blade to keep me on my two feet. The woods were wonderful.

Another postulant arrived: the fourth in two days. The prob-

---

*"*Cum omni humilitate et puritatis devotione . . . non in multiloquio sed in puritate cordis et compunctione lacrimarum*" (Rule of Saint Benedict, chapter 20).

lem of where all these people are going to sleep is becoming acute.

February 8

The other day Reverend Father announced in Chapter that I would make my solemn vows on the Feast of Saint Joseph. I thought perhaps it might not be until Easter, but the sooner the better.

And now it is really cold, for the first time this winter. The other night the holy water was frozen in the fonts of our dormitory cells when we went up to go to bed. But by the time we got up at two o'clock it had started to melt, because of the presence of so many monks in one room, with all the windows closed.

February 17 SHROVE TUESDAY

The Forty Hours ended today.

Yesterday morning I made my will. You always make a will before solemn vows, getting rid of everything, as if you were about to die. It sounds more dramatic than it really is. As a matter of fact, as soon as I had renounced all earthly things, I was called into Father Abbot's room and he presented me with a contract with Harcourt, Brace for the publication of *The Seven Storey Mountain*. So after making my will I put my living signature on this contract. The royalties of the dead author will go to the monastery. Meanwhile, I spent the afternoon writing business letters and making all kinds of mistakes.

This morning, before the Blessed Sacrament, it seemed to me that these vows will mean the renunciation of the pure contemplative life. If Jesus wants me to be here at Gethsemani, as my Superiors insist He does (*Qui vos audit me audit*), then perhaps He does not want me to be a pure contemplative after all. I suppose it all depends what you mean by a pure contemplative.

I soon came to the conclusion that I could not think straight about the problem anyway. Perhaps this is not the most perfect vocation in the Church, *per se*. Well, what about it? It seems to be *my* vocation. That is the thing that matters. What is the use of having some other vocation that is better in itself but is not your own vocation? But how can it be my vocation if I have such a strong desire for some other vocation? Don't ask me. Our Lord wants that sacrifice. How do I know? I don't know. That is what I am told. Do I have to believe them? I do not have to, I suppose. But something tells me that there is no other way for me. My conscience is on the side of my Superiors and anyway, when I have a moment of lucid thought on the subject, experience reminds me that these feelings will go away just as they have gone away before. No doubt they will come back again and go away again many times before I get used to forgetting them.

I was thurifer at the Solemn Abbatial Mass of reposition. On top of all my other troubles, I could not get a decent fire going. The grains of incense we use are so large and so coarse that as soon as they are put on top of the charcoal they melt into a solid mass that gives off no smoke and only puts out the fire. I was working and blowing on the charcoal all through the Canon and got my hands covered with coal and when it was all over I forgot to empty out the censer and put it away.

February 20   LENT

I went and talked over the whole business of my vocation again with Father Abbot and he assured me once again, patiently, that everything was quite all right and that this was where I belonged. In my bones I know that he is quite right and that I am a fool. And yet, on the surface, everything seems to be all wrong. As usual, I am making too much fuss about it. *Concupierunt concupiscentiam in deserto. . . . Numquid poterit parare mensam populo suo?*

February 28

This is the second day of a three-day retreat before I receive the last of the Minor Orders—that of acolyte. I had been expecting it since last December. I was ordained exorcist on the Feast of Saint Michael and All Angels last September, lector on the Feast of Saint Dominic in August, porter on the Feast of Saint Paul in June. I was tonsured last Easter Monday. The rite of ordination of acolytes in the Pontifical is full of appeals for light and of promises of it. The order elevates me to the steps of the altar, reflecting on the blood and water that flowed from the side of Christ on the cross as I minister part of the matter for the Eucharist of Christ's Blood. More than anything else, more than ever before I beg You, my God, to kindle in my heart the love of Christ and teach me how to give myself to You in union with His Sacrifice. It will not be the first time I have reflected on the marvelous prayer the priest says when mingling a drop of water with the wine in the chalice.* But I want that prayer to symbolize all that I live for. I want my whole life to be an expression of those words and of that rite.

March 1   FIRST EMBER SATURDAY IN LENT
Last night it snowed again and there is a fairly thick blanket of snow on the ground and on the trees. The sky looks like lead and seems to promise more. It is about as dark as my own mind. I see nothing, I understand nothing. I am sorry for complaining and making a disturbance. All I want is to please God and to do His will.

March 8

I continue writing this journal under obedience to Dom Gildas, in spite of my personal disinclination to go on with it. It is sufficient to have the matter decided by a director. If it is tedious to keep a journal, it is still more tedious to keep wondering whether or not I ought to give the thing up. I do not know whether it will give glory to God: but my writing of it has been disinfected by obedience. I need no longer apologize either to God or to myself for keeping a journal.

And now it is three days before I go on retreat for my final vows.

The wardrobe keeper went up to the attic and brought down

---

*"O God who most marvelously created the dignity of the human substance and re-made it in a more wonderful manner still, grant that by this mystery of wine and water we may be made partakers of the Divinity of Him Who deigned to share our humanity, Jesus Christ Thy Son . . ."

the suitcase that came into the monastery with me five years ago. It is in our dormitory cell. I am supposed to check over the clothes to see that everything is there, before formally renouncing that blue woolen sweater, those four striped sports shirts, those tweeds and the dark blue suit I was wearing. The whole job took about half a minute. But the suitcase remains in the cell. It still looks shiny and new and has a blue and white Cuba Mail Line label on it, with the letter M. It still has the rich new smell which, as I remember, impressed me when I first unpacked it at a hotel in Florida. It is almost impossible to believe that that was seven years ago. But what is more impossible is to believe that I ever wore those clothes. I do not believe in myself as a layman at all. I was never definitely meant to be one. That, at least, is good to know.

By my vows I desire to get rid of everything that I can get rid of by any official act, so as to dispose myself for getting rid of all the other attachments that are harder to escape because not even vows can sever them.

Concerning solitude: most of the accidents of community life need not seriously concern me—differences of opinion, other people's ideas of the spiritual life, the kind of organ music that seems to please many. Why should I bother about all that? It is none of my business.

March 10

Yesterday I read a couple of chapters of the *Cloud of Unknowing*. Every time I pick up a book in that tradition, especially Saint John of the Cross, I feel like the three wise men when they came out of Jerusalem and out of the hands of Herod, and once more saw their star. They rejoiced with great joy. They were once more delivered from questions and uncertainties, and could see their road straight ahead. In this case it is not even a question of seeing a road. It is simpler than that. For as soon as you stop traveling you have arrived.

I can remember other passages of other books that have hit me with the same impact. They bear witness to moments when I knew, right down to the very depths of my being, that I had found the thing that God wanted for me. I remember, for instance, Saint Teresa's chapter on the real unimportance of involuntary distractions in the prayer of quiet, in *The Way of Perfection*. Then, four years ago, in the novitiate, I discovered all that section of *The Living Flame of Love*, in the third Stanza, where Saint John of the Cross talks about the "deep caverns" and about prayer. More recently there was a chapter in *Le Paradis Blanc*, about the interior life. The chapter is called "*Un Chartreux Parle.*" But it applies just as well to us. In a different mode, I have been deeply impressed by Duns Scotus's distinction on beatitude, the 49th, in the IVth book of the *Oxoniense*, and by all Saint Bonaventure has to say about desire, especially in the *Itinerarium*. These things have gone deep into me and have shaped my life and my prayer. They have not only arrested my attention, they have transformed my soul. And yet I think that they have only been the last step in processes that grace was working secretly before. They have made me realize what had been going on inside me without my having been quite aware of it. For I read much the same things before I came to Gethsemani, and they did not transform me at all. In fact I was barely able to grasp what they were all about.

Another book that had a powerful effect on me in the novitiate was Father Philipon's study of Elizabeth of the Trinity and of her prayer.

March 11

The martyrology in Chapter first announced tomorrow's feast, that of Saint Gregory the Great. It called him the "apostle of the English." Then came a commemoration of a Saint Peter, martyr in Nicomedia, who, having been scourged, had his wounds filled with salt and vinegar and was roasted on a gridiron. Following that I made my promise of obedience.

My intention is to give myself entirely and without compromise to whatever work God wants to perform in me and through me. But this gift is not something absolutely blind and without definition. It is already defined by the fact that God has given me a *contemplative* vocation. By so doing He has signified a certain path, a certain goal to be mine. That is what I am to keep in view, because that is His will. It means renouncing the business, ambitions, honors and pleasures and other activities of the world. It means only a minimum of concern with temporal things. Nevertheless, I have promised to do whatever a Superior may legitimately ask of me. That may, under certain circumstances, involve the sacrifice of contemplation. But it seems to me this sacrifice can only be a temporary thing. It can not mean the sacrifice of the whole contemplative vocation as such.

However, the important thing is not to live for contemplation but to live for God. That is obvious, because, after all, that is the contemplative vocation. That is why it is best to take religious obedience quite literally. As soon as obedience is tempered with conditions, the mind becomes unfit for contemplation. It falls into division because it has to choose between its own solicitudes and the will of the Superior. It has reserved to itself a whole useless field of interior activity (that of judging all the commands that come to it) and this will inevitably interfere with contemplation. If activity becomes too intense—there is no reason why you should not ask your Superiors to have a little pity on you.

March 12   FEAST OF SAINT GREGORY THE GREAT
What I wrote yesterday is ambiguous because it assumes that the Rule of Saint Benedict is ordered to a life of pure contemplation. As a matter of fact, it is not. The Fathers would perhaps have said that the Benedictine life was active, in so far as it involved labor, asceticism, active glorification of God in the office, and even a certain amount of teaching and preaching, at least within the monastic community.

Nevertheless, work in the fields helps contemplation. Yesterday we were out in the middle bottom, spreading manure all over the gray mud of the cornfields. I was so happy I almost laughed out loud. It was such a relief to get away from a typewriter.

March 13

It was wonderful walking home from work at the lake, alone, yesterday afternoon. You do not see the Cistercian life in perspective if you do not look at your abbey from the fields.

March 16

I went to see Father Abbot yesterday. Once again I asked him if I could stop writing poetry and he said that he did not want me to stop altogether. As soon as I got in the room I had brought up the subject of avoiding too much activity and remaining in solitude and being a contemplative and he said "No" to everything. By this time it ought to be quite clear to me that Reverend Father is set on my writing books. So that is that.

March 18

Tomorrow is my profession day. Reverend Father seems to be ill. Last night, after collation, I saw him in the corridor on the way to his room. He was walking very slowly, with his hand on the wall. It was rather dark and I did not know, at first, whether he was feeling his way along or trying to support himself. Besides, he was at the other end of the corridor.

There are several very important things for Reverend Father to think about, at the moment. All of them are more important than two solemn professions, and I wish he would conserve his strength to deal with other things. The Abbot General is coming from France for the Visitation of the house. Father Alberic is dying in the infirmary. The deal for the property in Utah is about to be closed. He has his private counsel in his room now (after Sext).

It is not necessary for me to make any pious speeches about my dispositions.

Here I am, on the point of making solemn, perpetual vows in a Trappist monastery. I ought to be astonished. If I were the same person I was ten years ago, I certainly would be astonished. But I am not really the same person, except in appearance. *Vivit vero in me Christus.*

So yesterday I made my solemn vows.

I do not feel much like writing about it.

This does not mean that I am not happy about profession. But I am happy in a way that does not want to talk. One thing I will say: that the stamp of grace is on the memory of yesterday. And by that I mean that I am left with a sense of deep union with all the other monks. I do not know what I expected to feel after my profession. But afterwards I was left with a profoundly clean conviction that I had done the right thing and that I had given myself as best I could to God. And beyond that the nearest thing to sensible consolation was a deep and warm realization that I was immersed in my community. I am part of Gethsemani. I belong to the family. It is a family about which I have no illusions. And the most satisfying thing about this sense of incorporation is that I am glad to belong to this community, not another, and to be bred flesh and bone into the same body as these brothers and not other ones. Their imperfections and my own remain as obvious as ever, but they no longer seem to make any difference. I do not mind the thought that they will perhaps begin to bother me once more, when the pleasure of the day has worn off. All that will be taken care of when the time comes: and I think that at least I will be able to handle the temptation differently.

I prepared for profession by praying over the *Cautions* and *Counsels* of Saint John of the Cross. For the rest of my religious life I would like, by keeping these *Counsels*, to dispose myself for the work God wants to do in me and to which I am now completely consecrated. They are very simple, the *Cautelas*. It is because they are simple that they are difficult. They do not leave you a chance to compromise. And so it probably takes a lifetime to clear away the obstacles they are designed to remove. Nevertheless they seem to me to be the most detailed and concrete and practical set of rules for arriving at religious perfection that I have ever seen. From a certain point of view they may seem cold and negative. I think, however, that they can be taken as complementing Saint Benedict's chapter, *De Zelo Bono.**

> *March* 25   FEAST OF THE ANNUNCIATION

Yesterday was a gray, muggy day and we were sweating in our winter robes, but this morning snow began to fall.

Father Alberic died Saturday night.

While I have been writing this, the snow has stopped. Now there is a bright sky full of clouds, chased by a wind that lashes the building and sounds cold. I have not been out in it yet. Queen of heaven, I love you.

> *March* 27

Snow has been falling steadily ever since last night. I first noticed the storm after the night office, and now there is more snow on the ground than I have ever seen in Kentucky. It must be close to a foot deep.

The Abbot General, Dom Dominique Nogues, arrived on Tuesday afternoon (Our Lady's Feast). It was cold. We stood about in the bare front garden. There were flurries of snow between bursts of cold sun. There was some movement in the gatehouse and we knew that the visitors had arrived and were getting into their robes and cowls. Dom Benoit, the little Breton Abbot of our monastery in Japan, came running out through the whole group of monks and hastened to the main building for something that must have been very important.

Then the General appeared, with a miter on, looking as if he meant business. He stood in the shadows of the gate, reading prayers from the Ritual and sprinkling holy water over us, as we shivered in the wind.

Opening the Visitation in Chapter, yesterday morning, he said drily: "I believe you have a good Abbot, but in any case we will know in a few days."

This morning I served his Mass, and afterward I handed him his cowl the wrong way, so that when he put it on it was inside

*Rule of Saint Benedict, chapter 72, "On the Good Zeal which Monks should have."

out. But he was not in the least upset. He is not the kind of person to get excited over trifles—or to be moved by the monkey-business of any religious community.

March 30 PALM SUNDAY

The Visitation is in full swing. If I had kept my resolution about following the *Cautions* of Saint John of the Cross and "not seeing" anything that goes on in the community, I would not have found out, by sign language, which of the monks were closeted with the Abbot General for over two hours.

The General seems to be as wide as he is high. He has a face like a picture by Daumier and on top of his head he wears a black skull cap. On the whole I think he is quite capable of handling anything Gethsemani can offer, but he is also capable of doing so with diplomacy and kindness.

I went up to speak to Dom Benoit, who is traveling with the General and serving as his secretary, although it turns out that I am going to do the translating and typing and all the rest of the secretarial work during the Visitation.

We talked about the spirit of the Order, and the Cistercian monasteries in Europe. Dom Benoit confirmed my impression that there was a new spirit developing in the Order. Gethsemani has been out of contact with the centers of Cistercian life in Europe for about ten years. We tend to think here that the monasteries in America are the only ones that exist, and that everything in the universe revolves around Gethsemani. In other monasteries contemplation is coming to occupy the place that belongs to it in our life. There is a shift of emphasis from the old, narrow, and rather frigid insistence on ascetic exercises and practices of devotion.

Still, there is danger in the other extreme. It would be easy enough to fall into a feeble spiritual dilettantism, and flatter one's senses with easy excursions into quietude. It is not hard to be frivolous and cheap, in this matter of contemplation. If it does not grow out of humility, our contemplation will necessarily be superficial. We need to be emptied. Otherwise, prayer is only a game. But all that is cheap will go out with pride. And yet it is pride to want to be stripped and humbled in the grand manner, with thunder and lightning. The simplest and most effective way to sanctity is to disappear into the background of ordinary every-day routine.

Dom Benoit said there was a monk of Thymadeuc who went to try the Carthusian life for ten days. He was at the Grande Chartreuse. He said the life did not seem to be very serious but the scenery was pretty.

I asked Dom Benoit what he thought about my writing poetry and he said he did not think it would do any harm, but that it might do much good. That seems to be the common teaching of theologians around here. I wonder what the General will say.

April 1

Yesterday, Monday in Holy Week, it was my turn to talk to Dom Dominique, the Abbot General. Now I see that I was un-fair to criticize those who stayed with him for two hours. I was in there for more than an hour before I even realized it, and had a very good time too. I had simply written down my remarks about the state of the house on a bit of paper, which I handed to him, and then we proceeded to talk about everything under the sun.

Dom Dominique said, first of all, that he was very pleased with my writing, although he did not understand the poems. He told me emphatically—in fact it was the most emphatic thing he said, and the only thing that seemed like an official pronouncement, an *ex cathedra* fulmination—that it was good and even necessary for me to go on writing. He said specialists were needed in the Order—writers, liturgists, canonists, theologians. If I had been trained in a certain profession, I should make use of my training. In any case, he concluded, it was a matter of obedience.

He told me many funny stories, including a long involved tale of Charles de Foucauld's nephew who was a Cistercian at Thy-madeuc for about five years. He left, and taught at Laval Uni-versity, Quebec, and was finally killed in the war. His mother used to send Dom Dominique three bottles of Pommard every Christmas—for he was abbot of Thymadeuc until last year, when he was elected to replace Dom Hermann Joseph Smets as Abbot General.

Dom Dominique said that sanctity, for a Cistercian, consisted in allowing oneself to be formed through obedience. He also said that our vow of conversion of manners amounted, in practice, to a vow to do always what is more perfect. That is not altogether easy.

April 3   HOLY THURSDAY

I began translating the Visitation Card yesterday. It is a very solid and even inspiring document. Dom Dominique handled it in a way that impressed me deeply. I was especially interested in one page he had crossed out—he had changed some ideas and re-introduced them in another form, so that the meaning remained more or less the same, but the language was more serene and more objective and more profound. All the things he eliminated were good in themselves, but in the end the document was better, and included everything he wanted to say. And so I have seen how the Holy Ghost works in the machinery of a religious Order. How peacefully and smoothly He produces His effects! The atmosphere of the house is all tranquillity and happiness.

Meanwhile I have been thinking about my own interior life.

Once again, it seems to me that I ought to give up all desire for the lights and satisfactions that make me too pleased with myself at prayer. I should want nothing but to do all the ordinary things a monk has to do, regularly and properly, without any special thought of satisfaction in them.

I am thinking especially of Holy Communion. Today is a good day to think about it. Everything I came here to find seems to me to be concentrated in the twenty or thirty minutes of silent and happy absorption that follow Communion when I get a chance to make a thanksgiving that seems to me to be a thanksgiving. I like to remain alone and quiet after Mass. Then my mind is relaxed and my imagination is quiet and my will drowns in the attraction of a Love beyond understanding, beyond definite ideas. However, Dom Gildas insists that when I serve Mass at the second round I must receive Communion at the Mass I serve. This means I must go directly to choir for Lauds and Prime. As soon as I get to choir I am overwhelmed by distractions. No sense of the presence of God. No sense of anything except difficulty and struggle and pain. Objectively speaking I suppose it is more perfect to thank God through the liturgy. The choral office should be the best way of continuing one's Communion. For me it is the worst. No doubt Dom Gildas thinks I ought to be detached from the pleasures of the other way of prayer. I am content to sacrifice those pleasures and go to choir, but I cannot honestly maintain that it is much fun.

Today I am thurifer. That means I make my thanksgiving after the General Communion, stripping the altars with the General, who is celebrating all the functions of Holy Week.

April 4 GOOD FRIDAY

I had a pious thought, but I am not going to write it down.

It is raining. The best place to hide, this afternoon, was in church. It rained hard and you could hear the rain beating all over the long roof.

I had a thought about the Psalter, too—but I will not put that down either. The thoughts that come to me are stupid.

Father Renatus and I helped Father Prior dismantle the baldachin that was used in the processions of the Blessed Sacrament. This ceremony was not in the liturgy, but it was a kind of descent from the Cross. It meant that everything was over. It was a very prosaic *consummatum est*. The meaning of it came home to us because we were both tired and clumsy. In any case Father Prior could hardly have picked two worse helpers in dismantling a baldachin. Father Renatus is one of the holiest monks in the house and one of the most impractical. He is thin, angelic, and Polish, and talks in his sleep—in Polish. He is awkward and shy and intensely zealous. I am very fond of him. Together we started fumbling with the screws and strings that hold the baldachin together. For a long time we could not seem to make anything come undone. Then, suddenly, all the poles and parts began to fall to the floor with a great clatter.

A guest of the monastery, a big fat man, was half-kneeling, half-sitting at the benches and I looked at him out of the corner of my eye to see if he jumped. But he was very placid. He did not jump. Speaking of guests, I am reminded that the man whose feet I washed at the *Mandatum* definitely did not need the dollar I placed in his hands, with liturgical kisses. On the whole, both Father Renatus and I were very proud to have been asked to take apart the baldachin. It made us feel as though we were really efficient after all.

Yesterday, when I was thurifer, I had a sore knee and had my bows and genuflections all mixed. Father Abdon, who came to Gethsemani from Malta a long time ago, was deacon and he and I went about incensing first one abbot then another. There were four abbots in the house, including Dom Gildas. Father Abdon forgot Dom Gildas and I gave him a nudge and we spun around again and hastened to the presbytery step and Father Abdon started praying out loud, which is, with him, a sign of panic.

I feel knocked out, but I can think of no good reason for wanting to feel otherwise. There is not much use in making long speeches to Jesus about our pains, especially on Good Friday.

Yesterday the Abbot General told me that we ought to desire infused contemplation, and that the way to dispose ourselves to receive it was to live our Rule simply and without fuss. It is good to have this from someone who comes to the monastery with credentials from the Holy Ghost written all over him.

April 6 EASTER SUNDAY

Good Friday, Holy Saturday, Easter Week are all tremendous expressions of the truth that Saint John of the Cross was teaching. The *Exultet* is the key to the whole business. *O vere beata nox!* This is the blessed darkness in which Christ has risen from the dead and raised us with Him to the life of heaven! "A night in which heavenly things are united to those of earth, and things divine to those which are human."*

*"*Nox in qua terrenis coelestia, humanis divina junguntur*," Roman Missal.

On a dark night, kindled in love with yearnings—o happy chance—
I went forth without being observed, my house being now at rest!

In darkness and secure, by the secret ladder, disguised—
O happy chance—
In darkness and concealment, my house being now at rest!*

Humanly speaking, our efforts to show our love for God by
purifying our hearts, refresh and delight Him. It is for this that
He "thirsts." His *Sitio* is for the purity of our hearts, the emptiness of our hearts, that His joy, His freedom and His immensity
may fill them. If He can be said to thirst it is because He thirsts
to do us good, to share His infinite Life with us. But we prevent
Him by our selfishness from doing so. Detachment will procure
for us the greatest good, the pure love of God for Himself alone
because He alone is good: *amor amicitiae*. That is the bond of
perfection that unites us to Him. "Above all things have charity,
which is the bond of perfection and may the peace of Christ
exult in your hearts, in which you are called unto one Body. And
be grateful."† It seems to me that all mystical theology is contained in those two lines. *Super omnia:* this love is above all
things because it is the end for which we were created. It is perfection and sanctity. It is the only thing necessary. It is beyond
all mode and all law. It is the bond that unites us to God. It
unites us immediately to Him and it unites us to one another in
Him. And so we become one in Christ and Christ lives in us and
His peace exults in us. There is no other true joy. *Plenitudo legis
est dilectio.*‡
    Thus we can love God as He loves Himself, with His own love.

April 16
A big day. Father George celebrated his sixtieth anniversary in
the Cistercian Order. He shuffled out to the High Altar in the
beautiful new white vestments, was lifted up the steps by the
deacon and sub-deacon, and sang the votive Mass of the Im-

---

*Saint John of the Cross, *Ascent of Mount Carmel*, Stanzas.
†Colossians, 3, 14–15.
‡"Love is the fulfilment of the law," Romans, 13, 10.

maculate Conception with great emotion and with all the fervor of his Trappist heart. He is very happy, full of energy, kept a better Lent than I did, since I had the indulgence for the last ten days on account of that pain. He has been getting up at two in the morning with the rest of us.

The Seven Storey Mountain has been rejected by one of the Censors of the Order: not on theological grounds, but as unripe for publication. Our censors are also editors. They determine whether or not the Order will benefit by the publication of the books submitted to them. This time the decision is no. I am held to be incapable of writing an autobiography "with his present literary equipment" and I am advised to take a correspondence course in English grammar. Urged by Father Abbot, I sent back the manuscript with three pages of single-spaced self-defense, pointing out that Harcourt, Brace did not agree that the book was unripe for publication. Another objection was that I had been too frank about my past. Dom Dominique can decide that question, since he is on the spot.

Secretly I am delighted to have a cross that I can understand. It falls into a nice flattering literary context: I am a misunderstood author. However, I would not be sorry if the book were thrown into the ash-can. It would deliver me, perhaps, from many worries.

If, in the past, I have desired to stop writing, I can see that it is much better for me to go on trying to learn to write under the strange conditions imposed by Cistercian life. I can become a saint by writing well, for the glory of God, denying myself, judging myself, and mortifying my haste to get into print. Writing is a moral matter, and my typewriter is an essential factor in my asceticism.

It will do me much good to learn to choose my words, to think and re-read and correct, and to pray over a manuscript. At present I pull the sheets out of the typewriter and read them over once and send them away. I am working more carefully on *The Waters of Siloe*. It is a history of the Order. I have to do a lot of reading and rewriting. This slows me down.

April 20

GOOD SHEPHERD SUNDAY. DAY OF RECOLLECTION
It is a day of recollection. That means we are supposed to be
thinking about ourselves. It seems as though a year had passed
since my solemn profession. But it is only a month. The more I
think of my vows the happier I am. For there is only one thing
left to live for: the love of God. There is only one unhappiness:
not to love God. That is why I wish I did not find my soul so
full of movement, and shadows and cross-currents of dry wind
that stir up the dust of my human desires. Everywhere I turn I
find the stuff I write sticking to me like flypaper.

April 23

The Cistercian life is energetic. There are tides of vitality running through the whole community that generate energy even
in people who are lazy. And here at Gethsemani we are at the
same time Cistercians and Americans. It is in some respects a
dangerous combination. Our energy runs away with us. We go
out to work like a college football team taking the field.

Trappists believe that everything that costs them is God's will.
Anything that makes you suffer is God's will. If it makes you
sweat, it is God's will. But we have serious doubts about the
things which demand no expense of physical energy. Are they
really the will of God? Hardly! They require no steam. We seem
to think that God will not be satisfied with a monastery that
does not behave in every way like a munitions factory under
wartime conditions of production.

If we want something, we easily persuade ourselves that what
we want is God's will just as long as it turns out to be difficult
to obtain. What is easy is my own will: what is hard is God's
will. If I happen to desire something hard to get, it means that I
want to sacrifice myself to do God's will. No other standard
applies. And because we make fetishes out of difficulties we sometimes work ourselves into the most fantastically stupid situations,
and use ourselves up not for God but for ourselves. We think we
have done great things because we are worn out. If we have

rushed into the fields or into the woods and done a great deal of damage, we are satisfied. We do not mind ruining all our machinery, as long as we make a deafening noise and stir up a great cloud of dust. Something has been achieved.

April 25   FEAST OF SAINT MARK

Litany after Prime today. The weather has been very bad: cold and rainy, and we have hardly planted anything yet.

Typewriter broken. And now the infinite God has to compete, for possession of my mind, with the image of a beautiful new typewriter with French accents on it. . . .

I had to preach a sermon in theology class. Father Macarius refuses to comment on sermons or to give any advice. He lets the other scholastics write their observations, which he then takes and boils down and types out and hands to the one who has preached. You do not know who said what. But you can sometimes guess, by the style. The comments on the sermon I preached were interesting. I was praised for "avoiding his usual heavy philosophy." Another said I was in general "too scholastic." I was blamed for giving a lecture rather than a sermon. That was true. In fact, I felt myself sliding into the mannerisms of a ham radio announcer. This embarrassed me very much, but I could not seem to pull myself together and talk normally any more. Someone objected to the fact that I got into a critical discussion of Mersch's book *The Whole Christ* and asserted that Saint Bernard *did* teach the doctrine of the Mystical Body.

All this, except the remark about my speaking like a lecturer, surprised me. It had not occurred to me to wonder about introducing controversy into a sermon. But now that my attention is called to it, I remember that the monks (myself included) get very restless in Chapter as soon as anything controversial is introduced. We seem to find argument oppressive beyond measure. The reason is, of course, that no one can answer back. After years of being unable to talk back, a Cistercian is apt to be nauseated by the mere suggestion of controversy. When a conference is really argumentative the atmosphere gets to be so tense that the monks cannot even seek solace by falling asleep. When it is all over they file out in silent dejection, dispersing, running outdoors on every side to find solitude and fresh air.

Also criticism by itself, even true criticism, does not do much good in a monastery. We stand much more in need of encouragement, of positive and clear direction. We know well enough what is wrong with us, but the monotony of the life sometimes makes us so dejected that we cannot seem to do anything about it. What we need above all are words that will make us love one another and advice that will strengthen us to overcome evil with good. However, when a Superior uses his authority to correct an abuse the effect is quite different. It is the Superior's business to correct abuses—tactfully, of course, but he must correct them. When he does so in the right way the whole community feels cleaner, and there is peace.

April 26

We have been rooting up cedar stumps and brambles from a field that has just been cleared to be planted with oats. We felled the trees there the winter before last. It was a nice day, for a change. All the hills are beginning to be clouded with green. Here and there in the pale green wash that covers the hills you see a little cloud of pink where there is a redbud tree.

April 28

On and off since Easter I have been playing a new game called insomnia. It goes like this: You lie down in your dormitory cell and listen to first one monk and then another monk begin to snore without, however, going to sleep yourself. Then you count the quarter hours by the tower clock and console yourself with an exact knowledge of the amount of sleep you are missing. The fun does not really begin until you get up at 2 A.M. and try to keep awake in choir. All day long you wander around the monastery bumping into the walls.

Insomnia can become a form of contemplation. You just lie there, inert, helpless, alone, in the dark, and let yourself be crushed by the inscrutable tyranny of time. The plank bed becomes an altar and you lie there without trying to understand any longer in what sense you can be called a sacrifice. Outside in the world, where it is night, perhaps there is someone who suddenly sees that something he has done is horrible. He is most unexpectedly sorry and finds himself able to pray. . . .

> *April* 29   FEAST OF SAINT ROBERT

I have been corresponding with a Carthusian—a monk of Parkminster—about some work. A letter from him came the other day, with a couple of pamphlets, including *Umbratilem* in Latin and English. The Carthusians seem to have no hesitation in declaring that *infused* contemplation is the normal end of the contemplative vocation. That is a point which, it seems to me, should be made clear. The contemplative life is not just a complex system of "exercises" which the monks go through in order to pile up merits. God has brought us to the monastery to reveal Himself to us, although it may only be in a very intangible and obscure way. "He that loveth me shall be loved of my Father: and I will love him and manifest myself to him. . . . My Father will love him and we will come to him and make our abode with him."*

Perhaps not everyone in the monastery will arrive at a real recognition of this intimate presence of God: but I hardly think it possible that God would allow men to devote themselves entirely to seeking Him without letting them in some way or other *find* Him. I think He wants many of us to find Him and realize Who it is that we have found. "We have found Him of whom Moses in the Law, and the prophets did write: Jesus, the son of Joseph, of Nazareth."†

Father Nathaniel, a very young priest who is infirmarian because he has been ill, preached in Chapter. It was a good sermon, all about the "night of the senses." In fact, it was the most intelligent sermon I have heard on that kind of topic since I came here. The monks usually preach well enough on trials and sufferings and abandonment. All that is quite well understood. But

*John, 14:21–23.
†John, 1:45.

trials in connection with contemplative *prayer* are not so well understood.

The little dogwood tree that was just planted in the garden is now in full bloom. This evening, after meditation, a humming-bird got caught in the cloister and was terrified of the monks walking in procession to the refectory for supper. Two candles are burning by the relic of Saint Robert's finger bone. In the refectory they are reading the life of some mystic whose name I cannot catch. Meanwhile I am reading Saint Paul's *Epistle to the Hebrews:* "Let us go forth therefore to Him outside the camp, bearing His reproach, for we have not here a lasting city, but we seek one which is to come. By Him, Jesus, let us therefore offer sacrifice of praise always to God. . . ."* "Laying aside every weight and sin which surrounds us, let us run by patience to the fight proposed to us: looking to Jesus the author and finisher of faith, who having joy set before Him endured the Cross, despising the shame, and now sitteth on the right hand of the throne of God. . . ."†

April 30

We had a moral theology exam and then my chest was X-rayed. The mystic in the refectory turns out to be the Venerable Maria Celeste Crostarosa. I had never heard of her. She is eighteenth century. She started the Redemptorist nuns—contemplatives.

May 1

Today I got two new jobs. Father Abbot gave me the notes that Father Alberic was working on, for the revised edition of his history of the Order. Then I am to write a new postulant's guide. That means I now have no less than twelve jobs in various stages of completion, not counting books by persons outside the mon-astery which I am supposed to be shepherding toward the printer, because they remotely favor the interests of the Order or of the house.

There is the life of Mother Berchmans; *The Seven Storey*

*Hebrews, 13:13-15.
†Hebrews, 12:1-2.

Mountain; the biography of Saint Lutgarde which is, I think, in
the hands of the diocesan censors, although I am never quite sure
where the manuscripts go when they get away from me; and I
have finished three chapters of *The Waters of Siloe.* The Archbishop still presumably has the translation and commentary of
The Spirit of Simplicity, which I finished in a big hurry at
the end of 1945 because Father Abbot wanted it "in print within
a month." I am not quite sure what has happened to the six- and
seven-hundred-page lives of Cistercian saints which I wrote as a
novice, freezing to death in the unheated library. *Figures for an
Apocalypse,* a book of poems, is being printed by New Directions. The General Chapter expects us to put out something
on Saint Bernard for his eighth centenary in 1953. Laughlin is
still after me for two anthologies which I do not want to do, but
I have also been thinking of a Spanish-English edition of the
Dark Night of the Soul, with a preface and commentary. Somewhere I have a few notes I scraped together for a life of Father
Joseph Cassant. And on top of all that Reverend Father speaks
of a new critical Latin edition of Saint Bernard for 1953. That
last one is definitely beyond me. Anyway, who knows what they
are doing in Europe? In the presence of all this I ask myself the
following questions:

Just because a cross is a cross, does it follow that it is the cross
God intends for you?

Just because a job is a nuisance, is it therefore good for you?

Is it an act of virtue for a contemplative to sit down and let
himself be snowed under by activities?

What am I doing in that room over there: piling up fuel for
Purgatory?

Does the fact that all this is obedience make it really pleasing
to God? I wonder. I do not ask these questions in a spirit of
rebellion. I would really like to know the answers.

Fortunately, Father Abbot's injunctions are always good-
natured enough to be quite vague and flexible. He gets an idea
and communicates it to me and I happily accept it, but it is

understood that if I cannot do it I will say so and it will be dropped.

May 4 DAY OF RECOLLECTION

All day I have been waiting for You with my faculties bleeding the poison of unsuppressed activity . . . I have waited for Your silence and Your peace to stanch and cleanse them, O my Lord.

You will heal my soul when it pleases You, because I have trusted in You.

I will no longer wound myself with the thoughts and questions that have surrounded me like thorns: that is a penance You do not ask of me.

You have made my soul for Your peace and Your silence, but it is lacerated by the noise of my activity and my desires. My mind is crucified all day by its own hunger for experience, for ideas, for satisfaction. And I do not possess my house in silence.

But I was created for Your peace and You will not despise my longing for the holiness of Your deep silence. O my Lord, You will not leave me forever in this sorrow, because I have trusted in You and I will wait upon Your good pleasure in peace and without complaining any more. This, for Your glory.

I am content that these pages show me to be what I am—noisy, full of the racket of my imperfections and passions, and the wide open wounds left by my sins. Full of my own emptiness. Yet, ruined as my house is, You live there!

May 14 VIGIL OF THE ASCENSION

Last night there were thunderstorms: but today everything is beautiful. The leaves on the hickory tree by the cemetery are small and the flowers fill the branches with fringes of green lace. I hear the engine running down at the mill: only that, and the birds singing.

Tomorrow is the Ascension, my favorite feast. At any time in the year I am liable to find the antiphons of Ascension day ringing in my ears and they fill me with light and peace. *Vado parare* *vobis locum.** It is the feast of silence and interior solitude when we go up to live in heaven with Jesus: for He takes us there, after He has lived a little while on earth among us. That is the grace of Ascension day: to be taken up into the heaven of our own souls, the *apex mentis*, the point of immediate contact with God. To rest on this quiet peak, in the darkness that surrounds God. To live there through all trials and all business with the *Tranquillus Deus tranquillans omnia.*† God be with me this day and forever.

May 17

There is a calendar in the Scriptorium with a pious thought for each day, in French. It reminds me that today is the anniversary of the canonization of the Little Flower. Ascension day was fine —full of recollection.

The inviolability of one's spiritual sanctuary, the center of the soul, depends on secrecy. Secrecy is the intellectual complement of a pure intention. Do not let your right hand see what your left hand is doing. Keep all good things secret even from yourself. If we would find God in the depths of our souls we have to leave everybody else outside, including ourselves.

If we find God in our souls and want to stay there with Him, it is disastrous to think of trying to communicate Him to others as we find Him there. We can preach Him later on with the grace He gives us in silence. We need not upset the silence with language. *Dabitur vobis in illa hora quid loquamini.*‡

May 20

Liberum est cor quod non tenetur aliquo amore nisi Dei.§

Art and asceticism. The artist must be free, otherwise he will be dominated by his material instead of dominating it. Hence,

---

*"I go to prepare a place for you."

†"The tranquil God Who makes all things tranquil" (Saint Bernard).

‡"It shall be given to you in that hour what to speak, for it is not you that speak but the Spirit of your Father that speaketh in you" (Matthew, 10:19-20).

§"That heart is free which is held by no love other than the love of God." (Saint Bonaventure).

art demands asceticism. Religious ascetics have something to learn from the natural asceticism of the artist: it is un-selfconscious, organic, integrated in his art. It does not run the risk of becoming an end in itself. But the artist also has something to gain from religious asceticism. It not only raises him above his subject and his material but above his art itself. He can now control everything, even his art, which usually controls him.

Asceticism may involve a total sacrifice of art.

The happiest consummation for the artist as such: his art may be integrated into an organic spiritual whole and become the most vital expression of a life of praise and worship.

A magazine called *Tiger's Eye* wants to give me ninety-six dollars for a poem. I do not think Saint Benedict would want me to take that much. However, by a peculiar irony, I am not allowed to decide. I have a vow of poverty which prohibits one from *refusing* money.

May 23 VIGIL OF PENTECOST

The little locust tree by the corner of the wall has died and spilled all the fragments of its white flowers over the ground until that part of the garden looks like a picture by Seurat.

The Carthusians at Parkminster sent me three volumes of the *Meditations* they use in the novitiate and I like them very much, although I thought at first that I was not going to find anything in them.

May 26 WHITMONDAY

During the meridienne Father Prior slipped a note into our cell saying that although it was a holiday some of the monks would be going out to make hay after None, and that I could come if I wanted to. We all changed, but Father Abbot canceled it and told us to stay at home and pray.

When I was at Oakham, Whitmonday was the only day of the year on which we were allowed to ride bicycles, and I remember once riding over to Uppingham and being overwhelmed by the big ugly buildings of the school. But I have never forgotten how lovely the country was. Riding eastward out of Up-

pingham toward Stamford, I seemed to be always on the tops
of hills and the distance before me was filled with a warm blue
haze full of light where lowlands lay. I am filled with a kind of
contemplative awe when I remember the beauty of early summer
in Rutland, when I used to go off into the hills alone.

After the Visitation I had to give up Dom Gildas as my confessor because the Abbot General insisted that the novice masters
were far too busy to hear confessions. Father Macarius who is
now my confessor, as well as theology professor and *censor
librorum*, has just given me a life of Cardinal Newman to read.
I think he wants me to see how much trouble Newman got into
with holy people. He thinks it would be salutary for me to know
about this, and I am sure it is so! However, what really fascinates
me about the book is the realization that I have absolutely nothing in common with Cardinal Newman except for the fact that
we are both converts and both wrote autobiographies. He writes
beautiful prose, I write slang (and incidentally the Abbot General said I could write all the slang I liked). But above all, I feel
utterly remote from Newman's society. One look into his life
makes me feel like a savage. He is completely foreign to me:
speech, attitudes, everything. I have none of his refinement. In
fact I have always scrupulously avoided refinement. If I am
drawn to mysticism, it is to a mysticism that has a certain earthy
side to it, like that of the twelfth century. And yet I love the
Fathers of the Church, as Newman did: but probably for entirely different reasons.

May 29

I am trying to tone down *The Seven Storey Mountain*. When I
wrote it three years ago, I don't know what audience I might
have been thinking of. I suppose I just put down what was in
me, under the eyes of God Who knows what is in me. But not
everything that I remember will please—or help—everyone who
may happen to read the book. Now I have suddenly thought of
all the different kinds of people who may some day read it: men
riding on the Long Island Railroad, nuns in Irish convents, my

relatives, secular priests, communists . . . and young girls in boarding schools, whom the censors are afraid to scandalize.

May 31 EMBER SATURDAY

Today at Mass we sang the beautiful Communion antiphon, *Spiritus ubi vult spirat* with its four alleluias, which marks the end of Paschal Time. "*Nescis unde venit aut quo vadat.* The Spirit breathes where it wills, and you do not know where it comes from or whither it is going." I don't know where Paschal Time has gone, either. We have not yet had any real summer weather, and that makes it seem unbelievable that we are already in the doors of June.

The sun is bright. Catbirds sing with crazy versatility above my head in the tree. Fasting is easy in nice weather.

June 8

The whole place is swimming in honeysuckle. The smell nauseates me.

Corpus Christi went off better than usual. That is to say, I finished our floral design in plenty of time and without getting in too much of a whirl. On the Feast when we are supposed to contemplate the mystery of the Blessed Sacrament, there is absolutely no time for any such thing as contemplation. You are lucky if you can get a minute to kneel down before the tabernacle and say a Hail Mary.

June 13 FEAST OF THE SACRED HEART

I ought to know, by now, that God uses everything that happens as a means to lead me into solitude. Every creature that enters my life, every instant of my days, will be designed to wound me with the realization of the world's insufficiency, until I become so detached that I will be able to find God alone in everything. Only then will all things bring me joy.

Even the consolations of prayer, lights in the intellect and sensible fervor in the will: everything that touches me burns me at least lightly. I cannot hold on to anything. The pain in all these things is the pledge of God's love for me, as long as I am

as weak in the spirit as I still am. This pain is the promise of solitude.

Today I seemed to be very much assured that solitude is indeed His will for me and that it is truly God Who is calling me
into the desert. But this desert is not necessarily a geographical
one. It is a solitude of heart in which created joys are consumed
and reborn in God.

James Laughlin of New Directions was here yesterday, for an
hour or so. He had been promising to come, and sending cards
from different parts of the country—California, Utah, Colorado,
New Mexico, saying that he was indeed coming. The other
evening when I was in Father Abbot's room, reporting at the
end of work and looking for mail, someone called up from
Paducah and I guessed it was Laughlin. Then he showed up
here after noon yesterday. I went up to the top floor of the
guest house and walked into a room where the shutters were
closed and everything was half-dark. There was a man sitting in
a low rocking chair. When I entered he stood up and became as
tall as a tree. I had heard Laughlin was tall and now I was convinced. So I shook hands with him and we sat down again and
started to talk. We talked about books and we looked at books
and we walked around the farm and he was shocked when I told
him that monks who broke things had to go and accuse themselves and show the broken objects to the abbot. Meanwhile his
wife was outside in the driveway painting a picture of the gatehouse. We went out there to see her and she turned out to be
very small. She did not stay to talk but, seized with panic, went
back to her painting at a safe distance from the monastery.

So Laughlin and I sat in the gatehouse and looked at a lot of
kodachromes of the monastery and talked about the new postulant's guide because Laughlin had some good ideas about layouts.
We talked about D. H. Lawrence, too, and about Kenneth Rexroth whom Laughlin had been seeing in California.

Laughlin is a fundamentally simple person. He is basically
religious because he is *mundo corde*, clean of heart. I suppose
that the last thing in the world that would occur to the super-

ficial observer would be that the publisher of Henry Miller and others was "pure of heart." But there are many different aspects of integrity and some of them escape the attention of religious people who ought to know better. And though I don't remember having liked Henry Miller, there is a kind of integrity about him too. He insists on saying exactly how he feels about things; namely that there is evil in the world and that he is unhappy. He is to some extent more honest than the people who think things are better than they are, or believe that all is well with the world for the wrong reason. But I still remember having been revolted by Henry Miller even in the days when I thought I could not be revolted by anything. The first chapter of Saint Paul's Epistle to the Romans has a great deal to teach us about the world we live in and it remains the only explanation for writers like Miller.

As for Laughlin, I like him very much. He is the kind of person I can understand. He may be wrong about D. H. Lawrence but he is wrong in a good way: because he is looking for God. And although it is bad to look for God where He is not to be found, it is nevertheless good to be looking more or less explicitly for God. So Laughlin has a kind of feeling for the sacramentality of nature and of human love and he can even talk about it in Christian terms.

June 14

Yesterday at the solemn profession of Fathers Felician and Meinrad a priest from Louisville preached to us about Adam. He is the pastor of the parish that Father Felician comes from. Once when Father Felician and I were helping the sacristan put out wine and water for the priests of the archdiocese on retreat here, Father Felician pointed him out proudly. "Priest-me-secular-church." It was a delightful sermon. All about what a great contemplative Adam was, before the fall: a subject that has always appealed to me. The preacher cried out so melodiously and his sentences got so much higher and higher that I thought he would start rising and fly away obliquely into the vaulting of the transept. He is a saintly priest and perhaps that has something to do with the holiness of Father Felician.

At all these pontifical functions they have been playing some weird music on the organ. It reminds me of the stuff you used to hear at the movies before the silent movies went out and the talkies came in. Now I discover that it is the hymn that the faithful sing at Fatima. Mother of God, why do you let these things happen?

June 21

The book about Mother Berchmans is to be published by the Bruce Publishing Company. About a hundred pages will have to be cut. I have no objection, I know that I talk too much. It is a vice Cistercian writers have—at least modern Cistercian writers. It means that we do not really know the meaning of silence and that we have not discovered the secret of the contemplative life.

At first I felt pleasure at the thought that the book was going to be printed. But the pleasure soon ended up in a dead, heavy feeling inside me. I have a way to get away from all that. I think about solitude. I think of the people who live for God alone, and of how happy they must be. I think of myself living like that. This is a natural pleasure, perhaps, but since it is higher than the other one, it leaves me a little cleaner.

In the four weeks since Pentecost I have found things I like in the little books of *Meditations* that were sent me from Parkminster. Not that there is anything new or especially deep in them, but their pages are full of simple and practical ideas about the contemplative life. I can always pick up some sentence from it and close the book and walk about the cemetery in peace, watching the sun go down behind the hills.

June 29   FEAST OF SAINTS PETER AND PAUL
This morning Dom Frederic announced the names of those who are to make the new foundation in Utah. He hates to make announcements. He began talking all around the subject, which made everyone nervous because we all knew what he was getting at, and wished he would come to the point. It looked as though he would never get up enough courage to come out with it. He was actually on the verge of revealing the secret when he made another bolt for it and began talking about a washout on the

railway line to Georgia. The community was livid. I thought he
had given up the idea altogether.

At last he got around to the list of names. My name was not
on it. He read them out in order of seniority. I began to fidget
when he got to Father Valerian. When he jumped to Father
Septimus, I stopped fidgeting and sat at ease. Afterwards he came
back and roped in Father Felician, who is almost next to me in
Chapter and who came to the monastery five months after I did.
We went through the novitiate together and I have always liked
him.

I will miss Father Valerian, the organist, too. Here I sit writing this, under the tree. He just walked by with a sort of home-
sick expression and made me a sign that he would pray hard for
me to be sent out there too. I made him a sign back not to pray
too hard. However, I would not mind going there—or anywhere
else God wills. I have no objection to living in the mountains and
I have always had a suspicion this Utah foundation would turn
into one of the best houses in the Order. Anyway, no one knows
who may get sent where. I might be on the way to Utah in another month, if Father Abbot feels so inspired.

They leave on July seventh. I am very moved by the expressions on the faces of those who are going. They show that they
will miss Gethsemani but they are nevertheless happy. Their
happiness is the pure happiness of people who really love God
and it makes you feel cleaner to see it. If there is excitement in
the house, it is a clean excitement. The Holy Spirit has filled the
place with quiet joy.

I am surprised that Father Robert (who was my novice master)
is being sent. He is one of the pillars of Gethsemani. With him
away the house may fall. At least one thing is certain: without
Father Robert, there will be difficulty finding things when they
are needed from the files. I was surprised to see Father Nathaniel
go, too, since he has bad health: but I suppose they are counting
on the mountains to set him up.

> *July 6*   FEAST OF THE PRECIOUS BLOOD
"*Parata sunt omnia* . . ." we sang at Benediction. The ones going

to Utah have now packed all their effects in cardboard boxes, most of which came from the stores in nearby New Haven and are still marked "Whiskey" in big black letters. Seagram's, Calvert's, Old Crow, and the rest. When the Mormons see those whiskey boxes, life in Utah will become much more interesting. The colony is supposed to leave tomorrow night but nobody knows just when, since Dom Frederic has not yet told us.

I have been working over the Mother Berchmans manuscript and find it depressingly bad, especially in the beginning.

It is raining again and there is danger of our losing the wheat crop.

For about an hour and a half this afternoon I just shut up and forgot everything and stayed with God, first outside the church and then inside it. All the things that have been bothering me vanished until Vespers. As soon as I started to sing, everything came back. I was once again irritated with the choir and with the work I am doing and with everything in general and went back to the old refrain about being a hermit. Distractions overwhelm me as soon as the bell for office rings and we open the books and stand there ready to sing. However, if it gives God glory for me to stand there in confusion, I have no objection.

July 9

The founders left for Utah the night before last and the monastery seems very empty without them—even though the house is still so crowded. The best ones in the house have gone. The foundation is a grace both for those who are going and for those who are staying at home. The effect of it is almost tangible. The whole house is full of peace and tranquillity and spiritual health.

The ones leaving for Utah received the blessing of "those going on a journey" after Canonical Compline. Thirty-three of them bowed at the presbytery step, in the semi-darkness. It was very impressive. We will miss them very much, and I will especially miss all those who were so close to me, who were novices with me. You get to be very fond of the people you live with in a monastery. I am certainly not detached enough from them to be immune to a little pain at the thought that I will never see them again.

Compline was early. We all went out to the gate about seven-thirty. It was almost dark. There were many cars, ready to take them to the station. Monks and brothers were milling around in front of the gatehouse, saying good-by in sign language and embracing one another according to the custom of the Order, and it sounded like wind in the leaves of the trees. Father Abbot was in a hurry to cut it short and he got his car to start off first but the others did not follow at once. I left before they were all on their way and walked back alone across the guests' garden, toward the big dark building of the monastery. I shall never forget that return into the tremendous, beautiful silence of Gethsemani, silence you could almost feel! Clean, holy quiet!

I lay awake for a long time in the dormitory, hearing every train that whistled in the valley.

July 16   FEAST OF SAINT STEPHEN HARDING
On top of all this year's rain we had a tremendous storm during Vespers. The mill bottom turned into a lake. So much water piled up against the enclosure wall that it burst it from the inside and swept away some forty feet of cement blocks. There were a hundred rivers running down every hillside. The novitiate garden was swamped. All the areaways were full of water and the tailor shop in the basement was flooded. The ducks are very happy.

When the rain stopped I went through the cemetery, jumping puddles, to look over the wall and see what had happened and Father Joel and the Prior were up on the roof of the laybrothers' dormitory looking around at the flooded country.

Late in the evening, after supper, after the proper time for sundown, there was a great red glare all over the northern sky and no one could imagine what it signified.

July 20
They have been having a hard time at the Utah monastery. None of the splendid things they were expecting were ready for them.

The Quonset huts will not be finished until "October," which means next summer. They had bought three army huts, to live in while waiting for the others: but of these only one was on their property when they arrived, and it was not ready to be lived in. And some of them are ill.

A few drops of rain just started spattering on the leaves, and stopped again. The sky is gray. Birds sing. Far away a bob white exults briefly in the fields where our wheat crop is rotting.

The day after tomorrow is the feast of Saint Mary Magdalen to whom I pray with fervor and pleasure because she is one of the few people who ever had any sense. *Optimam partem elegit.** I saw a woodcut of her, sitting outside her hermitage, in one of the volumes of our set of Denis the Carthusian.

July 27   NINTH SUNDAY AFTER PENTECOST
Since the monk who was regularly reading to the retreatants, in the guest house, during their meals, has left for Utah, I have been appointed to replace him. It disrupts things a little, but I am glad to do it. If I did not, someone else would have to. Besides, *caritas Christi urget nos.* You want to do something for all the people who come here looking for God. You get few enough chances to show the world that you love those who are in it, and want to help them to be happy. So after dinner when the other monks go off to the dormitory I take my volume of Monsignor Sheen and sit on the windowsill of the guest's dining-room and read to them. After that I help clear the tables and wander off to the dormitory to try to rest while the others are singing None and the organ is booming in the closet at the end of the line of cells.

August 8
Hot, sticky weather. Prickly heat. Red lumps all over your neck and shoulders. Everything clammy. *Paenitentiam agite!* It is better than a hairshirt.

Yesterday old Father George collapsed. I suppose the heat had

*"She has chosen the best part" (that is, the contemplative life).—Luke, 10:42.

something to do with it. The bells rang and we hastened to give him Extreme Unction in the middle of the afternoon work. I did not know who was dying. I thought it was Father Odo's room, that we were kneeling at. Only when the monks went away did I find out that Father George was lying there instead of Father Odo.

A letter from Bob Giroux, the editor of Harcourt, Brace, about changes that were to be made in *The Seven Storey Mountain*, never reached me. We have been sitting here for weeks, I waiting for the letter to arrive and he waiting for me to answer it. Laughlin sent some poems of Patrice de la Tour du Pin.

August 14 VIGIL OF THE ASSUMPTION

Heat. But it is not so bad, on an empty stomach. The air sings with the din of locusts. By a kind of accident I got a small pamphlet of Dylan Thomas's poems from Laughlin, who wanted me to look at the type and tell him whether I wanted it used in *Cistercian Contemplatives*.

Dylan Thomas's integrity as a poet makes me very ashamed of the verse I have been writing. We who say we love God: why are we not as anxious to be perfect in our art as we pretend we want to be in our service of God? If we do not try to be perfect in what we write, perhaps it is because we are not writing for God after all. In any case it is depressing that those who serve God and love Him sometimes write so badly, when those who do not believe in Him take pains to write so well. I am not talking about grammar and syntax, but about having something to say and saying it in sentences that are not half dead. Saint Paul and Saint Ignatius Martyr did not bother about grammar but they certainly knew how to write.

Imperfection is the penalty of rushing into print. And people who rush into print too often do so not because they really have anything to say, but because they think it is important for something by them to be in print. The fact that your subject may be very important in itself does not necessarily mean that what *you* have written about it is important. A bad book about the love of God remains a bad book, even though it may be about the love

of God. There are many who think that because they have
written about God, they have written good books. Then men
pick up these books and say: if the ones who say they believe in
God cannot find anything better than this to say about it, their
religion cannot be worth much.

Tomorrow's Gospel: "*Martha, Martha, sollicita es . . .*" Sometimes I catch myself drumming with my fingers on a book or a
table. That is the worst yet. I never sunk so low, in the monastery! I suppose the extra work and the retreats have got me doing
that.

August 15   THE ASSUMPTION OF OUR LADY
This afternoon I was in the library, haunting the corner of the
second room, where the books about different religious Orders
are found. With a secret and guilty sense of interior delight I
had procured a stepladder and was sitting on top of it, where I
had full command of the one little shelf devoted to books and
pamphlets about the Carthusians. I had hardly been there five
minutes when Father Gervase, who is very sharp and intuitive,
caught me there *in flagrante delicto*, ravished by the pictures of
all the Charterhouses that existed at the end of the last century.

Father Gervase has access to the most unimpeachable sources
of information since, as private secretary to Father Abbot, he
reads all the letters that come in from all the convents in America.
What is more he is a very intelligible sign-maker. Without any
trouble at all he was able to assure me that Dom Verner Moore,
the Benedictine, who preached our community retreat two years
ago, had become a Carthusian at Miraflores, in Spain. Father
Gervase did not have to climb the ladder to find a picture of
Miraflores in order to get this information across. He merely
twirled on his heel and snapped his fingers over his head as if he
were playing a pair of castanets. After that, delighted at my
amazement, he hastened away to read all the latest books about
the Little Flower.

I sat on top of the ladder, unable to move, feeling as if someone had punched me in the stomach. Not that I am altogether
surprised at Dom Moore's becoming a Carthusian. I remember

him describing a Carthusian at work, pruning a fruit tree in his little garden and frequently pausing to pray. He spoke of Carthusians several times in his conferences and when he was receiving the monks privately, all those with Carthusian temptations were buzzing around the door of Saint Gabriel's room like flies around a honey pot. I complained that I could not seem to get much more than three hours of private mental prayer a day here. Dom Moore said he thought that was quite enough and told me how the Carthusians had to say many extra vocal prayers and were always complaining that they had so little time for private mental prayer and contemplation. . . . And now, there he is, a Carthusian. And here I am.

No matter how much I might *like* to be a Carthusian or something else, I could never make a move to become one unless I had some positive indication that it was the will of God. And I have no such indication. Even when I try to pry some expression of approval or encouragement out of my director I find myself with a hole in my conscience that tells me clearly there is something wrong.

August 17 SUNDAY, DAY OF RECOLLECTION
The *Exordium Parvum* sums up the Cistercian ideal—or one aspect of that ideal—in terrifying language. "Let them go on struggling and sweating until their last breath." The Latin is more direct: *"usque ad exhalationem spiritus desudant."* In any case, that is what we are doing today.

Father George is a living embodiment of that sentence. Last week or the week before, or whenever it was, we gave him the Last Sacraments. Today, he was up for the feast and came to choir. You cannot keep him out of the community. He wants to follow all the regular exercises until his legs drop off. For generation after generation of Trappists, sanctity has consisted in just that.

August 31
Another August has ended and we will never see it again. It was hot and stuffy all day, but although it did not rain, after Vespers

the air was cooler and the sky had brushed up to look something like September. O frightening and beautiful month with Saint Giles standing in your door to be the patron of those who are afraid. Soon we will fight the fields of corn.

We have the biggest retreat of the year. There are eighty-two or more in the guest house that was built for fifty. One of them is an old man with a magnificent white beard and a big curled mustache. He must be one of the wonders of Kentucky and I am overwhelmed with awe whenever he appears.

Waiting in the empty guest house dining-room, amid the smells of hot soup and fresh pie, while the brothers bring more wagons of food from the kitchen I lean in the windowsill and read snatches of Paul Claudel's prose. I like his prose more than his verse. Especially a long prose poem about rain, somewhere in Japan. Someone ought to write a whole book full of things like that.

September 7

*Nativitas est hodie sanctae Mariae Virginis.** We have just come from first Vespers of Our Lady's birthday. I am full of those happy antiphons, and glad because of the feast and because of what it means, for through her we come to heaven. *Coeli fenestra facta es.†* I am glad that in our Order we still enter heaven through the window. I believe that line of the hymn was re-formed in the Roman liturgy so that the rest of the Church goes in more decorously through the door. But we Cistercians still get in by the window.

The brothers came out for Benediction with new torches sheltered in red glass. They looked as if they were carrying burning hearts upon the ends of poles. I do not say it was beautiful, but it was at least curious.

Between me and the shadow that is under the cedars, gnats dance in the sun. It is cooler. It is definitely September now.

---

*"Today is the nativity of Saint Mary the Virgin" (First antiphon for Vespers of the feast).

†"Thou art become the window of heaven" (from the hymn *O gloriosa Domina*).

This afternoon I was content looking at the low green rampart of woods that divides us from the rest of the universe and listening to the deep silence: content not for the sake of the scene or the silence but because of God. And now I hear a car in the distance, a solitary car coming down the road. The sound of action reminds me that I must soon wash my neck and go and read Monsignor Sheen to the retreatants at their supper.

That is how everything stands, Mother of God, after the first Vespers of your Nativity in the year 1947. *Dona nobis pacem** Keep us in your heart until next year and the year after and until we all die in peace, disposed in the four corners of America in new foundations, and myself perhaps you know where, alone with you and with God. His will is my cell. His love is my solitude. *Dona nobis pacem.*

September 12

The Abbot General has sent for a complete list of all the manuscripts and incunabula in our library and I am working in the archives, the vault where all the old books are kept, trying to get the list ready. The vault is a fascinating place, very quiet, full of the smell of mothballs because of the vestments that are also kept there. But on its shelves are things that make me very happy. Also there are other things that I would never have bothered to buy if I had been Dom Edmond. Most of the material is merely curious. Here are a few of the notes I wrote down for my own information:

A Feuillant *Rituale*. Starts out with a long section of quotations from Scripture and tradition, on the value of sacred ceremonies. The Feuillants were not allowed to lean on the arm rests when they stood in their choir-stalls facing the altar. These volumes came from Feuillant monastery of the Guardian Angels in Paris. Crest on cover. Mass—Roman rite, it seems.

Processionarius, Marnef, Paris, 1510. Belonged to Chiaravalle, Milan.

Beautiful woodcut of the Presentation of Jesus in the Temple. *Manuscript of Saint Bernard's Sermons In Cantica* done in his

*"Give us peace."

own lifetime at Parc, Louvain. One of the most beautiful manuscripts I have ever seen. Parchment, easy to read. Beautiful red and green initials. A fine gold and green "Q" at the beginning of Sermon VII. After Sermon XX the writing gets much smaller, different hand.

Manuscript of Saint Bernard's Sermons, XIVth century, Italian, vellum. Contains a life of Saint Hugh the Carthusian. An isolated sermon, last in the series, has a portrait of Saint Bernard in the initial which happens to be "I" so that the portrait is not very successful. *Inter Babilonem et Jerusalem nulla pax est sed guerra continua . . .* *

September 14   FEAST OF THE HOLY NAME OF MARY
The *Usages* say it is winter. The weather obligingly got a little cooler so that the sky is clear enough to suggest autumn. This week I am servant of the refectory because there is no laymen's retreat. The priests of the archdiocese of Louisville are here for the week and they have their own reader. The Archbishop is also here.

The Franciscan ideal of poverty seems to have something of the same function in the spiritual life as the ideal of silence and solitude in the purely contemplative Orders.

I have been thinking of *La Soledad,* Our Lady of Solitude, Our Lady in her greatest sorrow and dereliction. When Bishop Davis of San Juan, Puerto Rico, was here, Reverend Father brought him into the vault to look at some of the old books and I was speaking to him and began to ask him about *La Soledad.* I remembered her church in Camaguey, Cuba. This devotion is unknown here, but is loved in Spain and Spanish America. I wish I could find out more about her, or get a picture or a medal or something of hers to have about me. Really, Our Lady of Solitude sums up my interior life: if only I remember what solitude meant for her. It was not a luxurious solitude, full of comfort and relaxation. It was the solitude with which she was alone in a crowd, on Calvary.

* "Between Babylon and Jerusalem there is no peace, but continual war."

September 15

Working in the vault. For the moment, I have a solitude. It is a bit pedantic, but it is quiet. Here are some of the things that grow there:

XIIth century Cistercian antiphonary and hymnal. Done at the Abbey of Morimondo (Italy). It is prefaced by some very useful notes by an eighteenth-century Italian bibliophile, Carlo Trivulzio. When Dom Edmond bought it, it was the oldest musical manuscript in this country, and perhaps it still is. It was written before January 1174, the date of Saint Bernard's canonization, because the office of Saint Bernard's feast is inserted in a different hand. This volume has only the proper and common of the saints.

The chant is not written on a four-line staff, there is only one line but you can see where other lines were traced out faintly in pencil. The writing is perfect but so small that the monks evidently did not use the books as constantly in choir as we do. They must have used them mostly for learning the office by heart, practicing outside the choir.

It starts with the feast of Saint Stephen (December 26). A fine red initial "H" (*Hesterna die Dominus natus est in terris ut Stephanus nasceretur in coelis*) for the first responsory. The volume also contains the office of the dead, with a beautiful black, green, gold and red "C" for the antiphon *Clementissime.* There are many proper hymns for the saints which we no longer have in our Breviary.

Saint Bernard, *In Cantica.* Printed by the Brothers of the Common Life in Rostock, 1481. The book once belonged to the Charterhouse of Wurzburg, for inside the binding is written *"Pertinet ad Carthusienses in Herbipoli."*

Maybe it was one of the Carthusians of Wurzburg that spilled something all over the first folio. The book has quite a few marginal notes and underscorings made by readers—I suppose by the Carthusians too. In Sermon XXI there is even a rough sketch of a red hand in the margin pointing to this sentence: "Therefore, when thou findest thyself to be cooling in thy sense of devotion, or afflicted with acedia and weariness, do not on that

account lose heart and give up thy striving for spiritual perfection."*

Sermon XXIII inspired a number of marginal notes. All down
one folio someone listed the different "Cellars" of mystical contemplation. In Sermon XXX, the famous passage about the monks
who are more solicitous about their diet than their interior life,
"*observatores ciborum et neglectores morum*," is picked out for
special attention, but after that there are fewer markings. After
the colophon there is a globe surmounted by a Cross—the Carthusian trademark.

September 21   FEAST OF SAINT MATTHEW
Father Osee and Father Ezechiel were ordained to the priesthood
yesterday. For a year and a half I have sat with them in the laybrothers' common room, listening to Father Macarius expound
the mysteries of Sabetti's moral theology and Tanquerey's
Dogma. Then Father Meinrad was ordained deacon. I was thurifer at the Mass, which means that my turn is coming soon and
the Master of Ceremonies wants me to be in a good position to
observe all the ceremonies of the ordination so that I will know
what to do when my own time comes. Yet it still seems a long
way off. Perhaps two Septembers from now I will be singing my
own first Mass.

While the three *ordinandi* were lying on their faces on the red
carpet of the sanctuary, and the choir was chanting the litany of
the saints, a catbird flew in through the window and sat on the
carpet behind them and chirped modestly. Meanwhile, being
thurifer and not having too clear a picture of the ceremonies in
my mind, I had built a fire too soon and I was afraid it would
burn out. So I lit some more charcoal and ended up with the
biggest fire I ever built in my life—at least in a censer.

This morning—Sunday—they sang their first Masses. Father
Ezechiel was very shy. He made the sign of the Cross over the
chalice as if he had a broken arm. He turned to the people and
said *Orate Fratres* to the community very humbly. It is deeply

*"*Ergo cum te tepore, accedia vel taedio affici sentis, noli propterea
diffidere aut desistere studio spirituali.*"

moving to watch a new priest make his first consecration, and realize what is going on.

Yesterday the whole community assembled in Chapter after dinner and the Archbishop formally presented the medal *Pro Ecclesia et Pontifice* to Captain Kinarney who is the monastery's greatest benefactor. He is a sort of unofficial oblate. In fact, I remember when I was in the guest house, about to enter as a novice, he stopped me in one of the corridors to assure me that Dom Frederic would treat me with kindness. On solemn occasions, like Dom Frederic's Golden Jubilee, Captain Kinarney is usually invited to make a speech in Chapter and he is so fond of the monks that he spends the whole time telling them how wonderful they are, which makes everybody laugh. He, in his turn, usually finds it hard to keep from being overwhelmed with emotion. The monks love him quite as much as he loves them. Yesterday's affair made everybody happy.

Dom Frederic, like the holy and unworldly man that he is, is not good at being glib on formal occasions and his speech threw little light on what was about to take place. Fortunately, I already knew what was up because at the last moment Dom Frederic thought he had misplaced the medal and sent Father Wilfrid to find out whether I had seen it in the vault. So after Dom Frederic smilingly closed his cryptic address, leaving everyone in suspense, the Archbishop patiently stood up and made a speech in which everything was made plain. He was going to pin a medal on Captain Kinarney and the medal came from the Holy Father and it was an expression of gratitude for the fact that Captain Kinarney had been very kind to the monks. After that the Captain himself stood up to speak and became incoherent with emotion after the first three words, finally bursting into tears. The Archbishop said to him: "Captain, you are almost weeping," and the Captain replied, with tears streaming down his face, "Well, I can't help it."

September 24

This is one of those days when you feel scabby all over. *Iniquitatem meam ego cognosco et peccatum meum contra me* *est semper.** However, I am glad of it. It makes penance a delight. You look around for something that will kill this leprous image that you have discovered in your soul.

I have been reading about the Carmelites in the *Dictionnaire de Spiritualité*. There are some good notes on poverty in the article —something of the idea that struck me the other day: poverty conceived as a function of solitude or "nakedness"—detachment, isolation from everything superfluous in the interior life. Renunciation of useless activity in your natural faculties. All this is what a Carmelite understands by being poor. And I wish I were poor. Yet I do not want to wish I were poor in a way that might imply that I thought myself rich. I am not rich. I just sit in my little pawnshop of second-rate emotions and ideas, and most of the time they make me slightly sick.

The one thing I really feel like writing—*The Waters of Siloe*, a book about the history and spirituality of the Order—is lying there half finished, but every time I reach out to take it up again, something else interferes.

Meanwhile, the typewriter assigned to me has gone off to the shop to be repaired again. It is an old rebuilt machine and important parts—the letters, for instance—keep falling off when I am trying to write. I have Father Raymond's typewriter; if he suddenly needs it again I will have nothing to work with at all, because all the other typewriters are needed to handle correspondence.

September 28 DAY OF RECOLLECTION

There was supposed to be no weekend retreat in the guest house but a whole crowd arrived anyway right after the diocesan priests had gone. So I am reading to them about Our Lady of Fatima, although it is our Day of Recollection and we are supposed to be immersed in silence and prayer. The trouble with this reading is that the guests come up and ask me questions and sometimes I go ahead and answer them. One man tried to give me a dollar.

I made a futile effort to find some notes I was writing this time

*"For I know my iniquity and my sin is always before me" (Psalm 50).

last year, to compare the Days of Recollection then with the
Days of Recollection now—as if I could really learn something
important by doing so. Really, I do not need to find those notes
and I know it. What I was writing then is just about the same as
what I am writing now. And yet I know too that somehow my
interior life is deeper and that I have more peace and that I am
closer to God and more under His control. But do not ask me
how I got there because I do not know. Solemn Profession, for
one thing, had much to do with it. I could make a long list of the
other graces God has given me: but I would never know how to
say whether I had made use of them. Somehow, with God's help,
they have not been fruitless.

October 12 SUNDAY

All the hills and woods are red and brown and copper, and the
sky is clear, with one or two very small clouds. A buzzard comes
by and investigates me, but I am not dead yet. This whole landscape of woods and hills is getting to be saturated with my
prayers and with the Psalms and with the books I read out here
under the trees, looking over the wall, not at the world but at
our forest, our solitude. Everything I see has become incomparably rich for me, in the years since I made my simple vows
and emerged from the novitiate.

This morning I was out there again reciting the 118th Psalm
and the Gradual Psalms by heart, looking at the hills. I am finishing my Psalters for the dead, and this is the last time round for
this year. I am finishing early. Five days more to go. We have
a month in which to say the Psalter ten times over. And I like it.
It means a great deal to me. When I am a priest I will no longer
be obliged to say the Psalters, because the priests say some Masses
instead. But I sometimes think I would like to go on saying a
few Psalters during the Tricenary anyway. But I will probably
no longer have the time.

What is the use of my complaining about not being a contemplative, if I do not take the opportunities I get for contemplation?
I suppose I take them, but in the wrong way. I spend the time

looking for something to read about contemplation—something to satisfy my raffish spiritual appetite—instead of shutting up and emptying my mind and leaving the inner door open for the Holy Spirit to enter from the inside, all the doors being barred and all my blinds down.

October 16

Two or three times this fall the local doctor has been here to give us all injections to keep away colds and the 'flu. Now we all have filthy colds. The choir cannot sing. Everything is awful. In the midst of this, the doctor showed up again today to give us injections to keep away colds and 'flu. He began to work just as we went to dinner. So we all got up from table and ran coughing and snorting to the infirmary to take the needle. I offered it up for Father Alberic, because before he died he was the one who used to sit there and wipe your arm with alky before the doctor stuck you.

We have had extra work all week and I was out the other day picking apples and broke the branch off one of the trees. But now I am again writing *The Waters of Siloe*.

When I first looked into the pages of "The Dedicated Life and Poetry" by Patrice de la Tour du Pin and saw so many words like "solitude" and "virginity," I became extremely interested. But on reading it more carefully it began to depress me a little. Clever and obscure language in a context that I do not quite grasp—all the traditional formulas of the contemplative life transplanted into a garden of flowers that are no longer any fun for me and fruits for which I have lost all taste. The dedicated life he talks about is evidently "dedicated" in his mind, but I cannot quite understand in what the dedication consists. I am living on the inside of a wall where such metaphors have ceased to make an impression. Dedication, for us, is not romance, it is routine.

Yet perhaps if I paid more attention to Patrice de la Tour du Pin I might discover something about my own writing problem —as long as I do not end up writing quite the way he does.

It is evening. Hot and stuffy. Good-by, fair elements, good-by.

"What if this present were the world's last night?"

October 19 SUNDAY

Today's offertory: *Vir erat in Terra Hus.** Dom Gueranger talks about it in the liturgical year and we have an *Offertoriale* here which Father Reinhold sent us. It has all the old additions and versicles that were suppressed in the thirteenth century. I sang them over, by myself. They are a bit operatic but very effective.

One thing about the eremitical life. It is *hard*. Saint Peter Damian is always urging monks to be converted from the free and easy life of monasteries to the "narrow way" of the hermitage.

Charles de Foucauld had a terribly hard life in the desert. One look at his picture will tell you all you need to know about it. His diet was so frugal that the two Tuaregs who helped him cultivate the dates in his oasis could not subsist on the things he ate.

And I think of how easy things are for me. A straw mattress on boards can be very comfortable. I have warm clothes. I do not even have to do my own cooking. There is enough to eat here. Perhaps it does not always taste wonderful, but you can be reasonably sure that you will get *something* when meal time comes.

I do not think I would have been able to lead the life of Peter Damian's hermits—the first Camaldolese. They fasted four or five times a week on bread and water, recited the whole Psalter twice a day, besides their office. And they went barefoot all winter—and their cells were in the Apennines.

Now a beautiful yellow rose bush has filled with flowers. They stand before me like something very precious in the late slanting sun as I write. The evening is very quiet. I can no longer hear Father Apollinaris exhorting the retreatants in the novitiate

*"There was a man in the land of Hus"—opening words of the Book of Job.

chapel, so no doubt his conference is over. One of those postulants is going to receive the habit.

The crosses in the cemetery are all absolutely motionless. And yet it is as though I had been expecting them to turn to me and speak.

October 26 FEAST OF CHRIST THE KING
To suffer the indignity of being a member of the human race, as distinguished from a soul fully liberated in Christ! But we are free, at any rate, in faith and hope.

I have been spending more time praying in church or just staying there with the Blessed Sacrament or in the chapel of Our Lady of Victories. The best thing I can do. Better than reading a lot of books I do not need to read.

Correcting page proofs for *Figures for an Apocalypse.* I am disgusted with it. Father Abbot gave me a guarded and partial permission to stop writing poetry "if it is a burden." But he wants me to go on "reaching souls." It seems I do not have permission to drop poetry altogether. Last night, singing the *Salve Regina,* what I thought was this: "Lady, if you want this dubious talent returned, I am happy to give it back."

I asked Reverend Father if any monks of our Order had received permission to become hermits in our time and to my surprise he said yes. The one from whom he inherited the name Frater Frederic, when he came to Gethsemani, had been a hermit out here in the hills somewhere. But as soon as he got in his hermitage, people from miles around came to consult him about their spiritual problems. He was very glad to get back to Gethsemani, which he had not found sufficiently silent.

One day a hermit from one of our monasteries in Canada came in from his hermitage and started to tell the Abbot how to run the monastery, so the Abbot excused himself for a moment and went out and told the Cellarer to go and set fire to the hermitage. Then he came back and listened patiently to the advice that he was being given for nothing. When the hermit went back to his hermitage there was nothing left of it. So he returned to the monastery.

November 1 ALL SAINTS DAY

Feast days always upset me a little. I have a hangover from the wild coffee we drank at mixt, and from the hours of chanting and ceremonies. There were great functions. Three simple professions in Chapter and Frater Erasmus, a gay and independent child of Memphis, Tennessee, made his solemn vows.

November 6

Here I come with blackberry seeds in my teeth, to write down in great haste the precious thoughts that have occurred to me during collation. It is nice, sitting in the refectory, dipping a chunk of bread into a dish of blackberry juice and listening to the silence. I prefer frugal meals, without reading.

On Sunday I had my eyes examined. There was a lot of rushing around during High Mass, and I became involved in it. The oculists were setting up their apparatus in Saint Gabriel's Room and one of the brothers nearly broke his neck trying to black out the window with a woolen blanket. As a reward for having joined in all this fuss, I was one of the first ones examined. They put drops in my eyes. They must have put drops in my mind too, because I was in a cloud of stupidity for the rest of the day.

After my eyes cleared, I went back to the galleys of the Mother Berchmans book. Having finished that job, I was all set to get back to work on *The Waters of Siloe*, which I have been trying to write all year, when a great scourge of God descended upon me. I have to produce an official souvenir for the centenary of the Abbey which we are probably going to celebrate next year or the year after. The foundation date is in December, and the hundredth anniversary will be in 1948, but apparently one cannot hold a sufficiently complicated celebration in December because it is just about Christmas time and you cannot at such a season muster a crowd large enough to upset the entire monastery for weeks before and after the event.

I made every effort to persuade Father Abbot that there was someone else in the monastery—as indeed there is—who would be able to turn out just the kind of spectacular album that would delight everybody. Reverend Father, however, listened to all I had to say and then told me sweetly that I was just the man for the job. Now I am punished in choir with mental images of layouts that everybody will detest—including myself. And so I offer my pride to be slain on this particular altar.

November 10

We sing the office of the Dedication of a Church, in commemoration of the Dedication of Saint John Lateran, the basilica where, for the first time, a picture of the Savior appeared painted on a wall and was seen by all the people. That made me glad, in the second Nocturn. It reminded me of the function of art in the life of faith. It spoke to me of the wisdom of the Church. Rome taught me something of that wisdom, fifteen years ago.

November 11   FEAST OF SAINT MARTIN

To discover the Trinity is to discover a deeper solitude. The love of the Three Divine Persons holds your heart in its strength and builds about you a wall of quiet that the noise of exterior things can only penetrate with difficulty. You no longer have to strive to resist the world or escape it: material things affect you little. And thus you use and possess them as you should, for you dominate them, in making them serve the ends of prayer and charity, instead of letting them dominate you with the tyranny of your own selfishness and cupidity.

November 13

FEAST OF ALL THE SAINTS OF THE ORDER

Today began Father Macarius' experiment with the theological conferences. They are doing a series on Saint Bernard's *De Gratia et Libero Arbitrio*. Much less dull than the talks on Tanquerey's Dogma. They have also moved the organ console into the middle of the lower row of choir-stalls on the Abbot's side of the church to see if the organists can manage to keep more or less with the choir which they certainly have not been able to do out of sight, around the corner of the transept.

Everybody is busy with ideas for the Centenary. I had to stick my nose into it, like an idiot. It would serve me right if I got some terrible job as a result. But I wanted at least to make the suggestion that we do some praying when the time came to celebrate our existence. And I hope against hope that the celebration will not go on for three days.

November 16

FEAST OF THE DEDICATION OF THE CHURCH

Even when I cannot think straight, God straightens me out as soon as I get a minute alone in church. It is good to go and pray even when you feel washed out. The mere effort makes you feel better. You are giving something of your silly self away, and that always nourishes you. And it is comforting to realize, "Even if I feel rotten, I don't want anything but God and His solitude. Health and sickness do not matter, *unum est necessarium.*"*

Mr. Gans or some other friend of the monastery sent the library a book of pictures of the Cloisters in New York—the Cuxa cloister and all the rest, up in Fort Tryon Park. I was looking at them after dinner and they made me happy, although I seemed to be considering a place utterly unfamiliar and new. Just as if I had not been saved in those cloisters. The pictures suggested nothing of a former life I might once have led, outside this monastery, in a city called New York.

Tomorrow is the ninth anniversary of my Baptism. Nine years ago this fall my happiest days were in those cloisters, even though they are only a museum. I say I have forgotten my former existence. That is not true: it is only the way I feel today. When I was writing a book about it I remembered everything quite well. And now, too, sometimes, in choir, details of some of the things one could not possibly write about in a book come back to me. And I do not even have the consolation of thinking of myself as having been a great sinner—only as an incomparably vile sinner, small and hateful, without any sense of indignity. Yet with all the things God did for me, in His mercy, when I was the thing I used to be, can I ever even wrinkle my forehead with the

*"One thing alone is necessary" (Luke, 10:42).

slightest suggestion of anxiety, for fear that He might fail to make me the saint He created me to be, that He came on earth for me to become? Or that He will fail to use me for the salvation of those He intends to bring to heaven through an instrument as worthless as I am? That is what gives Him the greatest glory—the achieving of great things through the weakest and most improbable means. He has leavened the whole earth with apostles that He scraped off pots in the kitchens of the Greeks—*omnium peripsema usque adhuc.**

November 16

So I am nine years old.

The chief thing that has struck me today is that I still have my fingers too much in the running of my own life.

Lord, I have not lived like a monk, like a contemplative. The first essential is missing. I only say I trust You. My actions prove that the one I trust is myself—and that I am still afraid of You.

Take my life into Your hands, at last, and do whatever You want with it. I give myself to Your love and mean to keep on giving myself to Your love—rejecting neither the hard things nor the pleasant things You have arranged for me. It is enough for me that You have glory. Everything You have planned is good. It is all love.

The way You have laid open before me is an easy way, compared with the hard way of my own will which leads back to Egypt, and to bricks without straw.

If You allow people to praise me, I shall not worry. If You let them blame me, I shall worry even less, but be glad. If You send me work I shall embrace it with joy and it will be rest to me, because it is Your will. And if You send me rest, I will rest in You. Only save me from myself. Save me from my own, private, poisonous urge to change everything, to act without reason, to move for movement's sake, to unsettle everything You have ordained.

*"We are made as the refuse of this world, the offscouring of all even until now" (I Cor., 4:13).

Let me rest in Your will and be silent. Then the light of Your joy will warm my life. Its fire will burn in my heart and shine for Your glory. This is what I live for. Amen, amen.

November 18

Today it rains, and I put on a winter shirt before the Night Office although it is not yet desperately cold. The other winter clothes have not yet been given out.

Another one of those "little magazines" has just come out. The first issue reached me today. Probably Father Abbot did not look at it too closely. All those magazines are alike. Second-rate stories, bad verse, and pretty good—or even very good—criticism. And the criticism is sharp and bitter. They are all rather pugnacious, mean, and ugly except for one or two that are superlatively well done.

November 20 EVE OF THE PRESENTATION

Even my contacts with the outside—with the world of writers and of people who publish and of people who insult one another for the sake of art—have their advantages. To see how seriously men take things and how little they profit by their seriousness. Their tragedy makes our mediocrity all the more terrible.

November 23

By God's mercy I have found someone in the monastery who is willing and able to help me produce something acceptable as a souvenir for the Centenary. This providential helper is Brother Theodoret, the baker, who is also an artist and an architect. He has plenty of time to do things while he is waiting for the dough to rise, and so he has a drawing-board in the bakery, on which he draws up plans for new monasteries. He did a lot of work on the Utah foundation, for instance. He understands layouts very well and knows a fair amount about type. And he has ideas. And he does not believe that God can be glorified by the solidified molasses which some people call religious art. Once in a while we have to talk to one another, but it is worth it.

Two letters from the Utah monastery are full of good news.

It is rare for us to get detailed news from a daughter house, still rarer to hear it read in the refectory. The monks in Utah seem to be happy. They are not in the Quonset monastery, because the men who were supposed to be building it for them went off deer-hunting. However they sit in their barracks with six inches of snow on the roof and Father Denis stokes the hot-air heating system and they keep the Rule, singing to God in their huts.

December 4

Two French Abbots and one priest are stopping here on their way to the Far East. One of them is little Dom Benoit, the Abbot of Notre Dame du Phare, on a headland near Hakodate, who was here with the General this summer. The other Abbot is Dom Marie Joseph Marquis, of Bricquebec. Bricquebec has charge of most of the houses in the Far East. He is going out there to see what condition they are in and to try to help the Chinese monks get established. We just heard, the other day, in the refectory, what had happened to the monks of Our Lady of Consolation. The story was read in the middle of the annual retreat. It had a terrific effect on us all.

The Reds took over the monastery in July, imprisoned the monks, and put them through a lot of staged trials, more or less as a public show. The usual Communist tactics: let the peasants sack the monastery, give them the impression that they are getting something out of it, try to make them feel that they have been outraged in the past and that now justice has been done. Then the monks are put through their routine, become living instruments of propaganda. Beatings, a whole litany of charges yelled at them over and over again, day after day, until everyone present gets thoroughly used to the idea that the monks are tools of capitalist imperialism in league with Wall Street, and the rest. One by one the monks begin to die off, they are carted around North China from village to village. They become the menagerie in a traveling circus. It is still going on. They are not all dead. Some of them were set free in October and got to Peiping. The story came through from them.

When this was being read in the refectory, some of the monks could hardly eat. The news did more to us than anything the retreat master could say to us in Chapter, although he is preaching a good retreat. How can you help seeing your vocation, and its obligations, in a new light when you realize that monks like yourself, with the same weaknesses, the same problems, the same difficulties, are suddenly called upon to suffer things that belong to the Acts of Martyrs?

We tend to think of "the martyrs" as men of a different stamp from ourselves, men of another age, bred in another atmosphere, men somehow stronger and greater than we. But it turns out that we too are expected to face the same sufferings and confess Christ and die for Him. We who are not heroes are the ones God is choosing to share the lot of His great warriors. And one look into our own souls tells us that there is nothing there that invites the combats of the mighty saints. There is nothing magnificent about us. We are miserable things and if we are called upon to die we shall die miserably. There is nothing of grandeur about us. We are null. And perhaps we are already marked for sacrifice—a sacrifice that will be, in the eyes of the world, perhaps only drab and sorry and mean. And yet it will end by being our greatest glory after all. Perhaps there is no greater glory than to be reduced to insignificance by an unjust and stupid temporal power, in order that God may triumph over evil through our insignificance.

At the end of the retreat I had suddenly lost all taste for becoming a Carthusian. As if the dead Chinese monks, in the naked seriousness of their martyrdom, had killed the roots of this spiritual self-indulgence in my soul. It is no longer permitted to me to waste, in such a dream, the precious hours of my monastic life, given me by God to prepare the way for His coming!

On my way up to see Dom Benoit, I ran into the young Swiss Abbot, Dom Marie Joseph, in a corridor of the guest house. I had a package of holy pictures in my hand—a few of those pious pictures that some people seem to love so much. Dom Marie

Joseph immediately began telling me how terrible these pictures were and I was so surprised and delighted that I nearly fell over backward. He said he had removed thirty bad statues out of monasteries that come under his jurisdiction. By now I was convinced that I must have a long conversation with him and made arrangements to do so. He said our whole Rule is the service of Christ the King: *Christo vero Regi militaturus*. Every month, for us, belongs to Our Lady.

We were talking about architecture and he said that Orval was good but that it was too big and that, as a matter of fact, the monks had to spend all their time sweeping and dusting the monument, and keeping it clean. Sénanque, he said, is only inhabited by one or two monks of the Medium Observance, who act as caretakers.

Twenty-five out of fifty men in his community were mobilized in the last war. Now that they are back he gives them all kinds of reading in the refectory that keeps them in touch with what is going on in the Church outside. He lets them hear about the social situation and what the Church is trying to do—priests in factories, and so on. He does not believe in monks forgetting their vital connection with the rest of the Mystical Body of Christ.

Other Orders have their functions, he said. Our vocation is to live life to the full—life in its perfection, and the secret of this is the complete gift of ourselves to God. It is not something that is achieved by a collection of ascetic practices.

Dom Lambert Beauduin, a Benedictine, preached a retreat for them recently at Bricquebec. He had studied monasticism deeply, at Monte Cassino, Mount Athos. He complimented the Cistercians on their closeness to Saint Benedict.

He said, too: our Rule is the Gospel. He wants his exposition of the Rule to be at the same time a commentary on Scripture. Scripture is not something that is given us to help us understand theology—on the contrary, Saint Thomas, Duns Scotus, should only lead us to Scripture, and in the word of God we enter into an immediate spiritual contact with the Word, Christ. On this point he was very good.

Benedictine life is perfectly simple. It is simply the Gospel. It liberates us from ourselves by enabling us to give ourselves entirely to God. The things he said about our life answered all the deepest needs and aspirations of my own spirit. He said all the things I would have wanted to say long ago if I had been able to discover, somehow, that they were the things I also wanted to be thinking.

Finally he told me about a Jewish woman, a doctor, one of three who survived from among three thousand prisoners in a Nazi concentration camp. In that camp she had been a member of a powerful Communist cell that had been formed among the prisoners. On her release, she began to discover that Communism could not begin to satisfy her. She made a pilgrimage to Lourdes walking barefoot across France. She found her way to the Church. He baptized her.

December 16   TUESDAY IN EMBER WEEK
Upstairs in the infirmary, old Brother Gregory lies dying. Most of the time he is unconscious, so that he cannot hear the guns, beyond the hills, at Fort Knox, tuning up for war.

Reverend Father took the two visiting Abbots to Georgia to show them the immense concrete foundations for the permanent Abbey at Conyers.

Today I finished dummying *Cistercian Contemplatives*. The dummy is a terrible mess and will shock the men who are preparing to do such nice printing for us in New York. I am happy at the thought that the book will look pretty.

Yesterday Robert Lowell's book, *Lord Weary's Castle*, reached me. It is wonderful. Harcourt, Brace made me a present of it after I had gone begging all around the town. Lowell is a poet, and practically the only poet in the country. I wish I could write an article about him. You could compare the "Quaker Graveyard" with Hopkins's "Wreck of the Deutschland," to the great advantage of "Graveyard." Lowell has little of Hopkins's spiritual depth but he is often more of a poet—more fluent and more finished. Hopkins is *too* finished. Lowell can be much more perfect than Hopkins because he leaves you with less sense of technical struggle. All the emotional intensity is there. Hopkins's spiritual struggles fought their way out in problems of rhythm. He made his asceticism bearable by thrusting it over the line into the order of art where he could handle it more objectively. When fortitude became a matter of sprung rhythm, he could keep his sufferings, for the time being, at arm's length.

The poems of Lowell that I like less are those written "After Rilke" and "After Valéry." He has his roots in New England and not in Europe, although I do not mean that he is in any sense provincial. He does not talk the language of Rilke or Valéry merely as a tourist. However, glad as I am to have him write like Valéry, I find him more completely satisfying when he talks about Boston as "my city." No immigrant could write as he writes about Boston. On the other hand there is nothing of the bad New England about him. I do not merely speak of Dutchland Farms, but also of "Lord-Geoffrey-Amherst-was-a-soldier-of-the-King." You would not dream of insulting the man by expecting to find a shadow of that in him, even though he has grown up in the thick of it. Perhaps I have made a *faux pas*. Harvard higher than Amherst.

Lowell makes a little bit go a long way—but he is always licit and healthy about the way he does it. In him, New England avarice is clean economy after all. I am surprised and happy. For instance he returns, I forget how many times, to the man in Dante who was rolled away by the torrent while two angels fought with billhooks for his soul.

December 18

Yesterday—Ember Wednesday—Brother Gregory died. All the abbots returned from Georgia and I was thurifer at the funeral. I found out I was to be thurifer just before Lauds. Not knowing whether or not they would bring the body down from the infirmary after Chapter, I went to check the thurible, as I would need it at once. There was no thurible. The brother novices had it in the scullery. One of them was cleaning it there. The chains were all tangled up in a knot. I got them straightened out, with the help of the Brother Undermaster, but fortunately there was no hurry after all. They brought the body down later in the morning.

I was appointed to watch by the body from twelve to twelve-thirty—during dinner. And it was a black fast day. The two who were appointed to relieve us sauntered in to take over some five or ten minutes late, having eaten their fill. We rushed off to the refectory. I was so hungry I was about ready to go straight in through the wall, instead of passing around and entering at the door.

It was like that all day.

Today has been beautiful. The sun shines, it is warm. There are neat little clouds up in the blue sky. The brown dirt is piled high on the grave of poor Brother Gregory, who turns out to have been Swiss. The reason why he used to limp was that one day a bull tossed him over a stone wall and nearly broke his back.

Brother Gregory was a saintly old man, and in his last years everything he did cost him so much effort that he seemed to lose himself completely in the intense business of getting around the stations of the Cross or moving from place to place in choir or climbing up the altar steps for Communion. He had a great hooked nose and went about bent almost double, without however accepting the use of a cane.

I asked Reverend Father what made Brother so saintly. I don't know what kind of answer I was hoping to get. It would have made me happy to hear something about a deep and simple spirit of prayer, something about unsuspected heights of faith, purity of heart, interior silence, solitude, love for God. Perhaps he had spoken with the birds, like Saint Francis.

Reverend Father answered very promptly: "Brother was always working," he said. "Brother did not even know how to be idle. If you sent him out to take care of the cows in the pasture, he still found plenty to do. He brought in buckets of blackberries. He did not know how to be idle."

I came out of Reverend Father's room feeling like a man who has missed his train.

December 21 FOURTH SUNDAY IN ADVENT

Yesterday Father Meinrad was ordained priest. I was candle-bearer and got a close view of everything. My own time is two years away and it seems like a hundred. What impressed me most? The prominence of Saint John Baptist in the liturgy of the day (Ember Saturday). Then the great amount of oil the Archbishop smeared on his hands, ordaining him. When the priests came into the sanctuary to lay their hands on the head of the new *ordinatus* I looked up and saw Father Kemper, S.J., from Cincinnati who preached a retreat here three or four years ago.

I also remembered how, five and a half years ago, when Father Meinrad first came to the monastery, I was appointed to be his guardian angel and show him how to get around. It was Paschal Time, and that day I could not get any sleep during the meridienne because I was so nervous, fearing that I might forget to hand him a book for the antiphon of the Little Office, when we went to choir for None. And then that afternoon we went out and spread manure around the cornfields of the middle bottom.

Dom Marie Joseph reads Léon Bloy and likes him, above all because he understands suffering. He let his novices, at least the ones who had been in the war, read *The Woman Who Was Poor*. However he thinks that Bloy was wrong in trusting Melanie and accepting her "secret revelation" at La Salette.

He told me that the Abbey Church at Bricquebec has been renovated by an architect who was a converted Communist on modern and functional lines. I would like to see some pictures of it. He also said that his secretary, who is an artist, is very fond of Picasso. So there is at least one Cistercian in the world, besides myself, who likes Picasso.*

We spoke about my writing and he said I must work for excellence and not for publication. He told me he wished I had a good theologian to guide me in my writing: someone who would be able to tell me without any hesitation what to write

---

*A Cistercian priest reading the manuscript scribbled in the margin that he too liked Picasso's "pink and blue periods."

and what not to write. And finally he told me to realize that I was working in union with others scattered throughout the Order and that I should go ahead confidently, aiming very high, loving and studying the Cistercian Fathers of the twelfth century.

December 25   CHRISTMAS MORNING

After Chapter, when I was hearing Mass, Father Prior sent me and Frater Erasmus to the refectory to sort out letters and cards. This year we got our Christmas mail on Christmas morning. By the time I got to the refectory I found that the place was crowded with monks putting out the mail. Those who have come to Gethsemani recently got a lot of letters. Those who came a long time ago got practically none at all. Brother Owen's mail—one letter or maybe two—came from Ireland. Others had only one or two from Germany and Italy. But Brother Tiburtius the gatekeeper got a big pile of cards from everywhere. So did Father Largus, who used to be a parish priest in Indiana and who seems to know, personally, every Carmelite in the United States of America. I got four cards and a letter from Granny in New Zealand.

Here outside the window of the Scriptorium is a monstrous temporary heating plant, living under a shed. It has a high tin smokestack and it looks like an ancient locomotive, pugnacious, and ready to run away on the slightest provocation, just in order to be nasty. The brother novices worked day and night to get this thing installed in time for Christmas because the old boiler was just about ready to blow up, and only the special Providence of heaven had so far kept it from sending us all sky-high. This new furnace sends hot water in through a window by pipes that are all wrapped up in tarpaper and other things I do not know how to name. And steam curls up around the windows of the Scriptorium.

I like it when the laybrothers serve the Midnight Mass. Last night, old Brother Anscar (who got very few letters this morning) was one of the acolytes. He came running up the altar steps, in his white beard, holding his right arm fully extended before him with a wine cruet in his hand. His left arm was swinging in the air.

Humble George, the Negro pilgrim, is here again for Christmas and immediately after the Consecration at the Dawn Mass, when everybody else was bowed down to the floor, he raised his arm in the air and made three huge signs of the cross in the direction of the high altar.

Outside, the fields are full of hard frost. It was cold in bed last night and I went to sleep with the Hymn of Lauds echoing in my heart:

> *Praesepe non abhorruit*
> *Foeno jacere pertulit*
> *Parvoque lacte pastus est*
> *Per quem nec ales esurit.**

December 28 FEAST OF THE HOLY INNOCENTS

The perfection of twelfth-century Cistercian architecture is not to be explained by saying that the Cistercians were looking for a new technique. I am not sure that they were looking for a new technique at all. They built good churches because they were looking for God. And they were looking for God in a way that was pure and integral enough to make everything they did and everything they touched give glory to God.

We cannot reproduce what they did because we approach the problem in a way that makes it impossible for us to find a solution. We ask ourselves a question that they never considered. How shall we build a beautiful monastery according to the style of some past age and according to the rules of a dead tradition? Thus we make the problem not only infinitely complicated but we make it, in fact, unsolvable. Because a dead style is dead. And the reason why it is dead is that the motives and the circumstances that once gave it life have ceased to exist. They have given place to a situation that demands another style. If we were intent upon loving God rather than upon getting a Gothic

---

*"He did not despise the manger / Nor did He refuse to sleep in straw / And He who does not permit the smallest bird to go hungry / Was Himself nourished with a little milk."

church out of a small budget we would soon put up something that would give glory to God and would be very simple and would also be in the tradition of our fathers. That is why the best-looking buildings around Gethsemani are the barns. Nobody stopped to plan a Gothic barn, and so they turned out all right. If they had built the gatehouse on the same principles as the hog house it would have been beautiful. Actually it is hideous.

However, the twelfth-century Cistercians took good care to be architects. Saint Bernard sent Achard of Clairvaux out to study the village churches of Burgundy and see how they were built. And it is true that there was a clean kind of mysticism in the air of the age that made everything beautiful. One of the big problems for an architect in our time is that for a hundred and fifty years men have been building churches as if a church could not belong to our time. A church has to look as if it were left over from some other age. I think that such an assumption is based on an implicit confession of atheism—as if God did not belong to all ages and as if religion were really only a pleasant, necessary social formality, preserved from past times in order to give our society an air of respectability.

PART TWO

Death of an Abbot

This was a year of transition. The publication of The Seven
Storey Mountain *at the end of the summer brought a change in
my whole life. I still do not know how much of a change it was.
The reason why I do not quite understand what it means for
an obscure Trappist to become "an author" is that the thing
has almost never happened before. True, it had happened to
one of the other Fathers in the monastery but in an altogether
different way. And in any case we have no communication
with one another. When a man becomes "an author" in the
world outside, he adapts himself comfortably to the situation by
imitating the other authors he meets at parties. An author in a
Trappist monastery is like a duck in a chicken coop. And he
would give anything in the world to be a chicken instead of
a duck.*

*The way I have adapted myself to the fact that I am an author
is to forget that I am one, to act as if I had never written a book,
and to treat* The Seven Storey Mountain *as if it were the work
of somebody else. This is not completely reasonable or even
possible. But it keeps me from taking too seriously the letters
that sometimes reach me from people who say the book means
a lot to them. I love the people who say this, because they are
sincere and because they are after all giving glory to God and
not to me. The letters they write are mostly about God and*

about their rediscovery of a thing called hope, which almost seems to have died in the world they live in. This much is serious. But I do not have to delude myself that because they love God I am somehow important. The only thing I need to remember is my own greater obligation to find God and to lose myself in Him because He alone is important.

I suppose, since I was the author of the book, I must take responsibility for The Seven Storey Mountain. *But there was one man who was in a certain sense even more responsible for that book than I was, even as he was the cause of all my other writing. That man was Dom Frederic Dunne, my spiritual Father, the Abbot who had received me as a postulant, who had given me the habit of novice one cold Sunday in Lent when he himself was nearly dying of pneumonia, who had received me to simple and to solemn profession. It was Dom Frederic who had formed and shaped my whole monastic destiny. It was he, together with my novice master, Dom Robert, who decided that I should write books. It was he who firmly and kindly encouraged me and indeed ordered me to continue, in spite of my own misgivings. At the same time, he continued patiently and wisely to show me, in every way that he could, that this writing was not supposed to interfere with my life of prayer. On the contrary, it demanded a life of more intimate union with God on my part. And so, although I sometimes failed to see how this was possible, I now realize that Dom Frederic not only "made" me as a writer, but that he disposed my life, under the guidance of Divine Providence, in such a way that I had a greater opportunity to become a contemplative at Gethsemani. For Dom Frederic, though he was a very busy man, hated anything that savored of compromise. A monk, in his eyes, had to be a real monk—a man of prayer and a man of God. He could not abide activism and a secular spirit masking under a cowl.*

I really think Dom Frederic was more interested in The Seven Storey Mountain *than I was. He felt that God had been very good to me. He was glad that the book might find a way to convince men of the reality of God's love for us. In the ardor of his own charity, he seemed to sense, in a way that I did not, something of the effect the book might have. And he was happy, because it was precisely for this that he had made me write books.*

I shall never forget the simplicity and affection with which he put the first copy of the book in my hand. He did not say anything. He just handed me the book, amused at my surprise. But I knew that he was happier about it than I could ever be.

A few days later, he was telling me to go on writing, to love God, to be a man of prayer and humility, a monk and a contemplative, and to help other men penetrate the mystery of the love of God. It was the last time I ever spoke to him or saw him alive, because that night he died. He took the night train to Georgia. He had a bad heart. Twice before something had grabbed at his life and tried to put it out, when he was on journeys. The same things had happened in the monastery too. Finally, in the small hours of the morning of August 4th, death succeeded, and took him away, when he was on a Southern train, in the mountains of Tennessee.

Dom Gabriel Sortais, who was then the Vicar General of the Order, was in Canada. He was coming to Gethsemani anyway, to make the Regular Visitation. He arrived in time for Dom Frederic's funeral, and presided over the election of the new Abbot, Dom James Fox, who was installed immediately after the election.

The days when Dom Gabriel was at Gethsemani, in August 1948, were busy and eventful days for me since I had to do some interpreting and secretarial work for him. He does not speak English. It was because of this that I went out of the monastery for the first time in seven years and accompanied the Vicar General on an errand of charity in Louisville.

We drove into town with Senator Dawson, a neighbor of the monastery, and all the while I wondered how I would react at meeting once again, face to face, the wicked world. I met the world and I found it no longer so wicked after all. Perhaps the things I had resented about the world when I left it were defects of my own that I had projected upon it. Now, on the contrary, I found that everything stirred me with a deep and mute sense of compassion. Perhaps some of the people we saw going about the streets were hard and tough—with the naive, animalistic toughness of the Middle West—but I did not stop to observe it because I seemed to have lost an eye for merely exterior detail and to have discovered, instead, a deep sense of respect and love and pity for the souls that such details never fully reveal. I went through the city, realizing for the first time in my life how good are all the people in the world and how much value they have in the sight of God.

After that I returned to the peaceful routine of monastic life—I had only left it for six hours!—and the autumn descended upon Gethsemani. The cool weather came. Dom James, our new Abbot, went off to the General Chapter, and everyone settled down to wonder what kind of Abbot he would turn out to be.

For the first time this year it has been warm enough to sit out-side. After dinner I sat in the sun and read T. S. Eliot's "East Coker" and part of "The Dry Salvages" from *Four Quartets*. Eight years ago when we were at the cottage at Olean, Nancy Flagg had "East Coker" in ms., for it was still not published. We all said we didn't like it, but today I like it quite a lot except that I paused a bit at two or three lines of archaic English. I was surprised to find him drawing so heavily on Saint John of the Cross; I do not immediately see how it fits in. And in the second section I was brought up short by "That was a way of putting it" and the other self-conscious passage. Maybe I'll see the point later. But the beginning is fine and the rhymed sections are very beautiful—as beautiful as anything that has been written in English for fifty years or more.

> Thunder rolled by the rolling stars
> Simulates triumphal cars
> Deployed in constelled wars
> Scorpion fights against the Sun
> Until the Sun and Moon go down
> Comets weep and Leonids fly
> Hunt the heavens and the plains
> Whirled in a vortex that shall bring
> The world to that destructive fire
> Which burns before the ice-cap reigns.

I think this book is the best of Eliot. Also I admire Eliot's literary chastity. He is not afraid to be prosaic, rather than write bad verse. But when he is very prosaic he is weak. However, a word like "grimpen" can liven up the prose. Then when he comes to the part,

> Do not let me hear
> Of the wisdom of old men but rather of their folly

it becomes poetry again.

> The wounded surgeon plies the steel
> That questions the distempered part

is maybe the best of the whole thing, not only beautiful but deep and precise and poignant. It makes a good contrast with the cosmic bit about the triumphal cars in heaven—here everything that was then big, vast, universal, is brought down to the pointed, the moral, and the human. The heavens are indifferent, but here are real wounds in a real moral order. A real death.

> The chill ascends from feet to knees
> The fever sings in mental wires . . .

(And I think of Dylan Thomas's "The pleasure bird sings in the hot wires" but it is the same fever.) As a poet, I have got to be sharp and precise like Eliot—or else quit.

March 15

When I had begun to write all that yesterday, Father Placid who is retreat-master this year called me in to Father Prior because somebody was in the guest house all full of Marx and Freud and Kant. He wanted to argue. I was glad not to have to do so.

March 16

At Communion it is Christ in the garden Who prays in me. I don't feel like writing any more.

The Easter moon is up—thin and pale. Last night much rain. There are puddles to be seen, but not big ones. The rain drops off the window above me and lands on my head in choir. Mark Van Doren wrote a beautiful letter about *Figures for an Apoc-*

alypse, full of sympathy for the problem of poetry vs. contemplation. At the beginning of the year he wrote another, with the same sympathy for the problem of solitude.

They are painting the dormitory and we all shift around from cell to cell as the paint comes after us. The brown paint they put on the floor is like the stuff you see on the decks of tug boats and when you get to bed you feel as if you were going on board a tramp steamer.

I am reading over the manuscript of *The Waters of Siloe* and cannot tell whether or not it is dull.

Today in the Epistle an angel took up Habacuc by the top of the head and carried him to Babylon that the dinner he had prepared for the harvesters might be given to Daniel in the lions' den. And when they took Daniel out of the den and threw in his accusers, the lions ate them up quick. But in Jeremias I read how the bones of kings and priests are to be taken and scattered from their tombs and laid bare to the moon and stars that they had worshiped.

"They shall cast out the bones of the kings of Juda and the bones of the princes thereof and the bones of the priests and the bones of the prophets . . . out of their graves. And they shall spread them abroad to the sun and the moon and all the host of heaven whom they have loved and whom they have served and after whom they have walked and whom they have sought and adored; they shall not be gathered and they shall not be buried; they shall be as dung upon the face of the earth."

"Woe is me for my soul hath fainted because of them that are slain."

March 19 SAINT JOSEPH

I spend the anniversary of my solemn profession in the infirmary —a piece of great kindness on the part of Saint Joseph as I am beginning to realize. It has all the earmarks of a plot arranged for no other purpose than to give me a little recollection on this feast and make it a very happy one.

As soon as I get into a cell by myself I am a different person! Prayer becomes what it ought to be. Everything is very quiet.

The door is closed but I have the windows open. It is warm—gray clouds fly—all night and all day the frogs sing. Reverend Father sold all the ducks (Father Simon Stylites kept proclaiming the Duck Brothers in the Chapter of faults because the ducks quacked all night) and it is an improvement.

This is the way I happened to come to the infirmary. Tuesday I got a cold. It was warm and damp and when I walked into the church to pray in the afternoon interval before work something got in my throat and I have been coughing a lot. That night in the dormitory was no fun nor was the one after. Finally yesterday morning, Thursday, I came up to Father Gerard and found out I had a slight temperature—99 or so. Later it got worse. Yesterday was full of penance. I tried to finish going over the manuscript of *The Waters of Siloe*, and finally left it in a good enough condition to be sent off. Reverend Father told me to go up to the infirmary again toward the end of the afternoon work and since by that time the thermometer was up to 101 they put me to bed in the room marked Saint Gertrude. I was in this same room six years ago today—with the same thing: 'flu. It is the one Brother Hugh died in.

However, it does not look as though I am going to stay long.

But even with your eyes aching and your head spinning, how good it is to be alone, in silence.

How close God is in this room! The presence of people around me is always something that divides my attention between the world and God: well, not always either. At meditation or after Communion in church I generally don't know that anyone else is there. But in the intervals—people moving about are a distraction.

To have nothing to do but abandon yourself to God and love God! Silence and solitude are the supreme luxuries of life!

Anyway I woke up about the time the bell was ringing for Lauds. I was soaked in sweat and that meant most of the fever was gone. I lay awake and listened to the frogs.

How this silence keeps claiming you for itself! As soon as you start anything it says: "Come back for a moment! Pray! Be quiet! Rest in your God."

Plenty of time. Plenty of time. No manuscripts, no typewriter, no rushing back and forth to church, no Scriptorium, no breaking your neck to get things done before the next thing happens.

I went down to Chapter because Reverend Father wants you to go to Chapter if your temperature is less than 100. Mine was. Father Apollinaris preached vehemently on the sufferings of Saint Joseph—his mental sufferings when he discovered that Mary was with child. I should not have made funny faces when Fr. Apollinaris said Abraham was born 1959 years after the creation of the world, nor can I figure out why he imagined that this event should be commemorated next year—1949. But he says things like that; they come into his head and he says them.

Then I came back to the cell. On the table were bread and butter and a can of barley coffee, and before I said the *Largitor* Father Gerard came in with the bottle of Mass wine in which much was left because Father Odo could not say Mass. And he said "This is a *feast* day" and poured out half a tumbler of wine. He was not aware of any anniversary of mine, but it was then that I realized what was going on—and that Saint Joseph had arranged all this as a way of giving me some manifestations of God's love, and that I might have joy.

So I drank the wine and it was good and it gave me back my appetite, for last night butter was hateful and I could not eat it.

Then I moved the table to the window and ate looking out of the window as the Carthusians do. The clouds flew, and the huts of the ducks were empty and the frogs sang in the beautiful green pond.

Now it is evening. The frogs still sing. After the showers of rain around dinner time the sky cleared. All afternoon I sat on the bed rediscovering the meaning of contemplation—rediscovering God, rediscovering myself—and the office, and Scripture and everything.

It has been one of the most wonderful days I have ever known in my life, and yet I am not attached to that part of it either. Any pleasure or the contentment I may have got out of silence and solitude and freedom from all care does not matter. But I know that is the way I ought to be *living:* with my mind and senses silent, contact with the world of business and war and community troubles severed—not solicitous for anything high or low or far or near. Not pushing myself around with my own fancies or desires or projects—and not letting myself get hurried off my feet by the excessive current of natural activity that flows through the universe with full force.

March 20 OUR LADY OF SORROWS

I feel as if I were in a hotel in Cuba. The landscape has something of the gray-green-yellow nondescript color that belongs to Cuba. And the air is full of the sound of birds and water frogs and tree frogs—and crows too. As for those frogs, as I lay awake last night for several hours listening to them I began to get a bit bored with their lyricism. They are inexhaustible—and ring those same bicycle bells all day and all night. I began to think—don't they ever *do* anything—don't they even stop to eat? Then when I was just about to fall asleep they all stopped for thirty seconds and the silence was so astonishing that I woke up.

I woke up when the bell rang for the Night Office at 2:00 and got up at 3:30, but it turns out that I stay up here for today.

March 21 PALM SUNDAY

Palm Sunday on the Feast of Saint Benedict, 850 years to the day, from the foundation of Citeaux—for some time I got away from the frogs. Now I am back with them. The landscape is nice. White fluffy clouds. Late afternoon sky. Brother feeds the chickens. And for a wonder the frogs are all quiet. . . .

During the High Mass I kept thinking of the Christ Who is crucified in His Body—His enemies armed against Him in Europe and His voice singing in our church in Kentucky—*Deus, Deus meus ut quid dereliquisti me* . . .*

Unbelievably peaceful, here! I think of the church the way it was at the end of Benediction and the priest setting the monstrance back on the altar and all the brothers and monks getting

*"God, my God, why hast Thou forsaken me?"

up off their knuckles on the floor and some sunlight coming in on the newly varnished floor.

March 22 MONDAY IN HOLY WEEK

Last Saturday I sent the manuscript of *The Waters of Siloe* to Naomi Burton and another to the Censor at Our Lady of the Valley. I got Father George to bless the manuscript, which he did. It is a wonder it didn't explode, after the things I said about De Rancé.

Holy Week—well, there goes the bell ringer to ring his bell.

March 28 EASTER SUNDAY

Post transitum maris rubri
Christo canamus principi.

When we sang the *Benedicamus Domino* with two *alleluias* at the end of Lauds it seemed to me as if only three days had passed since we sang it the Saturday before Septuagesima, two months ago.

All the Easter *alleluia* antiphons come back to me with rich associations of the happiest days in my life—the seven Paschal seasons that I have had in the monastery—this being the seventh now beginning. The Sabbatical.

All the apple trees came out in blossom Good Friday. It rained and got colder but today is very bright, with a pure, pure sky. The willow is full of green. Things are all in bud.

On these big feasts you come out on top of a plateau in the spiritual life to get a new view of everything. Especially Easter. Easter is like what it will be entering eternity when you suddenly, peacefully, clearly recognize all your mistakes as well as all that you did well—everything falls into place.

In the library I looked at the marvelous book *The Faces of the Saints*—pictures as near as possible genuine portraits—contemporary—of saints. Mosaics of the Fathers were some of the most beautiful. Saint Catherine of Siena, too, and another I have forgotten. More modern ones—some of the death masks frighten me. Saint Vincent de Paul looks very real—very much of a Gascon peasant, and tough as he can be, terrific energy in his face, fiery black eyes, and a mouth like a bear trap. The one that most astonished me was Saint Francis de Sales—ponderous and unlike anything I would have imagined.

One that most impressed me—Saint Benedict Joseph Labre. One that scared me least—John Bosco. Also Saint Catherine of Genoa looked nice and normal for a mystic, and Louise de Marillac was a French housewife in her picture. Saint Mary Magdalen de Pazzi looked a little like my mother. Saint Aloysius Gonzaga was almost too beautiful. Saint Teresa was funny—a plump little Spanish lady, like an innkeeper's wife in that picture, with all due respect, but I love her. Saint John of the Cross I knew; looks surprisingly un-ascetic. The saint's face that to me is most completely the face of a saint is the child's face of Saint Francis of Assisi with big astonished eyes looking out from that over-ample hood—the thirteenth-century portrait.

Some saints I had never heard of I wanted to love as soon as I saw their pictures, like St. Catherine of Ricci. All of them had faces that had suffered: some more, some less, some very intensely.

One very sad thing: a plane crashed in our woods yesterday afternoon about two o'clock. Six people all killed, terribly mangled, bodies cut to pieces and then burned—a woman's hand up in a tree—two children in the wreck. They were going somewhere for Easter—just getting near Louisville. What a terrible Easter for some family—or two families! All day at the Collect I thought about them, and hoped they had found mercy with God.

April 4   LOW SUNDAY. DAY OF RECOLLECTION
We prayed for fair weather for our planting and lo, today was the fairest I ever saw. Clear sky and warm sun and when you came out of church and looked through the open cloister windows you saw the pale green flowers on the maples in the *préau* and all the shrubs in flower too.

During the week they lighted the orchard heaters to fight the frost and the farm looked like a valley in hell, until dawn when they put them out again and the pipes smoked as the sun rose on the hoar-fields, and the monastery smelled faintly of gasoline.

Father Cantor got a bad throat and I was cantor for three days. The first day I was unprepared and made a lot of mistakes. I had not realized that some of the Easter Week Masses were difficult—I knew all the *alleluias* because I had practiced them before.

Lambs bleat under the cedars by the sheep barn and the other day we looked at all the little pigs running around on the hillsides and charging upon the teats of their huge mothers.

More nourishment and strength in one hour of obscurity than in ten weeks of typewriting and reading and thinking. Nevertheless, every day love corners me somewhere and surrounds me with peace without my having to look very far or very hard or do anything special. God is Who He is and therefore my life needs nothing else but Him.

April 7   S A I N T   J O A C H I M

All our prayers for dry weather were not answered as fast as we thought for it has been raining cats and dogs for two days. Yesterday with hailstones hitting the windows like a war I finished the pamphlet on contemplation and today Father Macarius the censor made me signs that he was not pleased with it *at all.* Over the two feast days—Saint Benedict and the Annunciation, both transferred—I got practically no sleep—three hours and no meridiennes—and on Saint Benedict's day Father Cantor's voice went off again and I had to take over the choir.

For some reason *Commonweal* wants me to review Osuna's *Third Spiritual Alphabet* which appeared four hundred years ago.

Tonight was the first time in the six years I have been here that we sang the hymn for Saint Joachim. Usually his Vespers are eclipsed by Saint Joseph and Saint Benedict. I discovered only after Vespers that I had never seen the hymn before. Time came for me to give it out and I wondered, "What do all those black marks on the red lines mean?" So I gave it out wrong and went and fell on my face under the sanctuary lamp and offered up the *Magnificat* in thanksgiving.

April 25   SAINT MARK
The two volumes of Marcel Aubert on Cistercian architecture in France finally arrived. Father Anselme Dimier got them for us, and it is a wonderful book. Then I sent *The Spirit of Simplicity* off to the printer.

Thursday I went out and got a big blister on the palm of my hand digging mud out of a ditch along the west side of the upper bottom and everything was beautiful. The spring is in its first stages of transformation. All the trees are full of small leaves just beginning to unfold and work themselves out into something and there are flowers in the ditches and along the edges of the woods—and in the woods too, I suppose, but I haven't been there.

The more selfish you are, the more involved life becomes. As usual I have to check my appetite for books and work and keep close to God in prayer. Which is what He wants.

April 28
When Dom Eugene, the Abbot of Aiguebelle, was here I heard for the first time of the apparitions of Our Lady at Tre Fontane and at Bonate. At the moment, in the refectory, Father Cantor is trying to read a translation written by Father Odo, of an account of the Tre Fontane apparition. It is all on bits of brown wrapping paper and Father Odo's hand must be getting very shaky because there are a lot of long pauses in the reading.

Second set of galley proofs of *The Seven Storey Mountain*—up to about the middle. This thing is going very slow. It looks better with cuts and I cut some more, but not much.

It seems to me the most absurd thing in the world to be upset because I am weak and distracted and blind and constantly make mistakes! What else do I expect! Does God love me any less because I can't make myself a saint by my own power and in my own way? He loves me more because I am so clumsy and helpless without Him—and underneath what I am He sees me as I will one day be by His pure gift and that pleases Him—and therefore it pleases me and I attend to His great love which is my joy.

May 2

Wind and sun. Catbird bickering in a bush. Ringing bells and blowing whistles and then squawking in a lamentable fashion. Trees are all clothed and benches are out and a new summer has begun.

May 6 ASCENSION

Yesterday Father Macarius and I went out and blessed the fields, starting with the wheat and oats and coming around by Saint Bernard's field and Aidan Nally's and across to the bottoms. Out in the calf pasture we blessed some calves who came running up and took a very active interest in everything. Then we blessed pigs, who showed some interest at first. The sheep showed no concern and the chickens ran away as soon as we approached. The rabbits stayed quiet until we threw holy water at them and then they all jumped.

May 17 WHIT-MONDAY

A beautiful Pentecost.

O God, do not let me take away from You the time that belongs to You in contemplation.

May 22 EMBER SATURDAY

A tremendous bright sky. I let the warm sun shine on my back. The hills were wonderful. All the green of green things is clean and dark and fresh and the sun is so high on the ecliptic that the shadows of things are right under them. And under my feet is the richness of all the new crushed limestone or whatever it is that has been put on all the paths in the garden.

A little old man from Cincinnati, who is supposed to be printing *The Spirit of Simplicity*, was down here and we had some consultations and fingered paper samples and I pray for the pictures of Fontenay to hurry up and come from France.

(The clock strikes eleven. How clean the bell sounds in this quiet air!)

O God, I am happy to be in Your house! *Dilexi decorem domus tuae. Unum petii a Domino, hanc requiram, ut inhabitem in domo Domini omnibus diebus vitae meae.*

I am reading the Aubert book on *Cistercian Architecture* and it is fine. And I think of those monasteries. I am trying to figure out whether or not a village church Father and I looked at near Lexos was Beaulieu abbey.

I think that the church of Valmagne must have been big—for that part of the country. I think of how they ran the river through Clairvaux and Sénanque. I like the name of Vauluisant and the site of Valcroissant (in the Alps of the Drôme) and something fascinates me about Flaran. At Clairvaux, Saint Bernard's secretary worked in a cell under the dormitory stairs. The brothers had their own refectory next to the *Cellarium.* The guests had their own chapel. Fontenay must have been more influential than we think because the church at Kirkstall, in Yorkshire, was a copy of it.

Yet Royaumont and Ourscamp do not impress me. They were too fancy. I like l'Éscale Dieu in the Pyrenees and I think of the founders of Bonnefont-en-Comminges who had a hard time. They were all slow in building—from fifty to a hundred years in finishing the abbeys usually—and so during the twelfth century our saints all developed in half finished monasteries.

Silvacane is another one that intrigues me—down in the Rhone estuary.

And I wonder whether to believe the story that the monks of Leonçel moved out to a grange in a lower altitude—a warmer valley—in winter time?

I am second servant of the Refectory, and soon I will have to say None and go and put out the soup.

May 30 DAY OF RECOLLECTION

I just upset the whole house by spilling half a bottle of ink on our cowl and then running to Reverend Father for ink eradicator which didn't work and then trying to get another cowl from somewhere. . . . Father Modestus had an extra one because he preaches to the guests, and he lent it to me. It was in the room where he is making a shiny model of the new monastery in Utah to dazzle all the guests that come for the Centenary.

I have a hard time trying to imagine what it is going to mean for me to become a priest. Sometimes I am terrified at the thought. Ultimately the only solution to that problem is obedience. I go ahead under obedience. If my Superiors want me to be a priest, it is at least safe. God wants it and He will do me good by it although it may contain an unimaginable death.

Sometimes I want to run away and be a tramp and hang around on the roads without anything, like Humble George or Saint Benedict Joseph Labre.

June 6

Third Sunday after Pentecost—we are in the plain post-pentecostal liturgy and that always makes me happy. I have been reading the *Book of Kings* and understand that the life of the twelfth-century monks was by no means dull. They lived on the Bible. Those books fulfill all the instincts to which movies appeal much better than the movies themselves. And like Saint Teresa I like David "*et omnis mansuetudinis ejus.*"

Over and over again I have read Saint John of the Cross and seemed to understand him and yet the most elementary notions he teaches have failed to sink into my life. But all right, they gradually will. And that fact—I mean my blindness—is part of the poverty I want to love for the glory of God. I must not act as if I could somehow possess the secret of some knowledge or some technique for arriving at the possession of God.

I tell Him I do not care if He does not want me to be a priest. I leave that to Him.

And about books—the ones I write—let Him take care of them. I am not obliged to think about all that—except when the proofs come.

They gave me some kind of award for being a poet and it made me unhappy. But I want to be nice about it for the sake of those who wanted to be good to me in that way.

I wouldn't mind being recognized as a poet if I really were a *poet.*

But it gives me comfort to read poets who are poets. Eliot's "Little Gidding," and Robert Lowell.

. . . the flies, the flies of Babylon.

June 13   FOURTH SUNDAY AFTER PENTECOST
It is quiet. The birds sing and I hear the rams and the lambs and it is the Feast of Saint Anthony of Padua. I write (during the week) *Seeds of Contemplation,* and doing it I work more peacefully even if the work—to which I am attached—is interrupted by many errands.

Retreats in full swing. A Negro postulant for the laybrothers—looks good but today I was scared the place was getting him down—he was all hunched up at the *Asperges* procession.

June 16
Yesterday morning I woke up about one with the conviction that I had been singing the *Veni Creator Spiritus* very loudly in my sleep.

Then in the refectory were read Clare Boothe Luce's reactions to Freud in her articles on her conversion. It was rather curious to hear all that being read to an audience of monks—including Freud's notion of dream symbolism. They mostly laughed heartily but probably did not quite grasp the implications. On the whole I think it will do Trappists no harm to have heard about Freud, although the little there was probably won't have much effect on them one way or the other except to give them the complacent notion that psychoanalysis is much more crazy than it actually is.

Personally I have always felt that a clearer understanding of the subconscious mind would help priests to be better spiritual directors.

June 20   FIFTH SUNDAY AFTER PENTECOST
Bob Giroux had somebody do an index to *The Seven Storey Mountain*—the most peculiar collection of names you ever saw.

Starts off with Abbot, Father, and goes on to Advent; Adler, Alfred; Ellington, Duke; Fields, W. C.; but Smith, Pete is followed by Smith, Robert Paul, and there is Bob O'Brien the plumber at Olean House and Pierrot the teamster at Saint Antonin and the Privats at Murat and Brother Fabian who went to Georgia and Mary Jerdo, and Helen Freedgood, and Burton, Jinny and Flagg, Nancy and Wells, Peggy. (Peggy wrote to me from Hollywood the other day. I can't figure out if she is acting as well as writing.)

I was fascinated. The index is beautiful. It is like the gathering of all the people I have known at a banquet to celebrate the publication of the book—and it is like a pledge that they will all belong to me somehow as trophies in heaven—or I will belong to some of *them* as a trophy. Blake, William; Francis of Assisi, Saint; Bonaventure, Saint; Aquinas, Saint Thomas; Bernard, Saint. I think this index is a partial, optimistic preview of the General Judgment with the four Marx Brothers among the sheep.

So God is very good. *Sanctus in omnibus operibus suis.** Though the natural pleasure of success sickens me a little and I get smoke in my eyes from thinking about how the book will look, still I have to take all that on the chin and stay as tranquil and detached as God's grace will grant me to do.

June 24 FEAST OF SAINT JOHN BAPTIST
The heat has got us and we change our torn shirts and hang them out in the sun for the sweat to dry out of them, and we sleep in work blouses. Since the floor was painted I ended up with a cell next to a window. . . .

This is a great and happy feast. Yesterday, the vigil, was beautiful, and today, the Feast, is beautiful. God talks in the trees. There is a wind, so that it is cool to sit outside. This morning at four o'clock in the clean dawn sky there were some special clouds in the west over the woods, with a very perfect and delicate pink, against deep blue. And a hawk was wheeling over the trees.

We pushed the psalms a little in the Night Office, or rather *I* did, and the Head Cantor let me get away with it. The organist

*"Holy in all His works."

put up the tone a little and for once the office was bright and lively and the angelus rang at five to four instead of about five or ten after!

And the Epistle moves me—*Servus meus es tu Israel—posui te ut sagittam electam*—and the Kings and Princes shall rise up and adore God . . . And I think we need another Saint John Baptist to come in the spirit and power of Elias. Last week I was reading about Elias in the third *Book of Kings,* how he hid his head and covered his face when he heard God speak to him in a small voice. Deep tranquillity. But I am not poor. When I read the beginning of the *Ascent of Mount Carmel* I realize that my spiritual life hasn't even begun.

> *Para venir a saber lo todo,*
> *No quieras saber algo en nada . . .*
> *Para veni a ser lo todo,*
> *No quieras ser algo en nada . . .*
> *Para venir a lo que no gustas*
> *Has de ir por lo que no gustas . . .* *

Every minute life begins all over again. Amen.

July 2 FEAST OF THE VISITATION

Last evening, on the vigil of the feast, we had an unusually long interval after collation. It was a fast day, and so we weren't long in refectory in the evening and got out early. Since the sun was higher than it usually is in that interval I saw the country in a light that we usually do not see. The low-slanting rays picked out the foliage of the trees and high-lighted a new wheatfield against the dark curtain of woods on the knobs, that were in shadow. It was very beautiful. Deep peace. Sheep on the slopes behind the sheep barn. The new trellises in the novitiate garden leaning and sagging under a hill of roses. A cardinal singing

---

*In order to arrive at knowing the All
Desire to know nothing in anything . . .
In order to arrive at being All
Desire to be nothing in anything . . .
In order to come to that for which you have no taste
You must go by the way of that for which you have no taste

suddenly in the walnut tree, and piles of fragrant logs all around the woodshed waiting to be cut in bad weather.

I looked at all this in great tranquillity, with my soul and spirit quiet. For me landscape seems to be important for contemplation; anyway, I have no scruples about loving it.

Didn't Saint John of the Cross hide himself in a room up in a church tower where there was one small window through which he could look out at the country?

On the Feast of Saints Peter and Paul the first copy of *Exile Ends in Glory* arrived. So much was cut (and wisely so!) that it is a thinner book than I had expected.

There is certainly nothing in it to get excited about except the faults which are numerous enough to make me try to practice the sixth degree of humility. *Omni vilitate vel extremitate contentus sit monachus . . .* * Well, Dom Benoit told me, *"Il faut goûter les humiliations."*† I am smacking my lips over the second chapter of *Exile*. It is one of the worst pieces of cheese that has ever been served in our refectory or any other.

Anyway, it is being read in the refectory. Father Raymond told me in sign language how the sweat runs down his ribs when *his* books are read in refectory. I prayed a lot to Our Lady and find I don't mind it so much. When the reader gives the stuff a peculiar interpretation I feel that the book is still getting better treatment than it deserves.

Brother Processus and Brother Donatus are painting the outside frames of the church windows. The other day I was kneeling in church praying on the presbytery step. Up in the Saint Benedict window Saint Benedict sat making that gesture of his to Saint Scholastica. His crozier and miter lay falsely on the floor among those incredible Bavarian flowerpots. Underneath this scene in two open spaces, side by side, Brother Processus and Brother Donatus—just their faces, beards, and straw hats—busy painting the frames very fast, trying to finish before the end of work.

*"Let the monk be content with all that is worst and with the lowest extreme in everything."

†"You must have a taste for humiliations."

July 11 EIGHTH SUNDAY AFTER PENTECOST
All day it has been dark and hot and wet. Sweat rolls down your
back in church. It is a Day of Recollection. What was I thinking
about? The false joy I take in created things—people, books, my
own work.

Last Wednesday, the 7th, anniversary of the departure of the
Utah colony last year, I went to Reverend Father just before the
afternoon work to see if I couldn't go out into the fields. But he
handed me the first copy of *The Seven Storey Mountain* and told
me to look it over. It is a good job of printing, and I skipped
through it with the general feeling that it is, with *Thirty Poems*,
the only respectable book I have written. And if I had never
published anything but the *Mountain* and *Thirty Poems* I would
feel a whole lot cleaner. *Exile* continues to be read in the refectory
and people in general seem to accept it bravely. Nevertheless
there are parts of it that make my stomach turn somersaults.
Where did I get all that pious rhetoric? That was the way I
thought a monk was supposed to write, just after I had made
simple profession.

Thursday Reverend Father went away to make the Visitation
at the Valley and Father Emery, our present Prior, says he is also
going to take a look at some land that is being offered us for a
foundation in the Adirondacks.

(Drops of rain fall and I keep ducking in and out of the cubbyhole where the old abbots lie buried—and where it is very stuffy
too.)

About *The Seven Storey Mountain:* three book clubs have
guaranteed the sale of fourteen thousand copies. The second
printing is already under way.

And I tell myself, Look out! Maybe this business is going to
turn your whole life upside down for true!

I caught myself thinking, "If they make it into a movie, will
Gary Cooper be the hero?" Or maybe there is no Gary Cooper
any more. But anyway, that is the kind of folly I have to look
out for now. I am reduced to that. I don't dare listen too closely

for fear I might hear the second Abbot of Gethsemani, the terrible Dom Benedict, roll over in his tomb. But I pray to him to
help me be very simple and tranquil and quiet in all this, which
is God's will both for me and for Gethsemani. Here is the book
I couldn't make a go of ten years ago—now it is a success just
when I am at Gethsemani and Gethsemani needs money. . . .

Take care not to be poisoned in spite of yourself by the pleasure you take in your own work! You say you don't want it,
and it gets into your blood anyway. You don't taste the dish,
but the smell of it goes to your head and corrupts you; you get
drunk by sniffing the cork of the bottle.

July 18 NINTH SUNDAY AFTER PENTECOST
Very hot. The birds sing and the monks sweat and about 3:15
when I had just changed all our clothes for the fourth time today
and hung out the wet ones to dry, I stood in the doorway of the
grand parlor and looked at a huge pile of Kentucky cumulus
cloud out beyond Mount Olivet—with a buzzard lazily planing
back and forth over the sheep pasture, very high and black
against the white mountain of cloud. Blue shadows on the cloud.

Yesterday, when we celebrated the Feast of Our Lady of
Mount Carmel, Our Lady made me happy in many different
ways. At prayer—aware of God's purity surrounding my own
imperfection with purity and peace. Yet helpless to get myself
out of the way so that there could be nothing left but His purity.
No other solution but to wait in love and humility—and love
my imperfection. Father Memiad in a very good sermon for our
founder Saint Stephen, on the 16th, told of the Little Flower
being glad on her death bed, not only that she could be judged
as imperfect but that it actually was true. That struck me very
deeply.

All my desires draw me more and more in that direction. To
be little, to be nothing, to rejoice in your imperfections, to be
glad that you are not worthy of attention, that you are of no
account in the universe. This is the only liberation. The only
way to true solitude.

But yesterday morning, Our Lady's Day, after we had had our heads shaved, and I was trying to study theology out under the trees by the Little Flower's statue (which Brother Processus has just repainted in the wrong colors) Father Gervase came running out from Father Prior and gave me a big book. It was Denis the Carthusian, Volume 41—one of those we didn't have, and the one containing his *De Contemplatione*. I nearly got up and flew around the trees. A long time ago I began painful negotiations with the Carthusians at Parkminster to get at least this volume; I had given up hope of ever getting it. But Our Lady brought it along yesterday as a mark of her love and to remind me that she is my guide in the interior life.

Here come great slate-colored clouds. I hope there will be a storm and my animal will cool off. For the glory of God. *Vivat Crux!*

July 25 FEAST OF SAINT JAMES

At the Communion of the High Mass, before I went off as servant of the Church to put out the Sanctus candles, a thought struck me which I had known before, but it suddenly struck me deeply. It is this: the desire to love God, the desire for perfect union with God means nothing at all and is without any value or merit whatever in the sight of God unless it is inspired and guided by grace and in conformity with God's will. Someone will say: all desires for union with God are inspired by grace. That is not true. The devils desire to possess God. There is a natural desire for heaven, for the fruition of God, in us. There is a natural desire for contemplation which may never get to be explicit in most men, but it exists. All this is without merit or value. Our desire for God must come from God and be guided by His will before it means anything in the supernatural order.

And so it is not sufficient to rush into church with a desire for contemplation or to do a lot of good works and acts of virtue with a desire for sanctity. In all the aspects of life the supreme good which includes everything else is God's will. Without it, contemplation and virtue are nothing. The first movement in all prayer, together with faith in His presence, ought to be the *desire* to know His will and to abandon oneself entirely to all His dispositions and intentions for us.

Without that, the desire of contemplation will only lead you to beat your head against a blank wall. But with it—peace.

August 4 FEAST OF SAINT DOMINIC. WEDNESDAY
Dom Frederic is dead.

This morning when we came down to choir he was not there. I had forgotten all about his leaving for Georgia. When he did not show up all through the Night Office I began to worry and pray for him, imagining he was sick in bed. I was praying as much for him as for Dom Dominique, the Abbot General, whose feast it was. At Prime there was a lot of confusion and running around and in Chapter Father Emery, the Prior, told us that Reverend Father had died on the train last night before they got to Knoxville, Tennessee.

Yesterday afternoon I had a long talk with Reverend Father about work and books and so on. It was very pleasant and cheerful and he was exhorting me to write something "to make people love the spiritual life."

He has had a lot to suffer in the last two years. And he has done a tremendous amount of work. The house is sad. He will come back from Knoxville embalmed and in an ambulance sometime tonight. The funeral isn't supposed to be until Monday.

Meanwhile Dom Columban Tewes, Abbot of Achel, showed up here today and so did Humble George. Dom Columban was in choir for Vespers and wore a skull-cap and kept his head on one side; as he sang the *Pater Noster* he softened all the endings so you couldn't hear them at all.

And this afternoon I tried hard for the third time to rewrite the second chapter of *The Waters of Siloe*. James Laughlin sent three books on Saint John of the Cross from Paris.

I keep thinking about Dom Frederic. I suppose he is in purgatory. But I nevertheless feel that he is very close to me and will remain so all the rest of my days. I trust a lot in his help. His sympathy was deep and real all the time he was alive. I don't know who was ever kinder to me. His patience with this community was wonderful. He had a lot of crosses. One of the greatest was the ingratitude and insubordination of some to whom he had been very good. Even in the last few days. He felt them very much. He was sensitive to the way people felt about him and he was very hurt when they did not understand his motives.

I keep contact with God by the touch of a sort of interior hollowness and that counts as my prayer for Dom Frederic and for Gethsemani.

August 13

I have never been so busy in my life. But also very much at peace.

About the things said by various abbots who are here or have been here:

Dom Columban of Achel—I saw pictures of the new monastery at Achel—a good job, on the whole, and very good adaptation of modern methods to Cistercian style. Huge brick arches in the Scriptorium—very effective. Indirect lighting in the cloister. He and his companion thought our chant a bit rough. In Chapter (today) Dom Columban, speaking in French, made the point that it was not the strictness with which we kept the Rule that counted but the *love* with which we kept it—his logic being, I suppose, that generally strictness will be proportionate to love. But it is not necessarily so always. So he added that it is possible for a monastery to be very observant of the Rule and yet to have very little interior life—if the observance is based on imperfect motives.

Yesterday I had to go in to Louisville. It was the first time I was out of the monastery in seven years. I had to go in to act as interpreter for Dom Gabriel Sortais, the Vicar General, who has come to make a Visitation, and who was called in to the Good Shepherd convent because their Mother General from Angers was there and wanted him to talk to the community and then hear her confession. The sisters received us in a cool library with a lot of armchairs and carpets. The place was cool because all the buildings were surrounded by big shade trees and on the whole the convent is a pleasant one—and very big. Big police dog, a laundry, brick houses, porches. So he told them, in French, to love their vocations, and I translated his message into English. I think they were happy. One sister held the black hat I had been wearing in her hand while I drank a glass of ginger ale and ate a cookie, and was too shy to look at any of the sisters.

    August 14 VIGIL OF THE ASSUMPTION
Going in to Louisville the other day I wasn't struck by anything in particular. Although I felt completely alienated from everything in the world and all its activity I did not necessarily feel out of sympathy with the people who were walking around. On the whole they seemed to me more real than they ever had before, and more worth sympathizing with.

 The country was all color. Clouds. Corn in the bottom lands. Red rocks. A lot of rolling land and more hills between here and Bardstown than I realized. I had the impression of having remembered much on my first journey when I came to the monastery seven years ago, and now I realize I had forgotten practically everything.

 It was nice reciting the office in the car and saying the *Gloria Patri* while looking at the woods and fields. But Louisville was boring. Anyway, the whole thing was a matter of obedience. It meant losing a day's work. We were back at seven, ate eggs in the guest house, and I was on time for the *Salve*.

 When I got to bed I remembered I had forgotten to say the Nocturn of the Dead in the car; I got my seasons mixed. So about 8:45 I got up again and went down to church and said the Nocturn kneeling by Saints Peter and Paul's altar where the light wouldn't be seen. It was the wrong Nocturn too.

 Dom Gabriel gave a very funny account of the dinner in the guest house (here) with all the bishops after the funeral, Monday. Everything was on the table and the bishops were left to help themselves, boarding-house style. He said he found it very shocking but I said it was that way everywhere in America. One bishop reached out and grabbed two oranges and handed one to him saying "*pour vous.*"

August 20 FEAST OF SAINT BERNARD. FRIDAY
Dom Gabriel was talking about some of the people who tried to
be postulants at Bellefontaine. An American who ran after the
novice master with a pitchfork and wrote *"A mort le Père
Maître"* all over the dormitory. A Negro from Haiti called
Fritzy who showed up one morning in a tuxedo, registered as
guide to the Cathedral in Port au Prince, did not work, left the
novitiate, went to the Dominicans at Angers and got a job as a
gardener. While working in the friars' garden he started throwing
kisses at a maid in one of the houses that overlooked the place
. . . Then a man who was in prison for manslaughter wrote to
Bellefontaine asking for permission to enter . . .

Dom Gabriel told me not to let myself get roped in to any
magazine as a *"collaborateur,"* i.e., not to get my name on the
mast-head as a staff writer and be slow to accept magazine work.
They are all "commercial." They ruin you. He told me not to
write book reviews.

He advised me not to worry about suffering in choir—told me
how the cantors suffer at Solesmes! He said I should think of
Jesus going up to Jerusalem with all the pilgrims roaring psalms
out of their dusty throats. He is an artist but he says he has at
last progressed to the point where he can live in a room like the
one they have given him in the guest house without putting all
the statues and pictures in a closet. He says at Solesmes, where
they are good in art too, it took three years to get rid of a statue
of Saint Benedict in a magician's robe with moons and stars all
over it.

August 22 SUNDAY
It is the Octave of the Assumption—Feast, I suppose, of the Immaculate Heart of Mary outside. The Visitation was closed in
Chapter. Being secretary I read the Visitation Card which I had
translated and typed yesterday afternoon. It was a long session
in Chapter—finished at 8:30.

Tomorrow is the abbatial election. A table in Chapter with
pens, papers, and chairs with backs to them, looks very official.

This afternoon scrutators were elected and I turned out to be one of them. Father Abdon, one of the others, just made me a sign that he had a box of matches and there is a stove in the Chapter room to burn the ballots. Some expect Dom James to be elected on the first ballot. He arrived today with Father Nilus and Father Remy from Georgia as witnesses. Father Remy sat in choir as though he were in heaven. Afterward I gave him a good hug and he made me a sign that the work was hard in Georgia and that he had liked *Exile Ends in Glory* which was read in the refectory there. Well, he looks holier than ever. And I was glad to see him and Father Nilus too. Father Nilus had to look twice at me before he remembered who I was—if he did so then.

Tomorrow we choose the one who is to lead us for a certain time to God—to make saints of us. I got time to think about it and to remind myself of the vow I will renew when he is installed—that is to be tomorrow also. And all that it means. I read over Saint John of the Cross's remarks about obedience in the *Cautelas* and all I want is to carry them out, to let God guide me by the one He is choosing.

August 25 FEAST OF SAINT LOUIS

The election lasted from 7:45 to 12:45—and this included confirmation and installation of Dom James who, of course, was elected. It is easy to see from this end of the affair that he was the Holy Ghost's candidate—in more senses than one. When we were in there a photographer's bulb went off outside. A newspaper man had got into the garden and took a shot of the smoke coming out of the stove-pipe where we were burning the ballots. Dom Gabriel made some observations on this fact. They were not mild. The whole thing got to be quite impressive after a while. When the voting was over, the result was announced in Latin at the Chapter door, the doors of the church, and the monastery gate. The cloister was unlocked and the novices, young professed, and laybrothers came in. Captain Kinarney strayed into the cloister and sat on a bench and we went in disorder to church singing the *Te Deum*. Then everyone flocked

back to the Chapter room and the ones who had not voted sat
there in silence and waited, rather confused, for the long business
of installation, while all the professed made their promise of
obedience to Dom James.

It was very moving. Big room packed with people—all silent.
A long file of monks moving up to Dom James's throne. The
scrutators' table in a big mess and most of the chairs empty ex-
cept where Father Macarius sat writing furiously, being notary.
It was far past dinner time and we had not even sung Terce and
Sext. (These were recited after meridienne, with None.) Every
once in a while I had to run some kind of an errand for Dom
Gabriel.

When it was all over we had an Abbot. And a holy one too.
Now it is very consoling to go into choir and have our own
Abbot beginning things again. Dom James is quiet and humble.

September 7   VIGIL OF OUR LADY'S NATIVITY
The laybrother novices with pneumatic drills and sledge hammers are pounding and battering at the foundations of this wing
under the Scriptorium to make a hole big enough to get a new
heating plant into the cellar. The place sounds and smells like
New York.

September 12   FEAST OF OUR LADY'S NAME
Today they slipped some fancy coffee on us at mixt and I drank
it by mistake and knelt before the Tabernacle with my mind full
of visions of how we could easily build a very beautiful, simple,
white monastery with long windows and a low belfry, very
simple and clean, on the edge of the Cooper River. . . .

Here is what you need to do more and more—shut up about
all that—architecture, Spirit of the Order, contemplation, liturgy,
chant—be simple and poor or you will never have any peace.
Take what is atrocious without complaint, unless you are in some
way officially bound to complain. Otherwise keep still. But if
everything really gets awful . . . ?

Two contraries cannot co-exist in the same subject!

Para venir a gustarlo Todo / no quieras tener gusto en nada,
Para venir a lo que no gustas / has de ir por lo que no gustas.*

September 13 MONDAY

It is the last day of the summer season. Tomorrow the fasts of
the Order begin with shorter work and longer intervals and I
have been breaking my neck in the last week to clean everything
up in the hope of going out to work at least three times a week.
Seeds of Contemplation is finally off to the printer and *The
Waters of Siloe* is being more definitely edited. In the last two
months I do not seem to have done anything but write business
letters and run around in circles.

Evelyn Waugh wanted to edit the English edition of *The Seven
Storey Mountain* and has apparently already done so. I am glad.
Also it seems he is going to do a feature for *Life* on the Church
in America. The idea seems to be that there is a great Catholic
revival in this country and that the future of the Church depends
on *us*. That is all news to me. If we are supposed to be reviving,
where are our saints?

September 20 MONDAY

The last two Ember Days were like great feasts. Friday was in
fact a feast—the Stigmatization of Saint Francis, and I sat with
my empty stomach and prayed behind the church while the
wind moved the trees and nobody in the world was in sight and
the clouds crossed the sky with motion that was imperceptible
and those red wasps clambered all over one another on the wall
of the church. I don't know what this business is that they go
in for every autumn up under the eaves of the side chapels, but
every once in a while a gust of wind would blow a bunch of
them off into the bushes and they would struggle back up the
wall and start all over again.

Day and night I think about Saint Francis and about poverty
as I re-read the seventh chapter of Saint Bonaventure's *Itinerarium.*

The best thing of all is that at last I can get out to work. The

*See footnote above, page 108.

Tricenary has begun. Saturday after we got our faces shaved with electric shavers, we went out and picked up apples in the orchard, walking around bent double under the low branches like the woman in the day's Gospel. Today we shoveled dirt into ditches that the rain washed out of the sheep pasture, and out of the corner of my eye I could see there was much corn waiting to be cut in the bottom lands.

I know why I will never really be able to write anything about prayer in a journal—because anything you write, even a journal, is at least implicitly somebody else's business. When I say prayer I mean what happens to me in the first person singular. What really happens to what is really me is nobody else's business.

In the novitiate they practice the Gradual for the Feast of Saint Matthew, very loud.

September 26

NINETEENTH SUNDAY AFTER PENTECOST

Love sails me around the house. I walk two steps on the ground and four steps in the air. It is love. It is consolation. I don't care if it is consolation. I am not attached to consolation. I love God. Love carries me all around. I don't want to *do* anything but love. And when the bell rings it is like pulling teeth to make myself shift because of that love, secret love, hidden love, obscure love, down inside me and outside me where I don't care to talk about it. Anyway I don't have the time or the energy to discuss such matters. I have only time for eternity, which is to say for love, love, love. Maybe Saint Teresa would like to have me snap out of it but it is pure, I tell you; I am not attached to it (I hope) and it is love and it gives me soft punches all the time in the center of my heart. Love is pushing me around the monastery, love is kicking me all around like a gong I tell you, love is the only thing that makes it possible for me to continue to tick.

That was the way it was up in the apple trees yesterday morning with all that blue sky. The bulls in their pens were rumbling like old men and I thought it was Father Sub-Prior starting to sing under his breath—I say that not because Father Sub-Prior is old but because he happened to be working near, hidden in the leaves.

But O love, why can't you leave me alone?—which is a rhetorical question meaning: for heaven's sakes don't.

That was the way it was all week. In choir the less I worried about the singing the more I was possessed by love. There is a lesson in that about being poor. You have got to be all the time cooperating with love in this house, and love sets a fast pace even at the beginning and if you don't keep up you'll get dropped. And yet any speed is too slow for love—and no speed is too fast for you if you will only let love drag you off your feet—after that you will have to sail the whole way. But our instinct is to get off and start walking. . . .

I want to be poor; I want to be solitary; I had a tough time after Communion and I think I was twisting and turning too much, as usual. This business burns me. *Aruit tamquam testa virtus mea.** I am all dried up with desire and I can only think of one thing—staying in the fire that burns me.

Dom James put books about Orval in all the Scriptoriums and the flossiest of all was in ours. I looked at it and the buildings are gorgeous but I'd be afraid to proclaim anybody in that Chapter room. The sacristy looks like the circular bar on the promenade deck of the *Conte di Savoia* which is probably long since at the bottom of the ocean.

The most interesting thing Reverend Father told me after getting back from the General Chapter Wednesday was that he addressed the Citeaux community in his French, and was a terrific success. My guess is that it was his personality that went over. His message, however, was the usual one, "*Tout pour Jésus, par Marie, toujours avec un sourire.*" Did I already say he has a rubber stamp with that on it, for okaying things? Well anyway, one of the monks came in and nearly kissed his feet afterwards and said, "What a wonderful message," and wrote him a little poem about "always with a smile," in French though. And the poem was on pretty blue paper with a drawing of a smiling saint which

*"My strength has burned up like a potsherd" (Psalm 21:16).

was clever and a bit on the cute side. All the religious are in rapture.

The reader in the refectory has made something incredible out of an ordinary pious book about the lady who got the Pope to institute the Feast of Christ the King. His reading makes all the syntax completely surrealistic. He inserts periods in the middle of sentences and reads unrelated thoughts as if they were tied together and the whole thing seems to be moving under water. It makes the book almost interesting. Like seeing the life of a saint from an upside down diving-bell.

October 10 SUNDAY

Sooner or later the world must burn, and all things in it—all the books, the cloister together with the brothel, Fra Angelico together with the Lucky Strike ads which I haven't seen for seven years because I don't remember seeing one in Louisville. Sooner or later it will all be consumed by fire and nobody will be left—for by that time the last man in the universe will have discovered the bomb capable of destroying the universe and will have been unable to resist the temptation to throw the thing and get it over with.

And here I sit writing a diary.

But love laughs at the end of the world because love is the door to eternity and he who loves God is playing on the doorstep of eternity, and before anything can happen love will have drawn him over the sill and closed the door and he won't bother about the world burning because he will know nothing but love.

Today for the first time we tried a schola of eight, singing during the whole Mass, and I can see where it would one day help a great deal. That was one of the ideas Reverend Father brought back from Citeaux.

In Chapter he told us about how it was at Lisieux, and La Grande Trappe, and Port du Salut where they run a power station. At La Trappe our Father Bernard, the sculptor, has discovered a system for making plaques of pious subjects, four at a time, all different sizes, and the notion made me quiver.

But sooner or later the world must burn—and *The Seven*

Storey Mountain and *Figures for an Apocalypse*. And I have
several times thought how at the Last Day I am likely to be one
of the ten most abjectly humiliated sinners in the history of the
world, but it will be my joy, and it will fill me with love, and I
will fly like an arrow to take a back seat very far in the back
where the last shall be first. And perhaps if Saint Francis will
pray for me, and Saint John of the Cross, and Saint Mary Magdalen, I'll slide down off my high horse now and begin being the
last and the least in everything, but not out of injured vanity as
I was this morning in the eight-cylinder schola we had, that sang
so fast *vir erat in terra Hus nomine Job.*

Now it is a toss-up whether I should ask Reverend Father to
give me another and fatter book to fill with *Journal,* for we have
been talking about my writing less. In fact, I have begun to tell
him all about my temptations to become a Carthusian and he says
he doesn't see why things can't be fixed up right here.

But *nos qui vivimus benedicamus Domino* by love, love, love,
in the cloister and in the choir and out there in the presence of
the forest and the hills where all the colors are changing, and
under the steeple whose topmost cross has been painted with
yellow traffic paint by Brother Processus who swung up there
for days in the sky with his angel holding on to him. (He upset
a bucket of paint and I could see it flying upside down on
the end of a rope, and the paint turned to spray before it was
half way down, and a drop fell on our Psalter and there were
little yellow spots all over the stones and the bushes of the cemetery where today I saw a hawk.)

PART THREE

Major Orders

In these seven months my life began to change much more than I realized. My mind was occupied with the last and most important steps in my progress toward the priesthood. I did not at once become aware that my writing, which had once been a source of imaginary problems, was now becoming a real problem and that the problem was reaching a crisis.

During the time of my sub-diaconate and diaconate—in the winter and Lent of 1949—I suddenly discovered that I was scarcely able to write at all. It takes more than good will to write a book. What you write has to come up out of the depths of your being and if, in those depths, the instinct for self-expression has dried up or become paralyzed, there is no way of writing a book. I should say, there is no way of writing a good book. In this state of intellectual siege I might, quite possibly, have written a bad book. But the job I was trying to do was so deep that I was hardly able to write anything at all. I would laboriously cover fifty pages with typescript and then tear them all up and start over again. Such were my first attempts to write theology. No doubt I needed to learn my own limitations, for after all I had not yet quite finished the study of dogma. When the fruit of all these labors finally turned into a book, quite easily and rapidly, two years later, it was called the Ascent to Truth. I still do not know whether the result was *what I wanted. It was certainly not what I had been planning in 1949, when I dreamed of a great synthesis on the interior life drawn from Scripture and the Fathers of the Church!*

There were several reasons for this paralysis. First, there was the obvious fact that my mind was not on my writing but on major orders and the priesthood. That was just where my mind belonged. My whole being had always rebelled against division, and it rebelled now. Second, I was tired and stale. I had been writing too much, and the depths of my soul were sick of it. Third, I was ashamed of being famous. After all, a Trappist monk has left the world behind him. Public success, for him, inevitably takes on the character of a defeat. I had to find out that in the plans of Divine Providence there is no such thing as a defeat and that every step is, or ought to be, a step forward into the wilderness and that even publicity can nourish humility. It must be neither loved nor hated for itself, but simply accepted with indifference from the hand of God, that His will may be done.

Finally, I got into another quandary. I began to receive fan mail. This was a surprising and sobering experience. For one thing I discovered that the letters I received were serious and not ridiculous at all. Those who wrote to me wrote less about me than about themselves and about God, and what they had to say, believe me, was important. Is there anything more important than salvation?

These letters created several curious problems, for the monastery and for myself. Evelyn Waugh, who came to visit Gethsemani in December, shortly before I was ordained sub-deacon, thought that it would be a good idea for me simply to put books aside and write serious letters, and to make an art of it. For letter-writing is an art. But when I suggested it to Father Abbot he reminded me, to my great relief, that it was not an art provided for in the Cistercian usages. Monks scarcely write letters at all. At Gethsemani, we normally receive mail four times a year and at these same four times write two letters. The annual literary output of the average Trappist is then eight short letters, four of which must be to his family. Clearly I would have to exceed this sober limit. But for most of the fan-mail, I devised a printed card which explained the situation and which promised my prayers. I have kept the promise.

Yet there was another difficulty. In most monasteries, even of Orders less austere than ours, the mail is screened. When I first came to Gethsemani, the Abbot himself read all the mail. Dom James had renounced the quixotic ambition of holding all the offices in the monastery at once, and had handed this one over to Father Macarius, who was now Prior. But the Prior had other things to do, and with grim humor gave me the job of opening and reading my own mail. It was one of the biggest penances I have ever had. Later on, Father Abbot took pity on me, and appointed one of the novices to help me out as a secretary. Frater Amos had been a radio operator in the Navy and was also, I later discovered, a poet. He was a smart, sympathetic secretary and it was probably due to him that I did not cease altogether to be a writer or even a human being. I speak about him in the past tense because he has since been sent to our new foundation near Rochester, New York.

A deep spiritual reaction against all this involvement occurred when I was ordained deacon. It was a gesture that may or may not have had a profound meaning to me. I thought it had some meaning. What it meant, I am still not sure. But I decided to stop trying to be a poet any more. I did this first of all because I realized that I had never really been a good poet anyway, and it seemed to me that by continuing to write poetry I would only be imposing an illusion on the people who thought my poetry was good. In so doing, I would run the risk of coming to believe, myself, that it was good. What I was trying to do was, I think, all right. It was a movement toward integrity. If I could not write well, I would stop wasting words, time, paper, and get rid of this useless interference in my life of prayer. Since that day, in order to relax the element of pride that may have insinuated itself in this resolve, I have written verse where I thought charity demanded or permitted it—for instance some lines for Saint Agnes, which were never really finished off into a poem, which occur later in this book, and which are simply an expression of personal devotion to her. I have written two other poems besides, both of them on occasions which called for some expression of personal affection and gratitude. To write thus is not, according to my vocabulary, an attempt to "be a poet."

October 15 FEAST OF SAINT TERESA [1948]
The fire of love for the souls of men loved by God consumes you like the fire of God's love, and it is the same love. It burns you up with a hunger for the supernatural happiness, first of people that you know, then of people you have barely heard of and finally of everybody.

This fire consumes you with a desire that is not directed immediately to action, but to God. And in the swift, peaceful, burning tide of that desire you are carried to prayer rather than to action; or rather action seems to flow along with prayer and with desire, as if of its own accord—you do not think so much of what you are to do and write and say for souls: you are carried away to God by hunger and desire. And this hunger is exactly the same as the hunger for your own personal union with God, but now it includes someone else; and it is for God's own sake above all, though you do not reason and separate.

Here is a great hunger, and it has a direct reference to persons, to individuals rather than to abstract groups. Or if it is for groups, it is for groups concretized in a typical representative who is individual, real.

In this hunger there is pain and emptiness and there is joy and it is irresistible—and somehow it is full of the strong assurance that God wants to hear all your prayers.

Sometimes you get the feeling that when you are carried away by this desire of love for souls, God is beginning to pour out everything upon you, to deluge you with all that you need, to overwhelm you with spiritual or even temporal favors, because you are no longer paying attention to your own needs, but are absorbed in the torment of desire for the happiness of *that* soul—

that soul—or *that* other one. Always individual and concrete.

It does not always have to be that way. You can lose sight of them all in God and pray for them as well or better perhaps . . . but it is still a deep experience to be swept with the flames of this hunger and thirst for the salvation of others and with a strange, mysterious sense of *power* to obtain tremendous riches of joy for them from God. It makes you want to sing and songs come up from your heart and half smother you with joy: and at the same time there is anguish as if your heart would burst, giving birth to the whole world. *Rugiebam a gemitu cordis mei.*

Saint Teresa of Avila, ask our God to fill the world with rivers of the fires of salvation—*fluvius igneus rapidusque egrediebatur a facie Dei!**

October 17

TWENTY-SECOND SUNDAY AFTER PENTECOST

It is getting near the end of the world—at least in the liturgy. *Si iniquitates observaveris* . . . 3rd tone. Saint Hilary in the Night Office says that the best way to handle the problem of rendering unto Caesar the things that are Caesar's, is to have absolutely nothing of the things that are Caesar's and then he will have no claim on you.

October 31   VIGIL OF ALL SAINTS

Floribus ejus nec rosae nec lilia desunt—in a way the Feast of All Saints is a little sad, because I think: how many of them would have been much greater and simpler saints if the Holy Ghost had been free to make them what He wanted them to be. Many were, no doubt, pious robots and many were terrible to get along with. . . . And all that has ended up by contributing something to their beauty.

It is not the beauty of the saints' own glory that matters, but the beauty of their glory in so far as it is the crown of Christ the King.

Beautiful stuff in a letter of Saint John of the Cross to the

---

*"A fast-flowing river of fire came forth from the face of God" (Daniel, 7:10).

Nuns of Beas (Letter V): ". . . we shall see what wealth you
have gained in pure love and in the paths of eternal life and what
excellent progress you are making in Christ, Whose brides are
His delight and crown: and a crown deserves not merely to be
sent rolling along the floor, but to be taken by the angels and
seraphim in their hands and set with reverence and esteem on the
head of their Lord."

Nobody ever writes us Trappists a letter like that.

I spent the whole afternoon in the cubbyhole where it says
"*sepultura fratrum*" and watched the rain falling on the cemetery. Part of the time I held a book in my hand but I couldn't
read more than a few lines.

Yet I am deluged with books. Dom Moore, who is Dom Pablo
Maria at Miraflores, got another Carthusian novice to get me the
Burgos edition of Saint John of the Cross and that came in red
and green half leather, utterly splendid. It makes our untidy
workroom look like a palace.

Then Mother Paula Williamson sent me a life of Marie Vic-
toire Thérèse Couderc who started the Cenacle, and was pushed
around quite a lot, and has a face something like Madame Privat.
She came from down there somewhere in the Cévennes.

And the nuns at Laval lent me some manuscripts dealing with
the history of their house and with a lot of sisters whose feast is
tomorrow (Feast of All Saints) and I can't seem to get into
any of it.

This week was busy. First Laughlin came down, then the place
was full of priests of the Byzantine-Slavonic rite who, when
encouraged to sing, ended up by singing two Masses a day and
Benediction and the last night they were here they were still
singing when Dom James left the church after sprinkling everybody with holy water at bedtime.

The Eastern rite—we got a good look at it this time—is in
many ways impressive. I like seeing priest, deacon and sub-
deacon all praying together at the altar with their hands up in
the air like the *orantes* in the catacombs. I like the way they

give the Kiss of Peace at the Offertory instead of just before Communion. It is more theological. "But when thou goest to present thy gift, if thou remember that thy brother has anything against thee . . ." etc. Three priests co-consecrating also make the Mass more striking. Their Mass gives you a greater sense of the reality of the Mystical Body. There is a much more vital participation between celebrants and people. It is a more contemplative Mass. I didn't bother to follow it with any of the leaflets, but I like the wonderful triumphant thing they sing right after Communion. I like the Blessing of the People with the chalice after Communion and I like the "entries" or processions—especially the one at the Offertory. They make things so clear. As for pronouncing the words of consecration out loud or, in fact, singing them while everyone answers *Amen* —that is splendid! I wish we did that. It makes much more sense. Our liturgy is too private. And yet I admit that all the polyphonic music got so lush that it sickened me a little and at the last great Mass I was deliberately paying no attention to the singing or the movements of the ministers but simply uniting myself interiorly with the Sacrifice and trying to keep empty and at peace, without being dragged around by liturgical emotions.

For hours and days afterwards the monks have been holding their heads with polyphonic Ruthenian music chasing itself round and round their skulls. Last night one of them was singing their "Alleluia Alleluia" in his sleep.

Laughlin came and liked the Greek rite and took some poems I was not altogether ready to let go. He read a life of Charles de Foucauld, and had with him something by the Jewish mystic Martin Buber which Rexroth had lent him. He brought proofs of *Seeds of Contemplation* and said he was going to vote for Norman Thomas in the presidential election, as a gesture of despair.

He said Munich was terrible—I mean that the bombing had been awful. He said that the people outside seem to have an obscene hunger for violence and death—a craving to be destroyed. That was what Christopher Hollis said too, in *Horizon*. But I think, on the other hand, of all the happy letters from our monasteries in France and all the good Catholic writing that is being done. He said well, the monasteries are in the country.

I got permission to take him for a walk outside the enclosure, as if we were just going to stand on the hill behind Nally's and look at the view, but in the end we went all the way out to the top of the knobs, behind the lake. I did not know they were so steep. We seemed to be high and looking right down on top of the monastery, although we couldn't see it much because of the trees. We sat on the top where there was a fine view across the valley.

When we were climbing down again I stopped in the middle of a very steep place and explained to him about Theresa Neumann, how she never ate. When we got back to the monastery there was a letter from Sister Madaleva about the leaflet I wrote on contemplation. We sat in the garden and one of the Byzantine-Slavonic priests walked around and around reading *Cistercian Contemplatives* with his forehead all puckered up. Maybe he is the one who, as Reverend Father told us, wants to become a Trappist.

In the refectory we read *Mystic in Motley* but it was just interrupted and replaced by a translation of *Quas Primas*—the Encyclical on Christ the King, today being the Feast of Christ the King. And the more I think about it, the more I believe if we ask Him, He will give us peace—and that He is preparing great things for us but in His own way—*per crucem*.

November 9

It is the feast of Elizabeth of the Trinity.

I used to think it would be a good thing to die young and die quickly, but now I am beginning to think a long life with much labor and suffering for God would be the greater grace. However *in concreto* the greater grace for each individual is the one God wills for him. If God wills you to die suddenly, that is a greater grace for you than any other death, because it is the one He has chosen, by His love, with all the circumstances of your life and His glory in view.

It is beautiful to see God working in souls. I thought the letters about *The Seven Storey Mountain* were going to be a penance. In a way they are. And yet they are all very beautiful and spiritual and filled with the love of God. People write with great simplicity to me as though it were the most natural thing in the world, and I feel as if I had known them for a long time and I wish I could answer them. To most of them I send a printed card. But it is beautiful to see how really genuine people can be—not bitter or twisted or warped. The ones who *are* bitter, at any rate, haven't been writing to me.

But it is beautiful to see God's grace working in people. The most beautiful thing about it is to see how the desires of the soul, inspired by God, so fit in and harmonize with grace that holy things seem *natural* to the soul, seem to be part of its very self. That is what God wants to create in us—that marvelous spontaneity in which His life becomes perfectly ours and our life His, and it seems inborn in us to act as His children, and to have His light shining out of our eyes.

November 14   SUNDAY. DAY OF RECOLLECTION
Tomorrow is the Feast of the Dedication of the Church. I am servant of the church this week and went around lighting the candles on the anointed walls, reaching over the heads of the choir with a flaming taper on the end of a long pole. As I lit the one under Our Lady's window the choir was reciting *"Nisi Dominus aedificaverit domum"* and I asked Our Lady to bless this house and all of us with her peace.

Evelyn Waugh is supposed to be on his way here. Two telegrams from Harcourt, Brace said so, and several phone calls from *Time* said so. *Time* called all the way from New York to get J. Edward Hagan—the painter in nearby New Haven—to hold his car in readiness to drive Waugh to the airport when he leaves here. And Hagan said: "Gee, that man must own the whole of New York." But none of the telegrams or phone calls have said when Waugh is going to come.

November 30   FEAST OF SAINT ANDREW

It is already Advent. In the last minutes before the retreat the novices are practicing some sweet polyphony for the small centenary celebration we are supposed to be holding on December 21st. Bishop Cotton is alleged to be going to say the Matutinal Mass and Archbishop Floersh to sing the High Mass but nothing has been said about anyone being ordained sub-deacon by either of them.

Evelyn Waugh arrived Saturday night after everyone was in bed and left Sunday at noon in a storm of rain.

The first thing he did was to reproach me with the fact that the house was so hot. He said it plainly contradicted the things I wrote about the cold in *The Seven Storey Mountain*. The lay-brother novices have got that huge new boiler working now, and that is the cause of all the trouble. We are still wearing summer clothing and yet I sweat in choir.

Waugh said Hollywood was very dull. He expected great jewels and thought everything would surely be done with parades of elephants but found that the people were just business-men doing business, and that there was no real entertainment anywhere except in the cemetery which, he said, he visited every day.

He offered to send us books, but said that Graham Greene's *The Heart of the Matter* and his own *The Loved One* were not proper material for our refectory.

He said the lady on *Time, Life* and *Fortune* who arranged his itinerary tried to route him from Cincinnati to Louisville via Washington, D. C.

Also he said he couldn't read any poetry written since Tennyson. When I talked about pious art he said that at any rate the pious art that is going out of fashion now is far better than that which is coming in—saints fixed up "like motor mascots." He thought Gethsemani had character and that it looked Irish. I said perhaps that was on account of the weather, but he said it was on account of the pointed windows of the novitiate.

At his house in Gloucestershire he says he has a painting of a Trappist by Zurbarán, on the stairway. I argued hotly that it must be a Carthusian but we settled for "Cistercian." Privately I still think it is a Carthusian. Anyway the monk's name was Jiménez.

Waugh is doing an article for *Life* on the Church in America and he kept repeating that it would "necessarily be superficial." He said he was deliberately doing America the way Americans did Europe, by way of revenge! He is very careful about trying to do things well if possible and so he wants to prepare everyone in case this cannot be done marvelously well. He saw some "charming Negro nuns" in Baltimore, and saw Dorothy Day and was at Grailville. I forgot to ask him what he was going to see in New Orleans. Maybe the leper colony down there.

Also Dr. Law was talking to a group of monks—mostly confessors and the novice masters—Frater Zeno and I being the only non-priests. The talks were about psychiatry and ended in a general discussion as to whether the average novice could read Saint John of the Cross with profit or even without harm. I don't know the answer. Right now the novices are singing and singing and they have already begun to decorate the place for Christmas. Who says they *want* to read Saint John of the Cross anyway?

December 1   ON RETREAT

Tonight we will sing the commemoration of Saint Bibiana who stands in the doorway of the new liturgical year. She always meets you there. She is quiet and unobtrusive and generally has nothing to say. Her prayer is in the antiphonary and you notice it at the end of the old season, with a picture of an angel under it holding, I think, a scroll, saying *Deo Gratias*. The *Deo Gratias* is for the old season. Saint Bibiana belongs to the new.

I can judge retreats I make by the quality of what I write about them in the journal and I must say the quality of none of my notes is very high, especially when I am on retreat and pushing and pulling at myself to find out what is wrong with my interior life. But what I mean to say is that when my investigations look silly on paper then they *are* silly in fact. If my questions and examinations really had some point, they would also, I think, be interesting—at least to me. After all, I am the one they are supposed to concern.

Here goes.

During the past year—temptations to become a Carthusian have more or less subsided. It seems to me they began to subside the precise moment when, on retreat last year, I opened an envelope from France which had a thirteenth-century picture of Saint Louis in it, from Father Anselme Dimier, at Tamie. Dom Marie Joseph helped and Dom Gabriel helped and I am ashamed to say the success of *The Seven Storey Mountain* helped and Dom James got me to declare formally that I didn't intend to run off and be a Carthusian, before he would let me be a sub-deacon.

December 2 ON RETREAT

Today, unless I am mistaken, is the feast of Blessed John Ruysbroeck—or would be if he had one. The morning sky behind the new horsebarn was as splendid as his writing. A thousand small high clouds went flying majestically like ice-floes, all golden and crimson and saffron, with clean blue and aquamarine behind them, and shades of orange and red and mauve down by the surface of the land where the hills were just visible in a pearl haze and the ground was steel-white with frost—every blade of grass as stiff as wire.

The things that strike me most about sub-diaconate all remind me how incomplete and half-baked my notion of my vocation has been even until now. I am assigned a very definite duty—that of officially praising God for the Church and for the whole of creation, and doing it in public and doing it as well as I can for those who cannot do it at all. More depends on this than my own soul. The Church militant will be better or worse for the way I do things in choir—and the way I help others to do them. To be sub-cantor in a Cistercian monastery—and worse still, to be cantor—is to hold a position on which tremendous issues depend. I hope that patience and control of one's temper can contribute something to all this—and make up for what we don't give by singing.

If the choir is a cross—it is still not enough to say "Oh well, it is a cross" and freeze a smile on your face and try to bear it. You also have to make some attempt to *improve* things—and do them well.

Generally this is not much fun.

The Mystical Body comes into the Rite of Ordination very explicitly. The *Pontifical* is careful to point out that the ministry of the sub-deacon does not extend merely to formalities and rites concerning inanimate things—vessels, linen. The altar is the living Christ and the linens are the members of His Mystical Body. Bringing their gifts to unite them with Him on the Cross I am dressing Christ in His members and clothing His sacrifice in the glory of a saved Church. *Attendite quale ministerium vobis tradetur.*

I think that is why, at this precise moment, God has caused me to start getting so many letters from people who want prayers. I'll take all those people up to the altar of the God who rejoiceth my youth.

December 4   ON RETREAT

The only sign so far that there is any fruit in this retreat is that I am recapturing a great respect and love for the usages, the common life, subjection, in obedience, to a superior. I think it is very important that a retreat should help a Cistercian to recover a *taste* for the *Spiritual Directory*, if he has lost it a little—recover a little unction in his relation with his community—his brothers—if he has lost that. Apart from this the retreat has been a long string of temptations, which have not, however, affected my underlying peace. And I just had a very good, though somewhat extra-curricular, talk with Reverend Father.

The atmosphere of contemplation is the atmosphere of humility that pervades the Rule of Saint Benedict, and especially

Chapter 7. It is not an atmosphere of conflict and strain in which everyone is trying to get away from everybody else, and trying to get out of monastic or liturgical duties, but striving in all things *"ut nemo contristetur in domo Dei."**

Also read Dom Lehodey's introductory letter to the General Chapter report on means to increase the interior life (1922)— importance of detachment, especially of humility, of knowing how to use every incident of the Cistercian life as a means to detachment and love—sanctify all our exercises by a deep spirit of faith.

He also refers to the beautiful passage in the Directory where the monastery is described as a *Schola Divini Servitii* and he shows how Christ directs and teaches us through the Rule and our Superiors.

In all this there is nothing exteriorly very exciting and it has taken me seven years to really notice and appreciate it. However, the Rule and the common life untie all the knots of worry and trouble and unquiet that gather in your head when you are living on your own.

December 6 ON RETREAT

The sun is coming up between the garage and the hog house. The duck pond is nearly dried up. Yesterday, Feast of Saint Francis Xavier, it was so warm that I could sit out there in one of the alcoves behind the church, holding the *Usages* in my hand and squinting out through the fine rain at the branches of the whitewashed sycamores.

I went to the retreat-master (a Passionist, Father Cletus Mulloy) yesterday and he sat in that very old throne we still use for pontificals, and heard my confession. He told me he had read *The Seven Storey Mountain* and liked it. He told me to pray every day for humility. He told me to write books to help, for instance, nuns in mixed orders. And he said I ought to try to write on the contemplative life in the same style as the *Mountain*, if I could. About fan-mail he said I ought to have

---

*"That no one should be saddened in the house of God" (Rule of St. Benedict).

someone to screen it and sift it out. Dom Frederic used to. Father Prior has the mail now, but his tendency is to dump everything in my lap unopened. One of the first things I must fix is this mail situation. Without working out any solution of my own—put it up to Reverend Father and take the solution given by obedience. Father Mulloy also said—concerning poverty—that I ought never to ask for anything without first consulting Superiors—in other words not so much presuming of permission and making it OK afterwards.

Clare Boothe Luce sent us two volumes of records of Handel's *Messiah*. They arrived all of a sudden Saturday. That seems to me to be on the borderline of what Cistercians can't use. Then Laughlin sent a volume of linotype faces, for which I had asked; it is so fat it embarrasses me. Also in that room I have Pound's *Pisan Cantos* and Williams's *Paterson* and two copies of *Horizon* and a fourteenth-century martyrology I forgot to put back in the vault—and the record player and all those records and the new typewriter Clare Boothe Luce sent, and all the Burgos edition of Saint John of the Cross and some of the books Sister Thérèse sent.

The mere fact that the room is in a mess does not make me poor.

Yesterday Reverend Father announced I was supposed to be ordained sub-deacon on the Feast of Saint Thomas the Apostle which is also our hundredth anniversary.

I took a good look at the sub-deacon at Mass. I never realized what a difference there is between the sub-deacon and the deacon. The sub-deacon is really just a glorified acolyte. During all the essential parts of the sacrifice he is standing down there *in plano* hiding his face behind the humeral veil and saying, "I am excluded from the mysteries. I am waiting until some menial job needs to be done—some errand between the altar and the credence table. Until then I mind my own business and keep out of the way!" In short, he runs errands for the deacon. On the other hand, he is much more than the servant of the church, whose proper place is in choir. The sub-deacon is at least vested and localized in the sanctuary, and he has an epistle to sing. On the other hand, the epistle is only one step above a prophecy and if the conventual Mass were to be merely sung by the hebdomadary alone, someone would be appointed to go from the choir to sing the epistle, just like a prophecy. So you see the sub-deacon is pretty small potatoes.

December 13 SAINT LUCY

What do you think, you dope, after having been a Trappist for seven years? I think, Where did the time go? I caught myself wondering, Have I changed? Not that it matters. I have and I haven't. I'm balder. Somehow I have more of an interior life but I'd have a hard time trying to say how. But I know some of the things that account for it: solemn profession—theology— and minor forms of tribulation here and there concerning writing, singing, contemplation. What graces all these little crosses have been. They are the very best thing in our life here. It seems they are so small. They do their work. They are coming in greater abundance now. How God works on your soul by these obscure and unremarkable sufferings that cleanse and drain your wounds. I am glad of every kind of trouble I have had and thank God in advance for all the trials that are to come. Other more pleasant graces—minor orders—the writing job, to some extent. All the reading, all the hours of prayer. God has taught me to find myself more in Him or lose myself more: it comes to the same thing. And I am tremendously glad of the prayers of the people who have read *The Seven Storey Mountain* and I am glad to pray for them.

December 14

The most precious thing I had today was an hour of silence out behind the church. It has been warm and damp and the knobs are hidden in mist. It started to rain a little and I came in but the laybrother novices were practicing part-singing in the choir novitiate and were singing better than the choir novices who were practicing Gregorian chant in the professed singing room.

By that time I discovered that it wasn't really raining after all and so I escaped to my silence and stood out there all alone, drugged and happy, with a book under my arm.

Tomorrow: revolution. Self-shaving is to be introduced at Gethsemani for the first time in a century. Father Prior is going to give out brushes and safety razors and small bars of soap and (o horror!) mirrors. Father Abbot has received a letter of instructions from Our Lady of the Valley telling all about how to shave. We are supposed to shave twice a week. Such effeminacy! We shall rake and hack at our own miserable chins; in the end this is going to be more penitential—but faster than the communal electric shave: we won't have to sit around waiting our turn.

Apparently this is what they do in Europe. Dom Gabriel was shocked to see us so hairy.

I am invitator and I sing *"Tota pulchra es, Maria."*

Berliner and Lanigan sent us an Advent house—you open a window each day and lo! a picture symbolizing one of the "O" antiphons. Tomorrow is Ember Wednesday—O happy fast!— and the Great "O's" begin Friday.

December 19 FOURTH SUNDAY IN ADVENT
O Radix Jesse!

I was kneeling in Reverend Father's room while a stream of people kept coming in and out. One of the people was Father Prior with a program for the centenary celebrations on Tuesday and I realized how merciful God's Providence had been in getting me ordained sub-deacon on that day. I am on retreat and therefore have no part in this carnival. *Omnia cooperantur in bonum iis qui diligunt Deum.* There was once a passing thought of getting me ordained in September, but first Father Macarius was against it and then Dom Frederic died and finally all things conspired to make this the only sensible time. As a result I am dispensed from any part in the singing and charades or whatever is coming off to celebrate our founding. I will just sit still and fast and be smug and wait to receive the *tunica jucunditatis.*

Everett Hagan is going to bring a stove all the way over from

New Haven to cook (he says) some food. I remember the last
big banquet (Dom Frederic's Jubilee in the Order—1944). I was
reader in the refectory and the ice cream set aside for me melted
and I couldn't sleep during the meridienne either because I
thought I had insulted the Archbishop.

Today (it is colder) I walked about in the cemetery learning
the prayers you say when vesting for Mass. *Da Domine virtutem
manibus meis ad abstergendam omnem maculam . . .**
I write out on little yellow cards all the rules for what the
sub-deacon must do in all the different kinds of Masses and keep
them in the top left pocket over my heart to show I am disposed
to love the liturgy above everything. And I have put (or tried to
put) everything out of my mind except being a sub-deacon.
Parsch says the sub-deacon sings the Epistle facing the altar
because the altar represents Christ and the office of sub-deacon is
like that of Saint John the Baptist. . . .

December 20 VIGIL OF SAINT THOMAS
Today Father Vedastus and I had a day of recollection before
ordination—our regular retreat having been accounted as the
annual one.
Going up to the infirmary chapel for two short conferences
somehow made a deep impression on me. The little chapel has
filled up with the associations attached to all the retreats I have
made since receiving the habit nearly seven years ago—and what
is more, the three happy days last Lent when I was up there
listening to the frogs all came back with a rush. I looked at the
primitive perspective in Father Odo's decorations, and read the
curious letters that spelled out *Joseph Filii Dei nutritie* and the
melody of Saint Joseph's litany began to play over and over
again in my mind.
Father Apollinaris was the same old Father Apollinaris, but he
made a deep impression. After the last conference I stayed
alone in the chapel and let everything sink in—and steeped my
heart in the great warmth flowing out of the Tabernacle.

*"O Lord, give power to my hands to cleanse away every stain . . ."

In the cemetery I looked up at the sky and thought of the sea of graces that was flowing down on Gethsemani as her hundredth year is ending. All the crosses stood up and spoke to me for fair this time. It was as if the earth were shaking under my feet and as if the jubilant dead were just about to sit up and sing.

I got some taste of how much there is to be glad for in the world because of Gethsemani.

Father Apollinaris was speaking of the need for a concrete spiritual ideal. What strikes me is the need of something absolutely concrete and definite—poverty, humility: not something abstract, off in the heavens, but here, at Gethsemani. To make it a real ideal you work for, not just one you occasionally think and preach about. To ask God somehow to make me the quietest and meekest and most unobtrusive man in the whole house, the *poorest* man, the one with nothing. I am right at the other end of the pole from all that—but in the circumstances God has given me to work with there are still graces—and all the founding fathers of Gethsemani, whom I love, will pray for me.

Father Euthymius who was the first sub-prior; Father Theotime who was, as I believe, the cantor; Father Timothy who did the fancy woodwork; those who ran away once or twice and came back; Brother Theodoret to whom I prayed one cold Saint Thomas day when I was feeling sad in the woods—and later Brother Simon the shoemaker who gave me the Holy Ghost poem—all will pray for me.

There are little blue flowers on the grave of Brother Conrad, the cellarer, who used to run all around the fields swinging his arms to the great scandal of many, and died when I was a novice.

December 25 CHRISTMAS DAY

Yesterday the first snow of the winter fell and last night before the Midnight Mass someone made me a furtive sign that it was snowing again. And so this morning is very beautiful, not because there is much snow, for it is as thin as the sugar on the porridge of the monks under twenty-one who can't fast, and the gray grass comes through it everywhere. Nor is it beautiful under a bright sky, for the sky is dark. But it is beautiful because of Christmas.

Last night at the Midnight Mass I went on for the first time as sub-deacon. The thing that most struck me—in fact it amazed me: I felt as if I had been wearing a maniple and tunic all my life, and it seemed to me as if I had grown up in the sanctuary and never done anything else but minister at the altar and sing the Epistle, as if I belonged there and always had belonged there and as if anything unrelated to this were strange and difficult. Not that I didn't make mistakes. I chased the acolyte away thinking Reverend Father would not use any water at the ablutions because of the three Masses. I suppose he could have put his fingers in the little glass of water that was there, but since the MC emptied it for him to pour the wine in from the chalice . . . well, anyway he wanted water for the ablutions!

I felt somehow that I was given the kiss of peace with a new kind of authority, as if a special power to spread Christ's peace all over the world had now been vested in me. As I stood there with the paten in front of my face, the only unfamiliar thing was that my thumb got tired.

(Father Apollinaris walks through the Scriptorium smiling and making gestures and bumping into the desks. The brothers sing vociferously in the singing room because today we are to have another show in Chapter.)

In bed I was singing over and over to myself *"Exivit per clausam portam"*—I mean, the second time we went to bed. I served Father Macarius' Mass at Our Lady's altar (Immaculate Heart) in the brothers' choir and he had on the white chasuble which was part of the set his friends gave him when he made solemn profession: one of the few decent vestments. (Father Hermes had another good chasuble at the High Altar for his private Masses—that sort of ivory affair with a Byzantine-looking figure of Our Lady and four Evangelists.) Anyway on the back of Father Macarius' chasuble was written *"Mater humilitatis"* in blue, and after the Consecration I looked at Our Lord and got a terrific desire for His humility. I am humble after a fashion—but when people cross me up, although I give in, I am interiorly too sardonic and tough about it, and I resist, and try to get even by being secretly critical of them. But Christmas is given us to make us love the kind of humility that is *love* and embraces contrarieties and difficulties and all the rest with joy. Maybe He will give me some of His joy in being in the crib. How can I say I love Him until I like what He likes? So in the end I was thinking of Saint Francis—and his spirit. That made three saints I thought of and invoked especially in this night. In between Saint Augustine and Saint Francis came Saint John of the Cross—at the Matutinal Mass.

January 7 [1949]

When Dom Robert was here he advised me to pray that I would not be made cantor. I did and now I am not even assistant subcantor. I have reached my ambition of being nothing whatever in choir and it gives me a certain amount of peace. I don't mind the singing now that I am not responsible for it. I can spend the office praying instead of fretting. The job I got this year is Assistant Master of Ceremonies, which is just what I need. I couldn't have been given the job at a better time—just getting ready for the priesthood. It keeps me in the sanctuary and I am forced to learn all the ceremonies, at least the salient ones from the deacon on down. It all started yesterday when besides the Pontifical we had the blessing of a monastic crown, a minor order (Frater Gervase became an exorcist), and Brother Donatus, to celebrate his golden jubilee of simple profession, renewed his vows, this time in church. He is the first brother to have gone through the profession ceremony in church according to the statutes of last year's General Chapter.

Father Modestus, now cellarer, kicked me out of Saint John's room, painted it up in one day and threw out all the rubbish, and now it is a very efficient place rattling with the noise of business, with three or four brothers in there all the time. Meanwhile, of course, I am out. He wanted to send me up to room 14 on the third floor of the "hotel" (guest house), but I balked at that and ended up in the rare book vault. *Omnia cooperantur in bonum*

*iis qui diligunt Deum.** The place has two steel doors and is as
nearly soundproof as any corner of this noisy Trappist monastery. I have permission to take some of my intervals in there to
work on the manuscripts—and Dom James said with a spark of
encouragement, "Maybe this is the solution to your vocation
problem," i.e., the Carthusians. That has ceased to be a problem,
but the vault is nice and quiet and when I went from there to
second Vespers of the Epiphany with the folios of a fifteenth-
century manuscript—all about the presence of God and the
mysteries of Christ—fresh in my mind, the office was better
than it had been for months, and love, love, love burned in
my heart. Still does. Waves of it come and go. I swim on the
waves. It is beautiful.

How quiet it is in the vault. I open a top window and you see
nothing but a little square of blue Kentucky sky and the sun
streams in on the bindings of the codices and the big quartos and
the little duodecimos and everything is silent and you are steeped
in the presence of God until it makes you numb. And in the refectory they were reading about Saint Augustine. . . .

January 8

. . . and it nearly made me cry.

Today, Sunday within the Octave of the Epiphany, is the first
day of recollection for 1949. When I came here seven years ago
I knew I would have crosses, but I never expected that one of
the biggest would be mail. I am getting something like seven to
ten letters a day, and I am praying Our Lord to make them stop
before it gets any worse. One lady told me she had wanted to
write me but had decided not to, until she read an article in
Cosmopolitan which said, "If you like a book, sit down and write
a letter to the author." I have mixed feelings about the author of
that article.

I had some cards printed at the print shop and they all went.
The first batch said I had received the letters and read them with
deep appreciation; now the second batch just says thanks for the
letter—because I hope to work out a plan by which most of them

*"All things work together for the good of those who love God."

will not be given to me, but that only means trouble for somebody else. Besides, I feel like a heel, not wanting to read all the letters most of which are very kind and sensible and full of Christ's charity: and as a whole, they manifest such a thirst for God and for prayer that they make me feel good about the world outside.

Not that the world outside is, physically, any more lovely than it ever was.

Wednesday, the Vigil of the Epiphany, Reverend Father and Father Emery and Father Raymond and I were all driven in to Louisville by Senator Dawson. Father Raymond had to go to the hospital. Father Emery and I were making application for citizenship, vulgarly known as first papers. It is the second time for both of us. Our first papers lapsed while we were busy with the pursuit of perfection in the novitiate and then the idea came back to us both simultaneously last summer. We are still busy, of course, with the pursuit of perfection. That was what Father Willibrod's speech in Chapter was about, this morning.

Louisville was dull as usual. The only good thing about the trip was that we stayed two hours in the Cathedral waiting for Reverend Father to finish his business. It is the first time in years—since the novitiate—that I have had a chance to pray two hours at a stretch. And then we fasted all day. Got back to the monastery at four and gobbled the warmed-up bowl of macaroni they had saved for us, and rushed in to first Vespers of the Epiphany just as the invitator (a novice) was having a nervous breakdown over the first antiphon *"Ante luciferum genitus."*

In winter the stripped landscape of Nelson county looks terribly poor. We are the ones who are supposed to be poor: well, I am thinking of the people in a shanty next to the Brandeis plant, on Brook Street, Louisville. We had to wait there while Reverend Father was getting some tractor parts. The woman who lived in this place was standing out in front of it, shivering in some kind of rag, while a suspicious-looking anonymous truck unloaded some bootleg coal in her yard. I wondered if she had been warm yet this winter. And I thought of Gethsemani where we are all steamed up and get our meals, such as they are, when meal time comes around, and where I live locked up in that room with incunabula and manuscripts that you wouldn't find in the house of a millionaire! Can't I ever escape from being something comfortable and prosperous and smug? The world is terrible, people are starving to death and freezing and going to hell with despair and here I sit with a silver spoon in my mouth and write books and everybody sends me fan-mail telling me how wonderful I am for giving up so *much*. I'd like to ask them, what have I given up, anyway, except headaches and responsibilities?

Next time I start sulking because the chant is not so good in choir I had better remember the people who live up the road. The funny thing is, though, they could all be monks if they wanted to. But they don't. I suppose, somehow, even to them, the Trappist life looks hard!

(Evening, after supper.) I just read the Gospel of the Purification. (I am taking Saint Luke to meditate on in this interval, for a month, and it is so beautiful that I am all lighted up with lights inside and there is a feast in my heart.) And I hear the antiphons singing already. Also I think of Saint Ailred, who comes the day after. And I think of Adam of Perseigne's *Mariale* and of digging up buckberries in the calf pasture when I was a novice, and praying to Our Lady and Saint Ailred. The Purification is one of my favorite feasts. But it is poignant, too, because it means the Christmas cycle is over.

How beautiful the Mass of today: Jesus has manifested Himself to the whole world in His Epiphany and so now the Church sings "*Servite Domino in laetitia*" and Christ goes back to Nazareth with His foster father and His Virgin Mother "and He was subject to them."

January 12

It is the anniversary of Saint Ailred's death when he went to heaven saying "Christ . . . Christ" in English because he liked it better in English than in Latin.

Perhaps one of the functions of a contemplative is to help other people, by word or merely by example, to become aware of how much they are capable of loving God—or perhaps of how much they already love Him without knowing it.

Christ recognizes Himself when the souls that possess His like-ness in them by charity, recognize one another by some actual expression of His love in one another, and begin to praise Him and thank Him and move one another to greater love, in His joy.

It is a great thing when Christ, hidden in souls—and perhaps forced by the world to keep in hiding—manifests Himself unex-pectedly by an unplanned expression of His presence. Then souls light up on all sides with recognition of Him and discover Him in themselves when they did not even imagine He could be anywhere.

His one Image is in us all, and we discover Him by discovering the likeness of His Image in one another. This does not destroy the differences between us but all these accidentals cease to have much meaning when we find that we are really one in His love. It is great praise of Him when people rejoice at finding Him in one another—not by effort, not by mere blind acts of faith, but by the experience of a charity illuminated, perhaps, by Wis-dom—for it is "sapience" and fruition of God's reflection in the joy which is His mirror in souls.

January 29

Reverend Father is supposed to get home from Utah today. He had been gone for about two weeks—and the reason was that Dom Robert's abbatial blessing took place in Atlanta on the 18th and Dom Maurice was blessed a week ago today in Utah. Last night in Chapter Father Prior read us a very funny letter from Reverend Father describing Dom Robert trying to get to bed in the pullman berth, on the way from Georgia to Utah.

I am supposed to be studying up the immensely complicated functions of the Second Master of Ceremonies on Candlemas day. Being between the hammer and the anvil I never simply get a candle and hold on to it. No. People suddenly rush up and give me candles which I have to pass on to someone else. If they re-fuse, I use my authority and my permission to speak and mutter "*Take* it!" and then retire behind the pillars and whip out the little book of rules to find out what I really ought to have done.

Father Macarius in Chapter talked about Blessed Guerric and Saint Amedeus and quoted Gerard Manley Hopkins at least twice.

After Chapter it was trying to snow: but we have had practically nothing resembling cold weather all winter. In Utah it is supposed to have been the worst winter in 15 years. So there! It just goes to show you never can say anything sensible about the weather.

But the Purification is a beautiful feast. Here I sit and look at the big snowflakes flying around the window like feathers and my heart grows warm within me at the thought of those lights. *Lumen ad revelationem Gentium.* Candlemas is to me a feast of inexpressible joy—joy in the lights of the Holy Ghost that lead men to God, as Simeon was led to the Temple *in spiritu* at exactly the right time.

And God disposes us in the Church, bearing the lights of our proper vocations in the procession. Saint Bernard's sermons are beautiful above measure on this feast although they are very simple. He seems to say, by the way, that the Purification was the only feast on which the Cistercians had a procession in his time. The Feuillants started the procession with the abbot singing out *Procedamus in pace!*

I was reading in the *Rituel Propre de Citeaux* that at Citeaux they read nothing but Saint Bernard at the reading before Compline for "many centuries"—the reading lasted *"un demi-quart d'heure"* and was varied by the *Exordium Magnum* during the Octave of Saint Stephen Harding. Incidentally our Fathers also had an octave for the Purification.

(Evening.) Dom Robert and Reverend Father got here and Reverend Father's room has been cleaned up. The huge black desks and bookcases, that were a mountain of darkness in Dom Frederic's time, have gone and the floor and new chairs are pale and the desk is clean-cut and low and the whole place is so shiny it looks as if it were made of glass.

For my own part this evening I was thinking, "Maybe I am

finished as a writer." Far from disturbing me, the thought made me glad. Nothing seems so foolish as to go on writing merely because people expect you to write. Not that I have nothing to say, but fame makes me inarticulate. Anyway I certainly find it extremely difficult to believe in myself as a poet.

On the other hand I am haunted by beautiful thoughts—solitude, obscurity, emptiness, *munditia cordis*, a virgin spirit. That my spirit, which has been raped by everything stupid, could again become a virginal spirit in the clean, simple darkness of pure faith, with no more half-lighted shadows between myself and God and no more desires biting my will like a bed of thorns!

Theology? Do I have to be tough about it, like a Dominican? That is not our spirit. No question, of course, but that I must know it if I am to *write* it. But do I have to write it in the first place? If I have to, all right. I'll take time, because I see no more reasons for hurrying and a million reasons for taking time—if I *get* time.

It was supposed to be a penance for Saint Joseph of Cupertino to be locked up in a little obscure convent in the hills where nobody knew he could fly . . .

January 31

Dom Robert sang a Pontifical High Mass yesterday. We had no green vestments for all those people so we used "gold."

Today—after the Night Office we were discovered to be deep in snow. For that matter the holy water was frozen in the dormitory cells last night when we went up. In a minute we have the Pontifical requiem—Solemn Anniversary for the Superiors of the Order which means Dom Frederic and very likely also Dom Benoit.

February 1

Deus quem innocentes martyres non loquendo sed moriendo confessi sunt . . . I was thinking of that all during collation. It is our vocation. It is our innocence to die without argument. People

---

*"O God, whom the martyred innocents confessed, not by speaking but by dying . . ."

ask me advice. I suppose I shouldn't give it. I feel terrible when I do—not because they will think I am a fool, but because they might go ahead and take it.

(Father Osee goes by and signals, "You write too much—take a rest, take a rest.")

It was utterly beautiful out there in the snow this afternoon. Everything was blue. Plenty of snow in the branches of the cedars but it was melting fast in the sun. Before Vespers the shoulders of the hills were brown. But it was beautifully quiet except for a moment I could hear what might have been bombers, but not bombs or guns.

Why do I desire things that are not God?

Inside me, I quickly come to the barrier, the limit of what I am, beyond which I cannot go by myself. It is such a narrow limit and yet for years I thought it was the universe. Now I see it is nothing. Shall I go on being content with this restriction? If I never become anything but a writer, that is what it will amount to—sitting on my own desert island which is not much bigger than an English penny. Desire always what is beyond and all around you, you poor sap! Want to progress and escape and expand and be emptied and vanish into God.

How quickly my limits accuse me of my nothingness and I cannot go beyond. I pause and reflect and reflection makes it more final. Then I forget to reflect any more and by surprise I make a little escape, at least to the threshold, and love moves in darkness, just enough to tell me that there is such a thing as freedom.

February 2   PURIFICATION

The feast was beautiful. The only thing I did that was really bad was to walk away with the bookstand with the book on it while the candles were being distributed, not realizing that the book would be needed afterwards. The Master of Ceremonies reproached the sacristan rather sharply for this misdeed of mine.

In the refectory was read a short life of Saint Benedict Joseph Labre who is definitely one of my favorites. The only way he could find solitude was by being the most despised person in a crowd—going so low that everybody ignored him, although he had to work to keep himself there: refusing friendship, practically never speaking, regarding everyone who treated him kindly as a benefactor, not as a friend.

There is something in my nature that makes me dream of being a tramp but from what I know of my experiences at being one, sanctity does not lie that way for me. I was always strictly a tourist even when I traveled on foot or hitched rides. And a respectable one too, in the pejorative sense of the word respectable. Even as a Trappist I am woefully respectable, though not conventional. I have no fleas, either, because I don't like fleas and I suppose I'm not the kind that becomes sanctified by lice—although one never can tell what the future holds in store.

I don't really like to get my feet wet but does that mean that the only way for me to be a saint is to have only one pair of shoes full of holes? Of course I have only one pair of house-shoes and one pair of work shoes but Brother Cornelius fixes them up at once if they get holes in them—and if I don't draw his attention to their needs I get proclaimed in Chapter. . . .

I wonder if, after all, sanctity for me is tied up with that vault full of manuscripts, and writing, and poetry and Gregorian chant and liturgy. It seems absurd for a man to be sanctified by things he naturally likes.

The answer is, of course, simple. I have made my vows according to a certain rule which does not, *per se*, involve fleas: but on which my sanctity does depend. The essence of that Rule is obedience and prayer—the renunciation of your own will, community life, undivided and uncompromising love and adoration and praise of God.

Stop asking yourself questions that have no meaning. Or if they *have*, you'll find out when you need to—find out both the questions and the answers.

February 3   SAINT AILRED

The High Mass was quite beautiful—first the organ went dead, and that made the sanctuary (where I am sub-deacon for the week) utterly peaceful. Then—on the altar there were a few pink blossoms from those strange bushes in the cloister garden that have bloomed on and off all winter. They bloomed at Christmas too, but then the flowers were so anemic that they were greenish white—and they stayed on the altar for a couple of weeks, until the Epiphany. The other night the thermometer was somewhere near zero. There was still snow on the ground today. We went out to work in the woods at the foot of the Vineyard Knob, trimming the crests of trees that must have been felled two years ago because the wild grape vines were growing all over them.

Mother Lutgarde Henery, late Abbess of Laval, certainly had a vocation to be Abbess. She took the habit with her own name—Céline—and when profession came along her superiors changed her name to Lutgarde so that she would one day be Abbess with the name of a Cistercian saint. She prayed God not to let her get elected next Abbess of Laval and was spared, but Mother Antoinette was a cripple who had to be waited on by three or four laysisters and couldn't do anything, so Mother Lutgarde was finally elected Abbess unanimously and stayed that way for over forty years.

Pictures of the Convent at Rivet were posted—the nuns from Blagnac moved there.

The affair rigged up behind the apse of the church to throw a light through Our Lady's window at the *Salve* stands outlined against the sunset like a gallows but I am glad those blue bulbs around the statue are no longer used. I hope they will be taken down so that they can't be used at Pontifical Masses either. The window looks nice at *Salve* and the first time the new stunt was tried it made Brother Fiacre gasp with mystical love.

February 7

Dom Benoit finally died of his cancer on January 31, a week ago today, when we had the commemoration of all the Superiors *hoc anno defunctorum*. And the day before yesterday Father Raymond came back from the hospital in Louisville with his cancer all gone. He looks better than he did a month ago and might never have been ill at all. Gets up at 3, comes to choir, is in the community refectory.

Poor little Dom Benoit—he was a saint. He loved and under-stood contemplation—and practiced it. He was steeped in the spirituality of Elizabeth of the Trinity, a quiet, cheerful little man—Breton I suppose. He originally came from Thymadeuc and volunteered for the Far East like so many others from there. He never had good health. He looked like some of the more sprightly engravings of De Rancé. The first time I saw him, Dom Frederic was taking him around the house and he stuck his head in the door of the laybrothers' chapter room where we were having theology class and I remember his round eyes and his exclamation, "O! So many! . . . so many students! . . ." I sup-pose there were seven or eight of us.

He always gave me good advice and told me to pray for humility and to "*goûter les humiliations.*"* I can't say that I get very many to "relish."

When he came here the first time he had a beard—one of the last monks in the Order who still wore one, but I suppose the Abbot General was the one who made him shave it off because when he came back with Dom Marie Joseph he didn't have a beard any more. He wanted me to read Lehodey's *Saint Aban-don*—I have never completely done that yet. I hope he will pray in heaven for me to love Jesus with very great simplicity.

February 9

I had written to the Dominicans at St. Maximin, La Sainte Baume, for a book they put out about their place. Henry de Segogne recommended it as a model of its kind. The Prior wrote and said it was already out of print and reprinting was too expensive but he sent a little folder about the place, and some postcards.

I can think of no better place for a monastery than over the tomb of Saint Mary Magdalen. The Trappists had it for a while, under Dom Augustin, but it was a thirteenth-century Dominican foundation. The cloister seems huge. I had also asked them about the Camaldolese at Roquebrune (Var) and they told me that two

*"Relish humiliations."

years ago the hermits packed up and went home to Italy and that now Roquebrune was a Discalced Carmelite "desert" and this made me happy. I did not know they really had "deserts" to go to for contemplation any more. It is very comforting to know that they have. I wish *we* had.

My work has been tied up in knots for two months—more. I am trying to write *The Cloud and the Fire** which is a book about contemplation and the theology of contemplation at that. The theology of contemplation does not mix well with fan mail. Also it is difficult. It is certainly impossible to write such a book with a lot of other concerns on your mind—for instance at the end of January the printers gave me the dummy for the centenary book and I was busy for two weeks writing captions and finishing the copy for *that*.

It takes a tremendous effort of will to get back to *The Cloud and the Fire* and I am usually helpless when I try to move that typewriter and get something on paper. I have a huge mass of half-digested notes, all mixed up, and I can't find my way around in them. My ideas are not fixed and clear. I have been trusting more or less to see them work themselves out on paper as I type —and have in any case made up my mind to regard the whole first draft of this book simply as preliminary notes. On the other hand, when I rewrite anything I entirely revolutionize it, sometimes with no improvement at all, because I only lose the freshness of the original and am just as prolix over again, but in a different and duller way. It is hopeless for me to write without the heat of some new ideas.

Into the middle of this came Sertillanges' *La Vie Intellectuelle* which may have what I need to cheer me up and keep me organized. I have glanced at it here and there and it has on me the effect that Dale Carnegie's advice might have on a despondent salesman.

Definitely, I have to make time for this book I am writing and get at it and finish it, patiently, and not let myself be eaten up by mail or other chores that do not really count—always excepting what comes directly by obedience and there is a fair amount

*Subsequently published as *The Ascent to Truth*.

of that. Fan-mail is not the problem: but letters that need to be
answered out of charity or monastery business . . . For instance there is a monk at Aiguebelle who wants a map of North
America with all our monasteries and all those of the Common
Observance marked on it.

February 13

SEPTUAGESIMA. DAY OF RECOLLECTION

Last night we threw away the *Alleluia*, very loudly too. Today
we got the *massa damnata* in the second nocturn and purple vestments at Mass and we all made a lot of mistakes, and in Chapter
we heard about what happened to Cardinal Mindszenty in Hungary. Standing at the foot of the altar with the humeral veil
wrapped around the paten and up in front of my face I realized
that it was I who was in prison in Hungary, and that that was the
reason why I was standing there at that moment, because what
is done to Christ is done to me: what Christ suffers I suffer and
what I do in Christ's name Christ does and this Mass is part of
Christ's crucifixion in Hungary and Christ's triumph over anti-
Christ. And at the consecration I thought how much of me is still
like the Apostles before the Crucifixion, who only understood
glorious victories and didn't believe in suffering or defeat.

Cardinal Mindszenty's face with huge eyes popping out of his
head is posted by the Scriptorium door, next to a polite comfortable picture of what he looked like before the Reds got at
him with the needle.

Now—about *La Vie Intellectuelle* by Sertillanges—it would be a
nice feat to prove that it is *not* diametrically opposed to Saint
John of the Cross. I bet no one can do it. Maybe Jacques Maritain
can see how the two can be reconciled.

Yesterday I got to the part where he says that solicitude for
one's health is a virtue of the intellectual. I took to laughing, perhaps immoderately at sentences like this: *"Un travail manuel
doux et distrayant serait également precieux a l'esprit et au
corps." "Soignez votre alimentation." "Observez vous en matière
de sommeil comme au sujet de la nourriture trouvez la mesure*

*qui vous convient et faites en l'objet d'une résolution ferme. Il n'y a pas ici de loi commune."** No. Definitely not. I wonder how the Abbé de Rancé would like that book. He and Sertillanges are now capable of discussing it without undue heat, in heaven—for Sertillanges died last year on the Feast of Saint Anne, as suddenly as Dom Frederic, and a week or so before him. Dom Frederic wouldn't have agreed with this book any more than De Rancé— or Saint Bernard either.

It is all *true*. The monks in the Common Observance know that. But it is not our vocation, I suppose. You'd go crazy trying to practice that here.

There is a wonderful passage beginning, *"Au sortir du travail l'homme est comme un blessé, il a besoin d'enveloppement et de calme: qu'on n'aille pas le violenter; qu'on le détende et qu'on l'encourage; qu'on s'intéresse à ce qu'il fait . . ."* (p. 59).†

John of the Cross after getting out of that jail in Toledo, scrambling down a wall in the middle of the night and following a dog through the weeds and rubble on the river bank . . . *"Au sortir du travail l'homme est comme un blessé."* Well, he had in his pocket the manuscript of the *Spiritual Canticle* and the *Dark Night*, and he was certainly *comme un blessé*.

On the other hand there could be a way of being humble and following Sertillanges, and nobody can say whether Mabillon was not a greater saint than De Rancé. But I have long since given up the idea that working with the kind of intellectual steam prescribed by Sertillanges for his Dominicans could be any vocation of mine.

It seems to me that what I am made for is not speculation but silence and emptiness, to wait in darkness and receive the Word of God entirely in His Oneness and not broken up into all His

*"A light and distracting form of manual work would be equally valuable to soul and to body . . . Watch your diet . . . Find out what you need in the way of food and sleep and make this the object of a firm resolution. This is not a matter that falls under common law."

†"The man who comes away from his work is like one who has been wounded. He needs to be cared for in a calm atmosphere: do not treat him with violence! Help him to relax. Give him some encouragement! Show some interest in the things he does. . . ."

shadows. But the truth is, there is room for both. In what pro-
portions is there room for them in my life? That'll work itself
out in practice.

An intellectual here—old Father Alberic, how many years in
the infirmary? took what he got—paid for every page of his
Compendium very dearly—a careful censor and a good old man.
On the whole that was his way to sanctity. Could be mine.

In any case—the life of a Christian has meaning and value only
to the extent that it conforms to the life of Jesus. But Jesus lived
in poverty and hardship and died on the Cross. And all our lives
are offered with His to God in the Mass—if we are true
Christians. This can be fulfilled in any vocation, and Sertillanges
shows the particular way in which it is fulfilled in the life of an
intellectual, which he describes as "consecrated" and which he
doesn't need to tell me has crosses and an asceticism all its own.

February 15

I had been worrying and bothering for two months about being
unable to get anywhere with this new book, *The Cloud and the
Fire*. There were some forty pages of it, written mostly in blood,
since the end of the retreat. And they were terrible—great confusion. Too long-winded, involved, badly written, badly thought
out and with great torture too. Finally it has come to seem obvious that God does not want the book and that He has simply
blocked it by not giving me the strength, the sense, or the time
to write it.

Yesterday when I had to do a prefatory note for *The Waters
of Siloe*, it went like a breeze. I had six pages done in an hour
and a half, and time to spare to write to Bob Giroux before the
end of work. And besides that I had taken time out to read a long
letter from Laughlin and another from Sister Thérèse.

I had been thinking of tearing up *The Cloud and the Fire* for
a long time. I haven't done that, exactly, but I have simply stuffed
it into an envelope, plans and all, and reconsidered what it was
I was supposed to start.

About *The Cloud and the Fire*—I have in mind something that
needs to be done some day: the dogmatic essentials of mystical

theology, based on tradition, and delivered in the context and atmosphere of Scripture and the liturgy. In other words a mystical theology that is not a mere catalogue of "experiences" many of them outside the range of the ordinary economy of the Gifts —but a book that drinks contemplation *de fontibus Salvatoris* and exploits all the mysticism there is in the Liturgy and in revelation: an *objective* mysticism, integrated with the common intellectual heritage of the Church as a whole and yet with its full subjective application to the experience of the actual or potential mystic, the concrete and individual contemplative. The contemplation of the Mystical Body in all its members.

And this is what I seem to be incapable of writing at the moment.

February 20

More pages in Sertillanges that made me laugh: the ones about getting up in the middle of the night to scribble down the ideas that come to you. I'd hate to put down any of the notions that occur to *me* when I wake up in the middle of the night. Sertillanges is definitely not my tempo, and yet he has very good stuff about organizing one's work. Reflecting on my own position— I have exactly the two hours' minimum a day which he calls a minimum. These I have, I mean, for writing. I have other time for reading and prayer. In those two hours I have to take care also of correspondence, duties of charity (reading mss.) or obedience, proofs, contracts, photos for illustrations, talk to the printer on occasion—and I order books, and resist the temptation to read catalogues and scraps of magazines . . . it is a wonder I turn out anything at all. Yet with Our Lady's help the book— now changed and called *The School of the Spirit*—goes quite smoothly. I have to simply sit down at the typewriter with what I want to say planned out. That is the *sine qua non*—even if I write something completely different, as I did today.

It was like summer or late spring out behind the church. I stood in the sun and thought of the first time I came here, on retreat, that Holy Saturday, when the sun was warm and I made the mistake of arguing with those fellows from Notre Dame instead of keeping silence and loving God.

My complaints about the world in the *Mountain* and in some poems are perhaps a weakness. Not that there isn't plenty to complain about, but my reaction is too natural. It is impure. The world I am sore at on paper is perhaps a figment of my own imagination. The business is a psychological game I have been playing since I was ten. And yet there is plenty to be disgusted with in the world.

February 24 SAINT MATHIAS

Last night I read Bouyer's article on preaching in *La Maison Dieu* and it is tremendous. The preacher is not an apologist, not a professor, not a lecturer. He is a herald, an instrument announcing the salvation that God has decreed for men who accept it. The reaction of the Church to this is a thunder of apocalpytic *Alleluias*. The whole history of the world since Jesus ascended to His Father is simply marking time until the Gospel gets announced to all nations. Then the final purification and . . . *Parousia!*

Isaac de l'Etoile thought his monastery was at the ends of the earth because it was on an island in the Atlantic off the coast of France. All the same the monks must have felt pretty desolate, with nothing beyond them but gray sea. To this situation he applied the Quinquagesima text *"Ecce ascendimus Jerosolymam."**

February 27 QUINQUAGESIMA. FORTY HOURS

My own vocation to the priesthood has relation to the way all the other priests in France are living, the Ruthenian priests in concentration camps—the Jugoslavs like the two jubilarians from Mariastern who are in prison, among others.

Some men lead lives that cry out to heaven for vengeance and persecution and others suffer the persecution. And I, *in medio—* I write books.

*"Behold, we go up to Jerusalem."

I have given up wondering what lies ahead for Gethsemani and for myself—I mean I have given up doing it consciously although some time this morning I was speculating, in a fierce distraction, as to how long one would remain conscious if he were being martyred by having a spike driven into his head. Nice thoughts!

This week I am sub-deacon again. Going around the big house and sprinkling the cloisters and dormitories and other offices with holy water, at Tierce, I was very happy to be a sub-deacon. Coming down from the laybrothers' dormitory I caught a shaft of sun coming through the window and God was with me in the huge empty building—everyone being in church. However, in the refectory Brother Onesimus was working and Father Zeno the infirmarian was eating his mixt, because there was a very short interval. Chapter finished at 8 and Tierce began about 9, and there was a long line at the visit of the sick. The reason I know that is that I whipped up there with a note for a Psalter. We have to recite the psalter for Father Odo because Father Odo is dead.

He died on Friday afternoon just before a theology conference. He had been ill in the infirmary for years, anointed several times. His heart finally gave out. He had been sitting up saying rosaries all the night before because he couldn't sleep and he said Mass, sitting down, at 2 A.M. All morning he was painting pictures of Our Lady and the Sacred Heart of Jesus and after dinner he had a crisis and died.

He was guest-master when Dom James arrived, about 1925. I suppose Dom Edmond gave him the job to let him learn some English. He came here from Acey, in the Jura. He was Alsatian. I put down in *The Seven Storey Mountain* what he said to me in the confessional when I was a postulant, namely that many souls depended on my staying here. Several people have written to me since the book came out saying, "Father Odo was right."

After High Mass and Sext I suddenly remembered that last year on the first day of the Forty Hours I was being beaten up by violent feelings of repugnance at the thought of becoming a priest—disgust, fear, misgivings. Mixed in with all that, I remembered, was the question whether I would be alive *this* year and whether I would be a sub-deacon. Well, I am alive and I was sub-deacon at the Mass, and knew more or less what to do, and did it, and what is more I realize I am much better off for knowing and doing these things. Major Orders are definitely one of the great graces of my life. I have had very much peace since sub-deaconship—feel a greater interior *solidity* which comes from serving God in the sanctuary, in the liturgy, in closer contact with the immensely powerful action of Christ's Sacrifice. This power in me comes from a closer union with the whole Mystical Body. It comes from being united in sacrifice with a Body that is sacrificed along with Christ its head.

The difference between the person who stood there as subdeacon, this year, and looked over the top of the paten at Christ on the Cross, and the acolyte who stood between the pillars last year, gnawing his heart out with fears and strange questions, is very great indeed.

All the same, the wheel may well go 'round and bring back more questions. But it will still be different.

Deaconship is slated for the Feast of Saint Joseph. Saint Joseph is my great friend. And I have never been sensibly attracted to devotion to him as I am to Saint John Baptist, Saint Francis, Saint John of the Cross, Saint Augustine, Saint Mary Magdalen, Saint Agnes, Saint Teresa, Saint Bernard.

March 5   FIRST SATURDAY

Three long chapters in Exodus tell how Aaron was to be ordained priest. Then a chapter on the Sabbath—contemplation. Immediately after that is recorded Aaron's first known act as priest: he made the people a golden calf and had the heralds blow their trumpets and announce a feast for the idol and the people sat down to eat and drink and rose up to play. Chapter 32 is tremendous—for deacons. The sons of Levi are introduced—declaring themselves against the unarmed people standing among the victims offered to the idol.

Aaron: "I just put a little gold in the fire and what should come out but this statue of a calf!"

March 6 FIRST SUNDAY IN LENT
Yesterday *Seeds of Contemplation* arrived and it is handsome. I can hardly keep my hands off it. Laughlin says the burlap effect on the binding is a material they are using now in night clubs for wall covering.

Every book that comes out under my name is a new problem. To begin with, each one brings with it a searching examination of conscience. Every book I write is a mirror of my own character and conscience. I always open the final, printed job, with a faint hope of finding myself agreeable, and I never do.

There is nothing to be proud of in this one, either. It is clever and difficult to follow, not so much because I am deep as because I don't know how to punctuate, and my line of thought is clumsy and tortuous. It lacks warmth and human affection. I find in myself an underlying pride that I had thought was all gone, but it is still there, as bad as ever. I don't see how the book will ever do any good. It will antagonize people, or else make them go around acting superior and stepping on everybody.

Laughlin tells me a book club is taking it and advertising it as a "streamlined *Imitation of Christ*." God forgive me. It is more like Swift than Thomas a Kempis.

The Passion and Precious Blood of Christ are too little in the book—only hinted at here and there. Therefore the book is cold and cerebral. What is the good of trying to teach people to love God without preaching through those wounds? The reason I do not do so is because I am still selfish. I find myself thinking about what we ought to get for dinner in Lent; about how to distribute signed complimentary copies of the de luxe edition of this book. I should never have gone into such a thing as a boxed special edition. I must be crazy.

Ever since the death of Father Odo and the Forty Hours, my mind has been overactive and I didn't finally get back to resting

in God in silence until this afternoon when I got into the vault
for an hour and a half and once more became a rational being.
All week I had been underwater with the whole world swimming
between me and God, like a school of fish.

Sister James, in Malden, sent me her book on Emily Dickinson
and I am happy to dip into it and find one person in the world—
Emily—with my own aspirations, though in a different way. I
wish I had Emily's good sense.

March 12   FEAST OF SAINT GREGORY
Tomorrow I go on retreat for the diaconate.

Big pain in the back. Also a cold. It would be 'flu if I were not
so full of cod-liver oil. Also Father Macarius has badgered me into
taking the *frustulum* this year and it helps to take the edge off a
cold. Finally I have big red vitamin pills that go with the
frustulum.

The Lenten schedule has been changed this year and this is
a big relief. It makes much more sense now, with an hour's reading or more after Chapter, and Vespers in the evening where it
belongs.

We gave Father George extreme unction. He came down to
Church, and sat in his wheelchair up there in front of the Prior's
High Mass stall and I could hear him say *Credo* before he
received Viaticum. It was after dinner.

March 14   ON RETREAT
In Leviticus—*Iste est sermo quem praecepit Dominus, facite et
apparebit vobis gloria ejus* (9:6).*

If that is true of the sacrifices of the Old Law it is much truer
still of our liturgy.

A monk under solemn vows can still be concerned first of all
with his own perfection, his own sanctity—in other words he
can confine himself to seeking his own spiritual advantage. The

---

*"This is the word which the Lord has commanded, do it and His glory
will appear to you."

priest cannot legitimately put himself first in any way whatever: Christ is always first. A priest does not exist merely for his own sanctification but for the Sacrifice of Christ and for the Gospel, for the people, for the world. This implies his own perfection: but the perfection of a priest consists essentially in his offering of Christ's sacrifice perfectly, for himself and for the Church. He no longer belongs to himself, whereas a monk can very well belong to himself in a legitimate way, and be concerned almost exclusively with his own progress, leaving the salvation of the world on a secondary plane.

A priest must not put the salvation of souls above his own soul. There is no question of a choice like that. But he has to put God and the Mass before everything. He has the whole Church on his conscience, and he not only gives up his will in order to possess the virtue of obedience, he gives up his will in order to become an instrument for the salvation of the world and for the pure glory of God.

This afternoon we were out sawing up a lot of cedars that have been felled behind the wall on the east side of the enclosure. I came back in at three because of the retreat, paused in the cows' gate to pray, and came home slowly enough looking at the big hole in the hill that leads in to the new boiler-room under the Scriptorium.

I took the *Spiritual Directory* to read the chapter on "employments" (*Les Emplois*) because in point of fact that is what the priesthood means, in a Trappist monastery: employments, jobs, business. It is a good, sensible chapter. Don't desire them too much, don't fear them too much. Saint Francis de Sales' principle: ask for nothing, refuse nothing.

There was a slight shakeup in the house today because Father Cellarer needed to be relieved of his job as Master of Laybrothers. This shift occasioned many others, as usual. New sacristan, because the sacristan became Father Master. New refectorian because the refectorian became sacristan. New bookkeeper and so on all the way down to the shoemaker's apprentice.

The sun was warm. I stood by the wall and watched the lambs. I had not known of their arrival. Little black-eyed things, jumping like toys on the green grass. I thought: "Feed my lambs." There is certainly something very touching about lambs, until they find their way into holy pictures and become unpleasant.

Aiguebelle* wrote, giving me a chore for the history commission: to tell them exactly what is in those documents in our archives, about the abbeys of Theuley, Bithaine, Rosieres, etc. We have some eighteenth-century transcriptions of their cartularies. Today I did Theuley in summary fashion. It was founded by a gent called the Lord of Malregard who went to purgatory— as his name would have led anyone to expect—and appeared to a pious person with the injunction that his four sons had better build a monastery to get him out quick.

What impresses me is the fact that in the eighteenth century the monks suddenly got very interested in their history and copied out all their records just in time, before the French Revolution came along to burn down their houses and make a bonfire out of all those deeds. By that time I don't think the monasteries were entitled to all the land they had accumulated and had long since ceased to work for themselves!

March 15　ON RETREAT

The first thing about the Diaconate is that it is *big*. The more I think about it the more I realize that it is a *Major* Order. You are supposed to be the strength of the Church. You receive the Holy Spirit *ad robur*, not only for yourself, but to support the whole Church. You have got to fight the armies of the devil.

But Thou, O my God, shut not the mouths of them that sing to Thee.

I cannot write about martyrdom. I fear it and I do not understand it. And I was afraid the retreat would get around to that, and it did. That is why the Holy Spirit is given *ad robur* in this Sacrament. He is the Spirit of the martyrs.

Not that the Spirit of God is waiting to get everybody killed.

*Monastery in southern France.

He has His will for each one. For each one it means the highest liberty. *Ubi Spiritus Domini ibi libertas.** It does not seem to me that His will for me is a martyrdom of blood. But perhaps I only say that because I am afraid. Anyway, I do not ask one thing or another: only strength.

The Trappist life for me has never been a martyrdom. Sometimes I am ashamed that it has not. It makes me feel a little funny. I am supposed to be suffering. Well, I've had a pain in the back and shoulder. And a cold. So what. Father Prior makes me take the *frustulum.* So it is God's will for me to have breakfast. Round and round the mulberry bush.

Sufficient unto the day is the evil thereof. By now I ought to be getting enough sense not to care what happens tomorrow, after the way God has guided and tended me so far. Is He going to stop taking care of me, now that I want to love Him more? *Not a sparrow falls to the ground ...*

What I need from the diaconate—to realize that I can lack nothing. *Dominus regit me et nihil mihi deerit. In loco pascuae ibi me collocavit.* To trust Him—I wonder if I have ever really done that? What is the good of a priest who does not trust God, and who has no practical belief in His power? Say a lot of things about His power and then trust yourself rather than Him!

Pius XII said the Church needs witnesses rather than apologists.

Why should I be afraid of suffering martyrdom? I am already suffering it. My body is being killed in Hungary and Yugoslavia and China and it was killed before in Mexico and Spain and Germany. And in France a hundred and fifty years ago and in England and Ireland and Scandinavia before that. I am always being killed.

To become supremely unselfish. To become Christ's voice in the world. To announce His salvation, the acceptable year of the Lord. To build the walls of the Temple of Jerusalem in a world that has been destroyed. And may our Lady of the Apocalypse gain me the Spirit of God *ad robur.* This, I think, is essentially in order to preach Christ in the teeth of persecution.

*"Where the Spirit of the Lord is, there is liberty!"

March 20 THIRD SUNDAY OF LENT

Yesterday Father Vedastus and I went out to the ordination in albs so starched that they rustled like canvas and stuck out all around us like hoop skirts.

I don't think I have ever seen a day like yesterday, and I am still dazzled by a dazzle that comes at me from all sides and from a source that I am not used to and which I can't spot at all, not in the way I could spot the contemplation that I am by now used to.

First, kneeling in the sanctuary after ordination and during the Canon of the Mass, I realized clearly that I ought to stop trying to be a poet and be definite about it too. I went to Reverend Father afterwards and he said, all right. And I have recovered a great deal of interior liberty by that one thing. In the afternoon I tore up all the rough notes for a poem. They had been lying around for a few days.

So after ordination, in this respect and in others, I felt for the first time in my life, like a more practical person. All of a sudden I seemed to know just what to do about everything that is on my mind at the moment.

Today I was on as deacon at Benediction. The new sense of practicality did not extend to the ceremonies. I was in a fog, but very happy. All I could think about was picking up the Host. I was afraid the whole Church might come down on my head, because of what I used to be—as if that were not forgotten!

But God weighs scarcely anything at all.

Though containing more than the universe, He was so light that I nearly fell off the altar. He communicated all that lightness to my own spirit and when I came down I was so happy I had a hard time to keep myself from laughing out loud.

March 21 SAINT BENEDICT

Yesterday and the day before I felt as if I had found a new center. Something I could not grasp or understand: but nothing else in the world seemed worth trying to grasp or understand either. So I grasp nothing and understand nothing and am immensely happy. The miracle of three days in which to be quiet has made all the graces of the diaconate sink deep into my soul. Today— two hours in solitude, practically. The tentative Lenten sched- ule gives us all that between dinner and Vespers.

I did a little work on the eighteenth-century cartulary mate- rial (copies of documents) on monasteries in the archdiocese of Besançon for the History Commission, then I tried to go on to Saint Bernard, but in the end couldn't do anything but sit still and be dazzled.

March 27   LAETARE SUNDAY

Since the diaconate Our Lady has taken possession of my heart. Maybe, after all, *she* is the big grace of the diaconate. She was given to me with the book of the Gospels which, like her, gives Christ to the world. I wonder what I have been doing all my life not resting in her heart which is the heart of all simplicity. All life, outside her perfect union with God, is too complicated.

Lady, I am your deacon, your own special and personal dea- con. What made me want to laugh in the middle of the Gospel this morning was the fact that you were doing the singing and I was just resting and sailing along.

Because you told me that if I gave you my soul, it would be- come your soul. After all, if I give you a book it becomes *your* book and if I give you a picture it becomes your picture. So if I give you a soul—my soul—it ceases to be mine and becomes *yours* and you are the one who uses it and moves it. And believe me, Lady, that is all I want. Because everything that is yours is perfectly united to God in pure simplicity.

April 2   SATURDAY BEFORE PASSION SUNDAY

We sang the *Vexilla Regis* and I thought with a certain deep satisfaction, messed up by confusion on the surface, that I am probably going to be separated from all this writing to which I am attached in spite of my complaints about it.

The last week or two I have been trying to clean up the galley proofs of *The Waters of Siloe*. Then four crates of Migne's Greek and Latin Fathers came in from a bookseller in Melun and

I had to break them all open and see just what we got. I was surprised to find so many of the Latin Fathers practically brand new. Physically the Greek set was a little ratty but I was happy to see Saint Gregory of Nyssa whom we don't have here. The rest are for the South Carolina foundation.

April 3

PASSION SUNDAY. DAY OF RECOLLECTION

I wish I had in me, I mean permeating all my soul like oil in a fabric, that kindness of Christ which I sang in last week's Gospels—when He raised from death the son of the widow of Naim and Lazarus.

The sorrow of Martha did not make Him weep, but the tears of Mary made His own tears spring up and overflow from His eyes. And that is how much He prefers contemplatives, because they are closer to Him.

Gray day—apple blossoms on this side of the barns, but not yet on the other side.

To be led and moved by the love of God: indifferent to everything except that. This is the source of the only true joy. *Laetabor ego super eloquia tua sicut qui invenit spolia multa.* There is really no sense in seeking or desiring anything but His will. But when you have found that, you have everything, not because His will is just arbitrary and you love it blindly for its own sake: but His will is the expression of His wisdom and His infinite truth and it springs from truth and brings us all truth, and catches us up into itself and sweeps us away with the inexorable tide of truth. To have His will in your heart and in your mind and in your love is to have sanctity and happiness. It is the foundation of all vision. Without it, even what you know to be true is no use to your soul because you are divided from the truth and armed against it.

April 5 FEAST OF BLESSED JULIANA

Yesterday was a landmark in the history of Gethsemani.

In the Chapter room, before the assembled community, and

scrutinized by the portraits of Dom Eutropius, Dom Edmond, and, above all, Dom Benedict, Robert Speaight gave us some readings from *Murder in the Cathedral.* That was our "reading before Compline" last night. It ended at about quarter to seven and we got to bed late. The first time Gethsemani has stayed up to go to the theater.

It was very good.

But what was best about it was that I felt the community was responding to it far better than the New York audience in which I sat and saw *Murder in the Cathedral* years ago. Here there was plenty of laughter at the apologies of the Four Knights. The last time I saw it I thought I was going to get thrown out by the ushers for being so indiscreet as to laugh at a play which, to judge by the program, was obviously high art.

There were many who were deeply moved by the whole thing. I think the chorus about hell went over big. Even Dom Benedict's portrait enjoyed that. The Christmas sermon was beautiful. I had the feeling that it was fully appreciated—because it is so simple.

The thing that struck me was the thought "saints are not made by accident," "martyrs are not made by men's choice but by God's." That, after all, was the echo of what Dom Frederic used to say so much in that same Chapter room *"non vos me elegistis sed ego elegi vos."**

It all began when Reverend Father came into the vault in the middle of the afternoon work asking if we had a copy of *Murder in the Cathedral* in the house. Then he took me in to talk to Speaight. Since he is a member of the firm of Hollis and Carter, who are publishing the London edition of the *Mountain,* I gave him the fancy set of galleys of *Waters of Siloe* which had been sent for the General when he comes here.

Speaight said that half the people he knew had at one time or another tried to become Carthusians. One of them had been sent away after having been told kindly, "We never before kept any-one so long with such a bad voice as you have!"

*"You have not chosen Me but I have chosen you."

He was very pleased about the way the community received *Murder in the Cathedral*. He said the first night of the play in New York was the closest he ever got to purgatory.

He goes all over England telling people how, the last time he was here, Father Augustine, who heard his confession, told him that to inspire himself with high ideals he ought to think constantly of the illustrious English Catholics, Hollis and Lunn. The first two to whom he told this story were his friends, Hollis and Lunn.

Speaight wanted me to write a book about Saint Bernard. In fact he suggested it without my having had time to bring it to mind. But his suggestion was just what I had been thinking about for months now.

He said T. S. Eliot regards every poem as a temptation and resists it for years. Amen.

April 6

Yesterday a short but beautiful letter came from Dom Porion, the Procurator General of the Carthusians in Rome. I had written to him, at the suggestion of Jacques Maritain, telling him that a copy of *The Seven Storey Mountain* was on the way. Maritain thought he would like it and also told me to send copies to Father Paul Philippe at the Angelico and to Monsignor Montini.

This letter was very beautiful. It spoke directly about the possibility of a foundation in this country which, he said, was unlikely. But he said he was going to bring it up at the next General Chapter but that the idea would probably not be accepted. He said how difficult it was to find people who could live purely for God alone in solitude, occupied with nothing but Him.

The way it was put was so concrete and well stated that I saw at once very clearly how literally the contemplative vocation is taken by the Carthusians.

Really the letter tore me to pieces, and yet it made me happy.

It reminded me of my own longing for solitude, interior purity, perfect silence, a life for God alone. I haven't prayed in months as I have been praying since I read that letter: not praying to be anywhere but here (except of course heaven) but burning up with the desire of God and with shame at my unmitigated interior activity and the futility of so much that I do.

And yet since the diaconate I have a new attitude. Although it half kills me, I find myself accepting the idea that perhaps I do not have a purely contemplative vocation. I say "accept." I do not *believe* it. It is utterly impossible for me to believe any such thing: everything in me cries out for solitude and for God alone. And yet I find myself admitting that perhaps I don't know what that really means, and that I am too low in the spiritual scale of things to grasp it, and even that I am somehow excluded from it by God's love. The feeling is absolutely terrible—the power of attraction that seems to draw the whole life out of me, to tear out the roots of my soul—and then the blank wall against which I stop—dead.

Yet in the middle of all this I find not unrest or rebellion but happiness and peace, and I rejoice in it, because blindly something in the middle of me clings to the one reality that remains accessible to me. This is the supreme reality of all—the love of God.

Somehow, I have to give up this thing that I love above everything else on earth *because the love of God is greater*. It seems like a contradiction: because what I have to give up is, in the last analysis, what I am convinced is the most perfect way I could love and serve God! But that is *per se. Per accidens* there is something greater: to renounce the purest of all vocations simply because it is not the one God has chosen for me—to accept something in which it seems likely that my highest personal ideals will be altogether frustrated, purely because of His love, His will. He who loves me prefers it this way, and to accept His love is to send up to Him the incense of the purest prayer, the sweetest praise, without pleasure for myself—and yet in the end it is a supreme joy! *Adoremus Dominum qui nos redemit per crucem.*

April 14   GOOD FRIDAY

First I must copy out some words from Dom Porion's letter. Or rather from his first letter. A second came, saying the book had reached him. Anyway, here is what was in the first letter—among other things. He wrote in English.

"Most people find their balance in doing, in creating something, mere contemplative life requires a special grace and a special fidelity. It requires a ripeness too, a maturity of soul which is not often to be met (with)in converts." (He was not aiming this at me since when he wrote that he didn't know I was a convert. But it is true of me also.) "This seems to result at least from the experiments we have made. But to contemplate in the first meaning of the word; to look directly at God and keep quiet—calm and purity being at once the condition and consequence of the vision—this indeed seems to me the true life, the life everlasting we are made for. The modern world seems to fly from that ideal: but I am convinced that mankind in the end will find again the way of contemplation—nature and surnature, in their deepest, lead to this divine joy."

There are also a lot of good things in Tauler whom I like very very much—when he is explained by notes like those of Father Hugueny.

Father Cantor lost his voice and wrote me a note last night to replace him as "Evangelist" in the Saint John Passion. The only direction he gave was "in all movements you are in the middle." Got all muddled up on the movements but it went well otherwise.

This afternoon I tried to be as quiet as I could for two hours in the vault and came out with the conclusion that writing is something very low and insignificant, and that I, who seem to have become identified with writing, am also low and insignificant.

April 15   HOLY SATURDAY

The Night Office of this day is bewildering. The confusion of sorrow and joy is so complex that you never know where you are. Some of the responsories might have been composed by James Joyce. All the associations of terms and symbols are thrown into confusion. One responsory starts out with *Jerusalem* . . . and you are all set to be glad. But you are told to mourn. Then in the end, speculatively, you find that you are saved. This is the product of the historical circumstances through which the Holy Saturday liturgy has passed.

But there is no confusion about the *Exultet*.

I often wondered if I would ever sing the *Exultet*. Well, I am supposed to sing it today. I am going to sing the whole of theology. It is marvelous. The *Exultet* is real liturgy—except perhaps it is too speculative. But really, the deacon who sings that and does the things the rubrics say, is teaching all theology. And the people who hear it are learning all theology, and the Holy Ghost, Who operates what is signified, throws light in darkness upon the whole meaning of Christianity, on the Mass, on Good Friday and Easter—the center of everything.

April 22 SATURDAY BEFORE LOW SUNDAY
Well, I sang the *Exultet* and stuck the five red grains of incense into the paschal candle, in the form of a cross, and afterwards sang the *Ite missa est* with two *Alleluias*.

And now the week has passed and the two *Alleluias* after every *Ite missa est* and *Benedicamus Domino* are finished and I sang the Epistles from the Acts and from Saint Peter and especially the one about the eunuch of Queen Candace who was riding in his chariot reading Isaias, which he did not understand.

On Sunday and Monday afternoons I spent the time in prayer and came out feeling as if I had been pierced and baptized, and with new knowledge about prayer and I hope new humility, as if I had also passed some milestone and gone down lower, or, if you prefer, up higher, or at least out of myself.

How much I need to go out of myself!

On Monday morning it was announced in Chapter that the Archbishop would really and truly be coming here on May 26th, that is Ascension Day, to ordain me and Father Vedastus to the priesthood and ordain four new sub-deacons into the bargain.

Today Father Titus was trying to teach us how to say Mass. I put my hands on the altar, there—one of those little altars in the back sacristy. I stood there while he talked. I kissed the altar, genuflected with my hands on the altar. I turned around and made the movement you make with your hands when you say

Dominus vobiscum. I held the paten up on my fingers with an imaginary host and said the *Suscipe sancte Pater.* Afterwards I thought how the union of ceremonies and words in the Mass is the simplest and deepest and most fundamental and also the easiest and most perfectly satisfactory way of adoring God that could be imagined—even from our own subjective point of view, and apart from all that is in it *in se.*

So I think very much of Our Lady of Cobre and of the question I once asked her.

April 29 FEAST OF SAINT ROBERT

It is extremely difficult to write theology well. The main reason why I can't write it is that I don't know it. I don't know precisely what I mean to say, and therefore when I start to write I find that I am working out a theology as I go. And I get into the most terrible confusion, saying things which I try to explain—to myself more than to anyone else—and rambling off the track of the plan I had arranged.

I wonder how many plans I have made for this book, *The School of the Spirit?* Perhaps six—including the ones I made for it when it was called *The Cloud and the Fire.* So I sit at the typewriter with my fingers all wound up in a cat's cradle of strings, overwhelmed with the sense of my own stupidity, and surrounded by not one but a multitude of literary dilemmas.

I am supposed now to be working on the book three afternoons a week and I try at all costs to get something down on paper, terrified that if I merely stop and read and organize notes I will go around in circles for ever and ever. This business of "getting my notes together" is something that can go on absolutely interminably, because there exists an almost unlimited number of combinations in which you can arrange the statements you have jotted down so carefully on some eight hundred pages of various notebooks.

All that undigested material is utterly terrifying, and fascinating at the same time. Sometimes I try to "meditate" on this monster which I call "my notes" (I should say "our" notes, but skip it)—but the statements standing out of context and in my own crazy handwriting do not have the meaning and unction they had in Migne or Saint John of the Cross or wherever I first discovered them. . . .

They seem to divide and slacken the mind and leave my spirit in a vague state of anguish, at the thought that I have eaten the Fathers and produced nothing but this unhappy web.

But when I tell myself "I am no writer, I am finished," instead of being upset I am filled with a sense of peace and of relief— perhaps because I already taste, by anticipation, the joy of my deliverance. On the other hand, if I am not delivered from writing by failure, perhaps I may go on and even succeed at this thing, but by the power of the Holy Ghost—which would be a greater deliverance. But whatever happens, success or failure, I have given up worrying. I just wonder about the business on paper, on the assumption that it might mean something to me if I should ever re-read all this at another season.

Nor is "saying Mass" as easy as I expected. I practiced it again today, this time alone, in the back sacristy at the altar of Our Lady of Lourdes. It is all right up to the "consecration" and would be all right after it, too, if you did not have to be so careful about your fingers. Your thumb and forefinger, of each hand, are only for picking up and breaking the Host. You use the other fingers on everything else. But I find myself uncovering the chalice, taking off the paten with those forefingers and thumbs, and touching the Host and purifying the paten with all the other fingers. In fact, the moment you have "consecrated," everything gets in the way. Then the dry host is hard to swallow, too. I am glad I am doing all this rehearsing *before* ordination.

Saint John of the Cross, at his first Mass, asked God for the favor of suffering for Him and dying abandoned as an outcast of men. I asked myself what it was I was going to ask of God at my first Mass, and I think it is not that. If I did ask that, it would be an act of insincerity in me, because it is not what grace usually seems to move me to and it would, I think, be only a piece of natural vanity, at least in my present dispositions. What does

God want me to ask Him? He will tell me, and when I find out, He will also give me what I ask. And no doubt the best thing in the world I could do with it would be to tell no one about it, and thus to do one greater thing than all the worthies did.

PART FOUR

To the Altar of God

That which is most perfect and most individual in each man's life is precisely the element in it which cannot be reduced to a common formula. It is the element which is nobody else's but ours and God's. It is our own, true, uncommunicable life, the life that has been planned for us and realized for us in the bosom of God.

My priestly ordination was, I felt, the one great secret for which I had been born. Ten years before I was ordained, when I was in the world, and seemed to be one of the men in the world most unlikely to become a priest, I had suddenly realized that for me ordination to the priesthood was, in fact, a matter of life or death, heaven or hell. As I finally came within sight of this perfect meeting with the inscrutable will of God, my vocation became clear. It was a mercy and a secret which were so purely mine that at first I intended to speak of them to no one.

Yet because no man is ordained priest for himself alone, and since my priesthood made me belong not only to God but also to all men, it was fitting that I should have spoken a little of what was in my heart to my friends who came to my ordination. I did not take time to write about it in this journal and do not intend to do so here, except to make the following remarks.

First of all, the greatest thing that happens in priestly ordination is the most ordinary. That is why Holy Orders is, in its conferring, the simplest of the Sacraments. The Bishop, saying nothing, lays his hands upon the head of the ordinand. Then he pronounces the words of a prayer and the new priest receives the grace and indelible character of the priesthood. He is identified with the One High Priest, the Incarnate Word, Jesus Christ. He is a priest forever.

God never does things by halves. He does not sanctify us patch upon patch. He does not make us priests or make us saints by superimposing an extraordinary existence upon our ordinary lives. He takes our whole life and our whole being and elevates it to a supernatural level, transforms it completely from within, and leaves it exteriorly what it is: ordinary.

So the grace of my priesthood, the greatest of my life, was to me something far greater than a momentary flight above the monotonous lowlands of an everyday existence. It permanently transformed my ordinary, everyday life. It was a transfiguration of all simple and usual things, an elevation of the plainest and most natural acts to the level of the sublime. It showed me that the charity of God was sufficient to transform earth into heaven. For God is Charity, and Charity is Heaven.

To love God is everything. And Love is enough. Nothing else is of any value except insofar as it is transformed and elevated by the charity of Christ. But the smallest thing, touched by charity, is immediately transfigured and becomes sublime.

The two most characteristic aspects of divine charity in the heart of a priest are gratitude and mercy. Gratitude is the mode of his charity for the Father, mercy is the expression of God's charity, acting in him, reaching through him to his fellow men. Gratitude and mercy meet and blend perfectly in the Mass, which is nothing else but the charity of the Father for us, the charity of the Son for us and for the Father, the Charity of the Spirit Who is Charity uniting us to the Father in the Son.

After my first Mass I understood perfectly and for the first time in my life that nothing else in the world is important except to love God and to serve Him with simplicity and joy. I saw most clearly that it is useless and illusory to look for some spectacular and extraordinary way of serving Him, when all ordinary

*service immediately becomes sublime and extraordinary as soon
as it is transfigured by love for Him. I saw, too, that His grace
and particularly the grace of the priesthood had made charity the
easiest thing in the world. It requires less effort to love God
than it requires to eat, or sleep, or breathe, or to perform the
simplest and most instinctive acts of our natural life: because it
requires no energy at all to make an act of will, and when our
wills are possessed and moved always by His grace, charity
becomes as spontaneous and constant and continuous as breath-
ing itself. I live, now not I, but Christ liveth in me. What is
easier than to let God live in you, and to love Him Who loves
you?*

*Yet, without the priesthood, this easiest thing in the world
had still been, for me, comparatively difficult, although I had
thought it was easy even then. And without baptism (at least an
implicit baptism of desire), the easiest thing in the world would
be impossible.*

May Day ss. PHILIP AND JAMES
DAY OF RECOLLECTION [1949]

As soon as a monk writes a book and gets it published the rumor starts traveling around: "He has left his monastery, you know." It began with me as soon as I had published *Thirty Poems*.

Nevertheless, it is a danger—but not because I am a *writer*. I am proud and I am defectible because I am an ordinary human being. Plenty of people have left this monastery who were not writers, and in the old days when many monks could hardly write their own names, there were a lot more departures and even real apostasies.

May 5

Today is the feast of that Saint Sacerdos who was Abbot of Huerta and Bishop of Siguenza. The other day I was reminded that Huerta is still a Cistercian Abbey by a letter from Spain—but the letter was from Viaceli and it contained information about another magazine they are starting, again in Spanish. Father Prior wondered whether to subscribe to it for the new monastery in South Carolina of which he will be the superior.

But the reason I started talking about Saint Sacerdos was that there is a lot about the priesthood in his Mass, which is *Statuit* from the common of Confessors Pontiff. Also the second *Alleluia* verse surprised me by being the melody we have in all the *Alleluias* at Christmas time in the Masses of the great feasts: and here we are in the midst of spring and everything is green and saturated with light and birds sing and the air is perfumed with the smell of the burning cedar wood where we have been clearing out the grove in front of the Abbey to prepare for the centenary celebration which is to be on June 1st only, and not, thank heaven, on June 1st, 2nd, and 3rd.

The other day I was out there with an axe and there were big fires all down the side of the little hill where the wayside shrine is, and the secular cemetery. The flames were angry and high and one delicate sapling which was left standing in the midst of all the fires withered and was blasted in the burning air. I watched the shuddering of the leaves in the gusts of that furnace and it made me think of Saint Joan of Arc.

May 8

"*Modicum et non videbitis me* . . ." I sang the beautiful Gospel: "Yet a little while and you shall see me no longer, because I go to the Father . . . The world shall rejoice and you shall be sad . . . but your sorrow shall be turned into joy and your joy no one shall take from you."

Which means: Yet a little while, and it will be Ascension Day.

It seems to me impossible that I should live the next two and a half weeks without keeling over, dying of heart-failure, or having the house come down on top of my head. How can I possibly achieve such a wonder as the priesthood? To do the one thing that saves the world and brings health into it and makes men capable of being happy! To continue the Mystery of Christ's Death and Resurrection and do all those simple and easy things by which the work of our Redemption is accomplished!

The fact that the Mass is so easy seems to me to be all the more reason first, for saying it perfectly and second, for making it your whole life.

I love the prayers that go with the incensation at a solemn Mass—the prayers and the ceremonies. These too, are so easy and simple and happy! What could be more joyful than swinging the censer full of sweet smoke around the chalice and Host and praying that our incense may go up to God and His blessing may come down to us—and that the fire of His everlasting love may burn in our hearts!

Most of my troubles come from a subtle lack of poverty. I mean the troubles at work—the correspondence that keeps me from writing that book. I have wanted to acquire too many things— books especially. Of course it is all "for the monastery" or "for the foundations" and it is all "blessed by obedience" but in the end it is all my own idea and I am in actual fact exercising the appetites of proprietorship and acquisitiveness even though the acts are legally purified. Hence all these complications—bartering books with the librarian at Achel and the librarian at Viaceli and the librarian at Bricquebec and Father Anselme at Tamié and the monks on the History Commission at Aiguebelle. Still, some of it is unavoidable. And Dom Déchanet in Bruges came after me to dig out the variants in our manuscript of William of St. Thierry's *Golden Epistle* so that he can identify it by the "family" to which it belongs. He can tell.

From all this flow distractions and bothers of all kinds and it has been sapping my spiritual energy—or trying to—for months. And here I sit resolving to stop it, and the catbird mocks me up there in the cedar tree.

I was reading the manuscript from the archives of Laval all about the Trappistines there and at Ubexy a hundred years ago —simple, fervent, and tough. They make me ashamed of myself and my "literary career."

Brother Carolus comes up and asks me by signs when hundred year big day book come? And I signal back to him "plenty late, plenty late." He says "How full pages? Two hundred?" I say "Naw sixty." But he says "Two hundred pictures?" and I say "Yeah." He goes away, not sad but not altogether happy.

The General is on his way here "*pour une visite sérieuse*" but I don't know when he will arrive. Reverend Father spoke in Chapter about what a headache the centenary is going to be, and he has been promising that once that is over, down will come the iron curtain—I hope we get all the reporters *outside* before it comes down.

I think almost entirely about the ordination and not at all about the centenary. Once I get those oils on my hands I'll be ready for anything.

May 15 ·FOURTH SUNDAY AFTER EASTER

The sun is rising. All the green trees are full of birds, and their song comes up out of the wet bowers of the orchard. Crows swear pleasantly in the distance, and in the depths of my soul sits God, and between Him, in the depths, and the thoughts on the surface, is the veil of an unresolved problem.

What shall I say this problem is? It is not a conflict of ideas. It is not a dilemma. I do not believe it is a question of choice. Is it a psychological fact: any interior problem is a psychological fact. Is it a question that I can resolve?

This problem is my own personality—in which I do not intend at any time to take an unhealthy interest. But (I speak as one less wise) this problem is my personality or if you like, the development of my interior life. I am not perplexed either by what I am or what I am not, but by the mode in which I am tending to become what I really will be.

God makes us ask ourselves questions most often when He intends to resolve them. He gives us needs that He alone can satisfy, and awakens capacities that He means to fulfill. Any perplexity is liable to be a spiritual gestation, leading to a new birth and a mystical regeneration.

Here are a few points:

What is the Mass going to do to my interior life?

I am confronted with the fact of my past prayer. Acts, thoughts, desires, words, became inadequate when I was a novice. Resting in God, sleeping, so to speak, in His silence, remaining in His darkness, has fed me and made me grow for seven years. Now that too is likely to become inadequate.

The Mass will hold the key of this inadequacy, I hope.

I cannot explain more at the moment, except that Christ the High Priest is awakening in the depths of my soul, in silence and majesty, like a giant, Who means to run His course.

When practicing the ceremonies of Mass, when standing at the altar as deacon, I have been more and more impressed by the fact that it would be utterly insufficient for me, as priest, to stand at the altar and say prayers with great personal love and fervor to Christ in the Sacrament before me. I once thought that would be the consummation of all joy—to be united by a bond of love with Christ in the Sacrament of love—to be lost in His presence there as if nothing else mattered.

And now—there is much more. Instead of *myself* and *my* Christ and *my* love and *my* prayer, there is the might of a prayer stronger than thunder and milder than the flight of doves rising up from the Priest who is the Center of the soul of every priest, shaking the foundations of the universe and lifting up—me, Host, altar, sanctuary, people, church, abbey, forest, cities, continents, seas, and worlds to God and plunging everything into Him.

In the presence of this huge power, my own thoughts and words and affections cannot seem to mean anything! Not that they have no value whatever: but now they are lost and sublimated in a far greater and simpler prayer that is beyond my comprehension.

As I sit here and write this, at the end of the afternoon, the robins are making much noise but not half so much noise as the novices who are full of polyphony for the day of wrath that is to come upon us on the first of June.

Meanwhile the community has been purged by sickness and accidents. The temporary door of the horsebarn fell down on Brother Nereus and crushed two vertebrae of his spine, and Father Gerard the novice-master is in the hospital with something unidentified, and Father Sub-prior fell down on his head and got knocked out while he was nailing up a partition in the red house. And maybe there is going to be another accident right away in the novitiate because Father Protase, who is conducting their *oratorio,* is stamping so hard that I expect him to go through the floor and break his collarbone among the pots and pans and bottles in the darkroom.

Anyway, there have been some colds in the community and one of the worst was the one that hit me. For two days I slept late—that is until 2:45 A.M.—and I still have no appetite for food. For that matter I haven't much appetite for anything else either.

But in the vault everything was beautiful. The page proofs of *The Waters of Siloe* lay neglected on the table, and I expect them to lie that way more or less until after ordination. I come out of myself and look at books and at letters and am sad, but I return to God and know that my vocation is to be a priest and a contemplative, and that my vocation is PRAYER. This makes me happy.

Father Abdon comes by with his rosary and makes me a sign "eleven days."

I had resisted the temptation to count the days to my ordination, on the grounds that it might be an imperfection—or that it might turn out to be something like David's census.

The Epistle of the day, "*suscipite insitum Verbum.*" And the Collect: "that our hearts may be fixed where true joys are." Another beautiful letter came in from Dom Jean-Baptiste Porion He said he likes the last part of the *Mountain* and that he shared my affection for Blake. That reminds me that the only other Catholic (besides Maritain) that I remember impressing me by a really sympathetic interest in non-Catholic mystics, is Dom Humphrey, another Carthusian—the one at Parkminster.

May 23 ROGATION DAYS

In three days, if I am alive and if the Archbishop does not fall down and break his leg, I should be a priest. I keep thinking: "I shall say Mass—I shall say Mass." And I remember our Lady of Cobre, to whose basilica I went nine years ago this May. She has done well by me, and her love has followed me this far, and will take me to God.

I can't read anything but Saint John of the Cross. I opened the *Living Flame* at the line, "*Rompe la tela deste dulce encuentro.*" The priesthood as an encounter of the substance of my soul with the living God! I do not understand it yet. Perhaps I will know more about it on Thursday. Anyway, that will be my prayer:

that more of the curtain may be taken away, and that the servi-
tude of desires that burden my whole life may be diminished,
and that I may be liberated and come closer to Him in the Mass
—in every Mass I offer. That each Mass may lighten the atmosphere and be a step forward to heaven and to vision. That each
Mass may be an enrichment and a liberation to my soul and to all
those souls who, in the designs of Our Blessed Lady, depend on
these Masses to come to holiness and to contemplation, to find
liberty and joy.

Apart from Dom Casel and Bouyer, most of the writing about
the priesthood does not satisfy me, and now I cannot read even
them. They seem too technical, and I need not literature but the
living God. *Sitivit anima mea.* The strong living God. I burn
with the desire for His peace, His stability, His silence, the
power and wisdom of His direct action, liberation from my own
heaviness. I carry myself around like a ton weight.

May 24

The problem of the priesthood for me is among other things a
problem of poverty. I know that not all priests are necessarily
committed, by their priesthood, to absolute poverty. But for my
own part it seems to me that the two are connected.

To be a priest means, at least in my particular case, to have
nothing, desire nothing, and be nothing but to belong to Christ.
Mihi vivere Christus est et mori lucrum. In order to have everything, desire to have nothing.

That contemplatives have nothing to do with the active ministry contributes more to our utter poverty, making it more complete and more spiritual. It implies the realization that perhaps
we have practically nothing to give to souls in the way of
preaching and guidance and talent and inspiration. We are
ashamed of any active apostolate that might conceivably come
from us. And so we vanish into the Mass—*omnium peripsema
usque adhuc* . . .

My poverty in spiritual goods, my defects and imperfections,
all have their part in this too. I shall go to the altar remembering

that Saint Paul said God had chosen the weak things of the world: *infirma mundi elegit Deus ut confundat fortia.*

Also: in my prayer and all my interior life, such as it is, I am concerned with the need for a greater and more complete interior silence: an interior secrecy that amounts to not even thinking about myself. Silence about my prayer, about the development of my interior life, is becoming an absolute necessity, so that I am beginning to believe I should stop writing about contemplation altogether, except perhaps in the most general terms. It seems to me to be a great indecency for me to pass, in the opinion of men, as one who seems to have something to say about contemplation. The thought makes me feel as if I needed a bath and a change of clothing.

May 25 VIGIL OF THE ASCENSION

In the Martyrology, together with the announcement of the great feast which always makes me so happy—there came also the annual commemoration of the Saint Augustine who re-converted England. After all these centuries I am one of the children of his prayers and apostolic labors and sacrifices.

The liturgy of the Vigil is matched by the brilliant weather of the day. Not a shred of cloud anywhere in the deep blue sky. This morning it was rather cool—like September. A thin rind of moon hung high over the bottoms and I almost expected to see fields full of tall ripe corn.

Vocem jucunditatis annuntiate et audiatur, alleluia . . .

I was very happy to sing the Gospel—the magnificent triumph of Christ which is echoed and expressed in the ordination to the priesthood of a thing like myself that He picked up out of the wreckage of the moral universe and brought into His house. It is He Who looks up to heaven, in my own soul full of weakness and infidelity, and cries out: *Pater venit hora, clarifica filium tuum ut filius tuus clarificet te.* And the context reminds me to whom I belong—*dedisti ei potestatem omnis carnis ut omne quod dedisti ei det eis vitam aeternam.* My joy is in the great power of Christ. Once again I am glad of my deep moral poverty which is

always before me, these days, but which does not obsess or upset
me, because it is all lost in His mercy.

The truth is, I am far from being the monk or the cleric that
I ought to be. My life is a great mess and tangle of half-conscious
subterfuges to evade grace and duty. I have done all things badly.
I have thrown away great opportunities. My infidelity to Christ,
instead of making me sick with despair, drives me to throw myself all the more blindly into the arms of His mercy.

May 29

SUNDAY WITHIN THE OCTAVE OF THE ASCENSION
I could not begin to write about the ordination, about saying
Mass, about the *Agape* that lasted three days, with all those who
came down to attend. Perhaps some day it will come out retro-
spectively, in fragments.

A sense of the absolutely tremendous work that has been done
in me and through me in the last three days; each day bringing
its own growth. Ordination, anointing, ordination Mass—then
the first low Mass and what followed, finally the Solemn Mass
yesterday and the talking in the afternoon out under the trees of
the avenue. I am left with the feeling not only that I have been
transformed but that a new world has somehow been brought
into being through the labor and happiness of these three most
exhausting days, full of sublimity and of things that none of us
will understand for a year or two to come.

(I got that far when Father Vedastus told me we were to go
up and bless the sick. The sick are old Father George who was
up there leaning over the table thinking of something, and
Brother Nereus in his cast, with a great big grin.)

I wish I could explain something about the gradation that seems
to have marked the three days of my festival. Each one seemed
to represent some gigantic development that I am powerless to
grasp or to explain. In the end I had the impression that all who
came to see me were dispersing to the four corners of the universe with hymns and messages and prophecies, speaking with
tongues and ready to raise the dead because the fact is, for three

days, we have been full of the Holy Ghost, and the Spirit of God seemed to be taking greater and greater possession of all our souls—through the first three Masses of my life, my three greatest graces.

It is all unfamiliar to me. These graces belong to an apostolic order that are beyond my experience. Yet I cannot say, without ingratitude and stupidity, that they were outside my vocation since they were in a sense its crown: I mean they crown this portion of my history—my last seven years. For this I came into the world.

Friday I said that Mass I had promised to Our Lady of Cobre. I had been told one got so mixed up in the rubrics that the first Mass was no fun. I did not find that to be true at all. On the contrary, I felt as if I had been saying Mass all my life, and the liturgical text of the Votive Mass of our dearest Lady in this season became immensely rich. It was at Saint Anne's altar and the church was full of sun (after Chapter) and there was no one else saying Mass nearby so I could really *speak* it. Then there was a beautiful chalice Dan Walsh brought down, and I had an amice and corporal and purificator and even a finger towel, all of which came from some colored boys and girls in a Catholic High School in Mobile, Alabama; and I had a cincture given by a sister in a hospital in St. Louis. If I had tried to say all the names of all the people I wanted to remember at the *Memento* I would have stood there until dinner time: but I had kept forming intentions for them all days beforehand, so that they would all be included when the time came. Even then I took time to remember all those that God wanted me explicitly to remember over again at that moment.

So I gave Communion to Nanny and to Dan Walsh and Bob Lax and Ed Rice and Bob Giroux, who wore his U.S. Navy jacket, and to Tom Flanagan who came with Ed, and Rod Mudge who came with Dan and to McCauliffe who wrote here about poetry. But I couldn't give Communion to Jay Laughlin or to Seymour. And after the Mass I had plenty of time to make a good thanksgiving by myself at Our Lady of Victories altar and after that I went out and talked, or rather Someone talked through me. It was a marvelous morning under the tree that Father Mauritius once marked *Gingko Biloba*, though all the botanical signs are now gone.

Now I know that I had the whole Church in America praying for me and I am scared and consoled by so much mercy and by the sense that I myself have contributed practically nothing to the whole business and that I have been worked on and worked in, carried upward on the tide of a huge love that has been released in people, somehow, in connection with a book printed over my name: and on this tide millions of us, a whole continent perhaps, is riding into heaven. It makes me truly the child of our Lady (*Mulier, ecce filius tuus!*) to whom the greatest mercy was given. When she has produced in me something of her humility there will be no end to what God will pour out upon me, not for myself but for the whole world—even perhaps to make others very great while I remain in my nothingness; all this would be, to me, the greatest joy.

In a way the experience of these three days has been a reversal and contradiction of everything I was thinking about solitude, on retreat: or is it a fulfillment that I do not understand?

June 4   VIGIL OF PENTECOST

Hot day. Stomach empty. Beautiful cumulus clouds sail over the woods, and everything is quiet.

The Mass is the most wonderful thing that has ever entered into my life. When I am at the altar I feel that I am at last the person that God has truly intended me to be. About the lucidity and peace of this perfect sacrifice I have nothing coherent to say. But I am very aware of the most special atmosphere of grace in which the priest moves and breathes at that moment—and all day afterwards! True, this peculiar grace is something private and inalienable, but it springs also from the social nature of the Mass. The greatest gift that can come to anyone is to share in the infinite act by which God's love is poured out upon all men. In this sense the supreme graces of solitude and of society coincide and become one—and they do this in the priest at Mass, as they do in the soul of Christ and in the Heart of Mary.

What a joy it is to remember the people I pray for at the *Memento.* Once, before I was ordained, I thought their names would be a distraction. Yet they only intensify the glowing radiance that fills the depths of my soul.

However, this is a dark radiance—burning in the silence of a faith without images—all the more radiant because I rejoice that it is dark.

If I had held to my resolution, perhaps I would not have talked so much the other day, to those who came to see me, about what occurred to me and filled my mind after my first Mass last Friday, at Saint Anne's altar. I suppose that was one of those resolutions that end up by being swept aside by the Holy Spirit. We quite often decide on good things which are not good enough because they are only our own idea. When God sees fit, He lets us know that He ignores them in favor of what is obviously much better. The change is not to be taken as a basis for generalizations, and I still hold on to my desire to be reserved. So much self-revelation is useless, and, worse still, in revealing what you think you have found you reduce it to a common and tangible level and lose what was best, what was spirit and life in it.

The centenary celebration on June 1st was well arranged and everything was far better than we deserved, and I have to admit, along with everyone else, that I remember it as a pleasant experience—or at least as something not altogether terrible. It seems to have been a day of grace, for us and for others. But everyone is glad the affair is over.

It was a bright day, but there was enough of a haze to keep the sun from knocking everybody down. In fact it was just the precise kind of weather we had prayed for.

In the afternoon when we came slowly back from Benediction in the field, chanting the *Pange Lingua* and passing from the crowded world into the cool shadows of the church, all the

monks were sunburned flaming red from the backs of their necks
to the summits of their tonsured crowns. And thus the door
closed behind us, and the Blessed Sacrament passed through our
midst under a curious white umbrella, which is assuredly an
Italian invention, and we put away our *Laudes Vespertinae* and
hoped there would be no more commotion and no more speech
for another hundred years. The terrible day was over.

The men from WHAS captured our Kyrie and Gloria in a
little box and took them away to Louisville to play to the people
after we had all gone to bed. The Fox Movietone men, both of
whom were very plump, ran back and forth through the crowd
with their newsreel cameras. You see, Saint Mary's field is *outside* the monastery and outside the enclosure, and for the pur-
poses of this feast, Saint Mary's field has been regarded as the
wide world which belongs to everybody and where you just
can't stop people from broadcasting and making movies.

In the morning, delivered from the job of second Master of
Ceremonies, I sat in the press-box and answered questions and
saw Monsignor Sheen in the distance standing in front of three
or four microphones that did not work so well at first. But when
they got louder, he was discovered to be preaching very well
about our silence.

And I, a solitary cloistered contemplative, assured some four
score nuns and other people that I was neither allowed to speak
nor to sign autographs and that I could only speak with reporters. Then they made me bless them and their rosaries and let
me go, and I stumbled away with the cameras going clickity-
click on every side. *O beata solitudo!*

One of the most impressive people I have ever seen is Archbishop
Paul Yu-Pin, of Nanking, who was here for the centenary. In
fact he spoke in Chapter about China and the contemplative life
and Buddhist monasticism—and about the reproach that Bud-
hists fling at us, that is, we are all very fine at building hospitals
but we have no contemplatives. He spoke of the two million (or
was it five million?) Buddhist monks and nuns in China. He told

of whole mountains covered with monasteries, and then spoke of the immense influence exercised by a Christian contemplative community like Our Lady of Consolation, when it existed!

June 10   EMBER   FRIDAY

The big thing in my day used to be Communion. Now it is the Sacrifice of which Communion is only a part. The center of balance of my spiritual life has shifted from the half hour when I kneel in the dark by Our Lady of Victories to the ten or fifteen minutes in which the Body and Blood of Christ are on the altar before me and I stand with my hands sketching that cramped little gesture of supplication that we have come to substitute for the wide-flung arms of the *orantes*.

Yet a certain restraint seems to be the best thing about the Mass in our liturgy. The whole sacrifice is so tremendous that no amount of exuberance will ever get you anywhere in expressing it. To bend down, unnoticed, and kiss the altar at the *Supplices te rogamus* is a movement that lifts me out of myself and doubles my peace. Saying the *Pater noster* is like swimming in the heart of the sun.

For hours after Mass it remains most difficult for me to get interested in anything else. Even reading makes me feel ashamed. Later on in the day, at odd hours, the Mass comes back and seizes me and envelops me in a moment of recollection that makes me wonder why I am doing whatever I am doing.

The prayers before Communion are beautiful and I love them and yet they embarrass me a little by the contrast with what has gone before because now I am once again speaking for my own poor self—and yet it helps me to remember at that moment, that I exist apart from God in the depths of an awful poverty which is nevertheless loved by Him.

I am never allowed to forget that poverty. I wish I knew her beauty as well as Saint Francis did—for the external poverty he married was simply the expression of the nothingness which he loved in himself.

This week, the week full of the Holy Ghost—I found out once

more something of the joy there is in being nothing and in de-
pending on Our Lady for everything. This is the key to the
simplest and easiest way of the interior life: to have no greatness
or holiness or distinction that one can claim as one's own but to
rely entirely on her love and her protection—knowing that she
will obtain for us, at the right moment, grace to do the good
thing that God wills us to do. From then on the whole spiritual
life becomes nothing else but a question of looking to her in confidence and faithfully receiving everything that comes to us
through her without clinging to it or keeping it as our own, and
without reflecting on ourselves.

June 15

We have been praying for rain, and this has been the *imperata* at
Mass. So this morning around the Offertory a steady rain began
(it had been raining on and off for the last thirty-six hours anyway) and it has gone on pouring down ever since, floods of it,
in a constant and uninterrupted and very vocal cascade all day
long. The land is full of its rumor and all our fields have rivers
running through them.

Tomorrow is Corpus Christi and there are practically no
flowers in the house anywhere.

After None I sat in one of the windows of the Scriptorium,
next to a fresh piece of flypaper that wasn't doing much business,
and watched the rain. Out near the big sycamore, where swine
are usually seen, shorn sheep and lambs were standing in the
downpour, about twenty or twenty-five of them I should say.
They were all absolutely motionless. Not browsing, not looking
about, not considering the slightest change of position. They all
stood like sculptured things for at least half an hour, perhaps all
afternoon.

June 19

SUNDAY WITHIN THE OCTAVE OF CORPUS CHRISTI
Heat, flies, lilies. I am deacon and forget my genuflections. And
the word of God in His monstrance dries up all desire in me to
write, or to be anything but a priest.

Christ has come to stand among us, and our dust and our rugs. We surround Him with our ceremonies and our shirts cling to our soaked ribs, and I want to look up at the monstrance to ease the heat and the heaviness but I am conscious of the acolytes standing between the pillars and it upsets me a little and anyway I am tongue-tied. During the Canon a fly passed through the flame of a candle and came down giddily on the corporal and began somersaulting around with burned wings until it got under the missal and then disappeared altogether.

The Mass each day delights and baffles me at the same time. This beautiful mixture of happiness and lucidity and inarticulateness fills me with great health from day to day. I am forced to be simple at the altar. Our liturgy has a peculiar intensity of its own precisely because it is so straightfaced and non-committal. Never an exclamation! Never any outcry!

But in the middle of this beautiful sobriety the indescribably pure light of God fills you with the innocence of childhood.

Day after day I am more and more aware that I am anything but my everyday self at the altar: this consciousness of innocence is really a sense of replacement. I am superseded by One in Whom I am fully real. Another has taken over my identity (or He has revealed it), and this Other is a tremendous infancy. And I stand at the altar—excuse the language, these words should not be extraordinary—I stand at the altar with my eyes all washed in the light that is eternity, and I become one who is agelessly reborn. I am sorry for this language. There are no words I know of simple enough to describe such a thing, except that every day I am a day old, and at the altar I am the Child Who is God and yet when it is all over I have to say *Lux in tenebris lucet et tenebrae eam non comprehenderunt* and I have to fall back into my own, in *my* poor "*propria*" which cannot receive Him altogether. I even have to rejoice at being nothing but a shell; well, I have contained some echo of His purity, and it has meant something tremendous for me and for the whole world, so that at my *Memento* of the living, which is very long, I swim in

seas of happiness that almost heave me off my moorings and
float me away from the altar.

It is at Mass, by the way, that I am deepest in solitude and at
the same time mean most to the rest of the universe. This is
really the *only* moment at which I can give anything to the rest
of men. And I am the only one who can give it to them, for
unless I apply it to them, the special fruit of my Mass will not
be theirs.

June 27   FEAST OF THE SACRED HEART
Yesterday afternoon I went out to the woods. There was a wall
of black sky beyond the knobs, to the west, and you could hear
thunder growling all the time in the distance. It was very hot
and damp but there was good wind coming from the direction
of the storm.

(Before None, during the meridienne in the dormitory, I
dreamed of going out: and in the dream I crossed the field where
the platform still remains, from the centenary, and walked up
toward Aidan Nally's. Before I got to Nally's, in the dream,
the wagon road developed sidewalks and I came not to solitude
but to Jamaica High School, which we used to pass going up a
hill on the way to the movies at Loew's Valencia in the old
days.) But when I woke up and really went out it was nothing
at all like the dream.

First I stopped under an oak tree on top of the hill behind
Nally's and sat there looking out at the wide sweep of the valley
and the miles of flat woods over toward the straight line of the
horizon where Rohan's knob is.

The wind ran over the bent, brown grasses and moved the
shoulders of all the green trees, and I looked at the dark mass
of woods beyond the distillery, on those hills down to the south
of us and realized that it is when I am with people that I am
lonely, and when I am alone I am no longer lonely.

Gethsemani looked beautiful from the hill. It made much
more sense in its surroundings. We do not realize our own setting
as we ought to: it is important to know where you are put,

on the face of the earth. Physically, the monastery is in a great solitude. There is nothing to complain about from the point of view of geography. One or two houses a mile and a half away and then woods and pastures and bottoms and cornfields and hills for miles and miles.

I had a vague idea there was a nice place beyond the field we call Hick's House although there has been no house there for years. I went to the calf pasture beyond St. Malachy's field at the foot of the knob where the real woods begin. It is a sort of *cova* where Our Lady might appear. From there we started walking to get to the forest fire we went out to fight on All Saints Day two and a half years ago.

It was quiet as the Garden of Eden. I sat on a high bank, under young pines, and looked out over this glen. Right under me was a dry creek, with clean pools lying like glass between the shale pavement of the stream, and the shale was as white and crumpled as sea-biscuit. Down in the glen were the songs of marvelous birds. I saw the gold-orange flame of an oriole in a tree. Orioles are too shy to come near the monastery. There was a cardinal whistling somewhere, but the best song was that of two birds that sounded as wonderful as nightingales and their song echoed through the wood. I could not tell what they were. I had never heard such birds before. The echo made the place sound more remote, and self-contained, more perfectly enclosed, and more like Eden.

The black clouds meanwhile piled up over the glen, and I went to where there was a shed, down at the entrance to the wilderness, a shed for the calves to shelter in, in cold weather in the fall. And yet it did not rain.

I looked up at the pines and at the black smoke boiling in the sky: but nothing could make that glen less peaceful, less of a house of joy.

On my way home I turned to the storm and saw it was marching northeastward following the line of the knobs, over on the other side of them, following the line of the Green River turnpike that is far over there beyond the property in the woods, going from New Haven to Bardstown. I got in just after the first bell for Vespers. Only when we were in choir for first Vespers of the Feast of the Sacred Heart did it begin to rain. Even then it did not rain much.

Back in the refectory one of the novices read to us at supper an article, taken from the *American Ecclesiastical Review,* on the privileges of a minor basilica and all the monks were laughing themselves silly at the description of the half-open parasol and the bell on the end of a pole and the other incidentals which go to make life unusually complicated in a minor basilica. Today we are back in the middle of a book about Russia called *God's Underground,* parts of which I almost but not quite believe.

July 10

Here I sit surrounded by bees and write in this book. The bees are happy and therefore they are silent. They are working in the delicate white flowers of the weeds among which I sit. I am on the east side of the house where I am not as cool as I thought I was going to be, and I sit on top of the bank that looks down over the beehives and the pond where the ducks used to be and Rohan's knob in the distance. And that big wobbly step-ladder I nearly fell off, cleaning the church once, stands abandoned out there next to one of the cherry trees, and the branches of a little plum tree before me, right by the road, sag with blue plums.

In the Chapter Room they are finishing *Seeds of Contemplation,* reading a couple of pages each evening before Compline. It began when I was on retreat for ordination. I do not know what the general feeling about it has been in the house—as far as I know it is not unfavorable. Father Macarius told me: "Those who think they are intellectuals, like it." Once or twice I felt as if everyone were a bit exasperated—at passages that were at the same time excessively negative and subtle and obscure.

I am glad the book has been written and read. Surely I have said enough about the business of darkness and about the "experimental contact with God in obscurity" to be able to shut up about it and go on to something else for a change. Otherwise it will just get to be mechanical—grinding out the same old song over and over again. But if it had not been read aloud at me I might have forgotten how often I had said all those things, and gone on saying them again as if they were discoveries. For I am aware that this often happens in our life. Keeping a journal has taught me that there is not so much new in your life as you sometimes think. When you re-read your journal you find out that your latest discovery is something you already found out five years ago. Still, it is true that one penetrates deeper and deeper into the same ideas and the same experiences.

Saying Mass in the secular church these days has been very beautiful. Because of the heat the front doors are left open, and I stand and speak to God on the dark altar, and outside the catbirds shout and sing in the damp trees.

I have never sweated so much in my life, even at Gethsemani. The heat has gone on unrelieved for some three weeks. No air. Nothing is dry. Water comes out of you as soon as anything—even the air itself—touches your skin, and you kneel in choir with sweat rolling down your ribs and you feel as if you were being smothered, by a barber, with hot towels: only this barber doesn't leave a hole for you to breathe through.

Out at work the other day we got into some tomato plants that had been overwhelmed by bindweed, and the soil was full of broken bricks. I think it must have been on the site of the old monastery. Anyway we did penance that must have been like the days of Dom Benedict. Tides of sweat coming out of you, blinding your face, making your clothes weigh twice their ordinary weight. And yet somehow it is good and satisfying to suffer these things and to do some of the penance we are supposed to do, and at night when we stand in our boiling tunnel and shout our *Salve* at the lighted window, you feel the whole basilica swing with the exultation of the monks and brothers who are dissolving in this humid furnace.

In the refectory they finished *God's Underground* full of terror and beatings and tortures in a Red prison in Prague, and suddenly switched to a namby-pamby Italian biography of Sister

Benigna Consolata, "The Little Secretary" whom Jesus called
"my joy and my Benjamin."

July 11

We have a new mechanical monster on the place called a D-4
Traxcavator which is enormous and rushes at the earth with a
wide-open maw and devours everything in sight. It roars terribly, especially when it is hungry. It has been given to the laybrother novices. They feed it every day and you can't hear
yourself think in the monastery while the brute is at table. It is
yellow and has a face like a drawbridge and is marked all over
with signs saying it comes from the Whayne supply company
in Louisville, but really, as I know from secret information, it
was born on a raft in Memphis, Tennessee. There, the hippopota-
mus abounds: which this instrument greatly resembles.

Also we have bought fans. They are exhaust fans. You make
a hole in the building and put the fans there and they draw all
the hot air out of the dormitory. Nobody knows what happens
after that. My guess is that the hot air that went out through the
fan is then replaced by the hot air that comes in through the
windows. The fans are not yet running because the laybrother
novices have not yet made the holes in the building. However,
they have begun. They have a scaffold up on the roof of the
infirmary and they have been blasting at the gable of that wing
with jack-hammers, and two frail novices who are very young
were posted down on the ground floor near the doorways with
artistic signs which read "Falling Bricks." At first one of them
was standing at the precise spot where all the falling bricks
would land on his head. He was saying the rosary in an attitude
of perfect abandonment. Afterwards he got a stool and moved
inside the cloister and propped up the sign in his lap and took
to reading the immortal masterpiece of Father Garrigou-
Lagrange, *Christian Perfection and Contemplation.*

July 17

Today, in our Order, we celebrate the Feast of Our Lady of
Mount Carmel although to the world it was yesterday. But yesterday was our Saint Stephen.

The chief thing that happened to affect the history of my existence was this: I was on as deacon for the Pontifical High Mass. Everything was going along fairly smoothly, although it was a hot muggy day. But in the middle of the Gospel I passed out.

It happened this way: I started to sing, and suddenly found that I was very dizzy.

After that, I looked around and I was lying on the floor and people were trying to pick me up. It was a nice soft carpet. I might have landed on it like a feather. I think I remember starting to fall and being completely unable to do anything about it.

At first I was angry, believing that I had been thrown on the ground by the devil. I got up and finished the Gospel, and then when we started to mill around to get in position for the *Credo*, I got lost and started off in some wrong direction. The subdeacon got me straightened out and I was thinking: "Must recite the *Credo* with fervor and attention" in order to rectify this business of lying on the floor. I said what I could remember of the *Credo*, the central thought in my mind being *Christ! Christ!* While I was focusing on Our Lord and trying to get saved from what had thrown me down, the M. C. came and took me off to the sacristy, where a substitute (Father Gerard) was wriggling into a lace alb.

I thought about a lot of things, lying on the straw mattress in the dormitory afterwards. One of the thoughts was that I am glad to be at Gethsemani and that the way to be a saint is to give yourself up entirely to your rule and the circumstances in which God has placed you and work out the secret which is His will.

July 20

We are in the Octave of Saint Stephen. I have never thought so much about Saint Stephen before or prayed so much to him.

The other day—Sunday—on the Feast of Our Lady of Mount Carmel, I went and sat at the benches of the infirm during the Matutinal Mass. It was the first time in my life I had seen the Matutinal Mass from that angle and it gave me a new slant on the Community—and on God's Providence. There must be something like one hundred and forty brothers and novices and clerics going to Communion in that long line. Since the line was relatively short when I first came here, and since I was close to the head of it for the last four years of Theology, and since I had my eyes shut during my thanksgiving, I never realized what an enormous long line it was. It takes over twenty minutes for the whole business to form and file up to the Epistle corner and get back again in choir. . . . At the end of it are a number of great tall laybrother oblates who used to be paratroopers, "night jumpers."

Then it struck me with greater force than ever before that God certainly didn't bring any of us here without a reason— and least of all myself. I saw the poor little handful of priests and I thought of our poverty. . . . And the thought that I have wanted to withdraw myself from all this by my own choice began to appal me.

July 21

I said the Mass of the Seven Dolours again today, out in the secular church.

I am finding myself forced to admit that my lamentations about my writing job have been foolish. At the moment, the writing is one thing that gives me access to some real silence and solitude. Also I find that it helps me to pray, because when I pause at my work I find that the mirror inside me is surprisingly clean and deep and serene and God shines there and is immediately found, without hunting, as if He had come close to me while I was writing and I had not observed His coming. And this, I think, should be the cause of great joy, and to me it is.

The community has never been so big as now. I do not know the official figure but it must be around 185, including one or two in hospitals or non-stabilited in other monasteries of the Order. Three postulants arrived one day last week and five more on Monday—all these for the choir. One of them stands in the lower stalls in front of me in a very distracting shirt, printed all over with huntsmen and foxhounds in green and brown.

What disturbs me especially is that one of the huntsmen, on a very fat horse, is riding directly through the middle of the pack of hounds, at right angles to the apparent direction of the chase. And I say to him, "Where do you think *you're* going?" when my mind ought to be on the psalms.

Soon I will go to Chapter and a little novice with a calm and somewhat metallic voice will read a translation from the Hungarian about *Life Everlasting*. He will go peacefully through all those comforting sentences, and again and again the phrase will recur, "life everlasting . . . life everlasting." It fills the Chapter with a happy, evening charm while darkness comes down upon our hills and on our frogs and on our robins and on our wet grass that was freshly mowed this morning by Father Raymond and rained on this afternoon by the rain. *Life Everlasting!*

Tomorrow is the Feast of Saint Mary Magdalen. We sang *Ardens est cor meum . . . desidero videre Deum meum . . . quaero et non invenio . . .*

I have found many good things in Hugueny's Theological Introduction to his translation of Tauler. He is especially good on the psychological factors in contemplation and on natural contemplation. I have never read anything so clear and so sensible on the subject. At the center of contemplation is this complete, global apprehension of a truth not in its details but in its wholeness, not as an abstract matter of speculation but apprehended in all that appeals to our affective powers so that it is appreciated and prized and savored. This in the natural order alone.

That is what this book in the Chapter room is doing—it is an incantation of familiar sentences, stated in a way that is calculated to carry with it a certain enchantment to a Catholic, and to bring back this global and appreciative savor of the whole subject and all its associations—and you get a sort of low degree of contemplation out of it. I suppose many of them think they are acquiring arguments and convictions. Not at all. They are feeling good. The same book would mean practically nothing to someone outside the Church. Or it would have meant nothing to *me* when I was outside the Church. So many books are like that. I am not sure whether it is a good thing or a bad thing. Contemplation is OK. But whether or not you can get too much supernatural contemplation, the natural kind can certainly be overdone. As for the really infused kind it is not up to you to say how much you are going to get anyway.

July 27

Yesterday, on the Feast of Saint Anne, they put up a wallboard partition across the middle of the monks' Scriptorium and gave half the place to the novices to save them from bursting the walls of their novitiate. The old monks are staying down in the part that was left to us—and it is like a Turkish bath, being right over the bake-oven. I am writing this in the library. The younger element moved their desks up here and I have ours jammed up against the shelves full of old German collections of sermons that nobody would think of touching with a twenty-foot pole. I write this leaning on the broad windowsill looking over the *préau* that echoes robins and locusts, for it is still very hot, and the bell in the tower has just rung seven and the gray buildings are beginning to be in shadows.

July 31

It is the 8th Sunday after Pentecost and the Feast of Saint Ignatius Loyola and the Gospel says, "Give an account of thy stewardship," and I took up the Sapiential books beginning in the middle of *Ecclesiasticus* where I left off last year.

Give an account of thy stewardship.

The bier, the black open box with long handles in which we carry our dead out behind the Church and bury them, is parked in the drying room and I look at it on purpose every time I go by to remind myself of the happy day when, please God, I will go home.

Today Reverend Father gave official and general permission for the first time for the professed to go out into the orchard and around the wagon shed and out behind the old horsebarn in their intervals—or rather between None and Vespers on Sunday.

Our garden and the cemetery are intolerably crowded and it is hard to get extricated from the other monks.

Anyway, I made a bee-line for the little grove of cedars that is behind the old horsebarn and crowded up against the far end of the enclosure wall and it was nice. By the long time it took me to get completely recollected I realized that I have been awfully busy and my mind is terribly active. And if I had to give an account of my stewardship, I would have to fall upon God's mercy more heavily than ever, because it seems to me that since I became a great success in the book business I have been becoming more and more of a failure in my vocation.

Not that I haven't made efforts to keep my head above water: but in the spiritual life it is not so hard to drown, when you still imagine you are swimming.

August 3

Tomorrow—Saint Dominic. We sing a solemn Requiem for Dom Frederic who died a year ago. I said a Requiem Mass today and at the Consecration of the Precious Blood I was thinking how much I owed to Dom Frederic and I was glad I had here a way of repaying him for everything. There are many in the Order and in the world who owed him very much. He died alone on the train to Georgia: and I think it was because he was really a very lonely man. People might not believe that. He had many friends who loved him: yet he was isolated from everybody in a peculiar way, in spite of all his kindness and affability. There was a great deal of Dom Frederic that no one had access to—including, perhaps, himself. One reason for this was that he had buried a great amount of suffering inside himself and had forgotten it—with the help not only of charity, but also of his activity which, though tremendous, was perhaps, in his case, merciful.

Which leaves me thinking that although perhaps objectively he should not have killed himself as he did with overwork, things were perhaps best as they were. It leaves one thinking that all things eventually turn out the way they ought to, even though it seems they might have been much better.

Tonight at the evening meditation I remained with my eyes open, which I do not usually do. The altar was ready for to-morrow's Requiem. No flowers or bric-a-brac: plain candles and a bare wooden crucifix, the one we always have in Lent and adore on Good Friday. It was a comfort to me to look at the crucifix and presently (there had been showers of rain since Vespers began) a shaft of sunlight broke through a window somewhere and fell like gold on the head and arms of Christ on the crucifix and it was quiet and beautiful in the sanctuary with no one moving and light falling on the crucifix.

The Portiuncula always brings me great blessings—and that is the Franciscan side in me which continues to grow also. It was last year I first realized how much there is in Portiuncula Day for those who will take it. If we are granted indulgences, it is because there is so much in the feast, which they represent. They are counters. The feast brings graces of contemplation and spiritual joy, because every church becomes that tiny little church that Saint Francis loved above all others. Thus everyone in the world can share the bliss of his sanctity.

August 4   SAINT DOMINIC

Here I sit under the trees full of locusts, near Dom Frederic's grave, with my feet in the blue limestone gravel, and I think about the spirit of Saint Dominic. It is a spirit that has little or nothing to do with ours, but it is impressive and means much more to me today than it did four or five years ago.

I wish I had gone into my study of theology with something more of the mind of Saint Dominic. The thing I most lack is the outstanding Dominican characteristic of sharpness, definite-ness, precision in theology.

I admit that sometimes their precision is the fruit of over-simplification: but it is good, anyway. The sharp contrast between the Dominican colors—black and white—is a good symbol of the Dominican mind which likes clear-cut divisions and distinctions.

I admire Saint Dominic above all for his love of Scripture,

and for his respect for the *study* of Scripture. Scripture was the heart of his contemplation and of his preaching. I have often meditated on Scripture but I have never in my life seriously studied it and this is a lack that I ought to lament. Now that I am finished with the theology class and have four months or so to go on, by myself, in Scripture, to fill out the time required by Canon Law—I pray Saint Dominic to guide my study of Scripture in these months and for the rest of my life.

In Saint Dominic's first Friaries they were brief and quick about the office (just the opposite of the twelfth-century Cistercians) in order to get to their books, and the friars were encouraged to prolong their vigils in study. Study was not precisely the essence of the Dominican vocation, nevertheless each house was a house of study and the study was to lead to contemplation that would overflow in preaching. Honorius III I think refers explicitly to the Dominican life as essentially contemplative but without implying any contradiction between contemplation and activity. In any case what they studied was *Scripture*. The Bible was their textbook of theology.

I wish Saint Dominic would finally give me an understanding of this problem of contemplation vs. action—clear as the line of the landscapes of Southern France!

The Epistle, from Saint Timothy (*argue-obsecra-increpa . . .*) struck me with great power at the Mass. *Sana doctrina!* What an ideal! Clean and precise thinking—sweeping the world clean of the dust of heresy and bad theology. I need that *sana doctrina* and it will not hurt me at all to realize that everyone who loves Truth is, in this world, called upon in some measure to *defend* it. "*Divinas Scripturas saepius lege: immo numquam de manibus tuis sacra lectio deponatur. Disce quod doceas; obtine eum qui secundum doctrinam est, fidelem sermonem ut possis exhortari in doctrina sacra et contradicentes arguere*" (Saint Jerome, Ep. 52).*

---

*"Often read the Holy Scriptures, indeed, let the Bible never be out of your hands. Learn what you are to teach; gain a firm grasp on the truths of faith according to Doctrine, in order to exhort men in Sacred Doctrine and refute those who oppose the faith."

In the short Prologue of Saint Thomas to his *Summa Theologiae* is a very beautiful paragraph containing a whole discipline of study: his three points are that students—beginners, but it applies to all—are impeded from arriving at truth by (1) the great number of useless questions, arguments and articles, (2) the lack of order in the way doctrine is presented, (3) repetition which produces confusion and boredom.

The Dominicans and Cistercians had this at least in common —that they wanted to get rid of all non-essentials.

August 5   OUR LADY OF THE SNOWS

Here are some words of a Jesuit—the theologian Maldonatus— that ought to give all Cistercians something to think about:

"Where shall our morning and evening (theological) work begin if not among the riches of the Bible? I do not regard as theologians those who neglect the Scriptures spending their time and labor and wasting their strength and their talents in other books. . . . After your exercises of piety *devote an hour to the reading of the New Testament in the morning and an hour in the afternoon to the reading of the Old*. Read the New Testament in Greek and the Old in Hebrew. . . ."

This makes me hang my head considerably. Sometimes I get bursts of fervor and make a resolution to give the best of my intervals to Scripture but I never do, and even as I write this I find myself mentally defending myself against giving up the half hour after None to anything but Tauler or Rolle or John of the Cross. Of course, I have the morning study period and that is a wholesome chunk of the day but it has been *assigned* to me, not chosen. Then, at any rate, I can get my hour or more of New Testament, for the time being, but not, I fear, in Greek.

How little Scripture I used to read in the novitiate! I remember walking in the garden on summer mornings and reading Jeremias and also Saint Paul, but not very consistently. However, I *did* read the Fathers commenting on Scripture, more to get the thoughts of the Fathers than anything else. I read the

Canticle of Canticles several times—I remember that—especially the last few paragraphs.

This year I have been going along regularly with the Books assigned to the season by the liturgy and it has done me much good—I went through the books of Kings again and loved David more. Every time I read Kings, David grows in my estimation and Solomon decreases. Now I am in Ecclesiasticus and study the qualities of good women.

I find an interesting passage in Saint Thomas's commentary on Saint John (Chapter I, Lect. XIV), the place where Jesus turns to Andrew and John who have asked Him where He lives and He says, "Come and see." Thomas interprets this mystically as evidence that we can only come to know Jesus dwelling within us by experience. But I take this experimental knowledge of the presence of God in us to be contemplation. He then says there are four ways of arriving at this experimental knowledge. Two are, as one might expect, by interior quiet and rest, and by the taste of the divine sweetness.

But the other two are—first, by the performance of good works and second, *per operationem devotionis*. I don't know precisely what that means but in any case it is an activity. Hence it is easy to see that for Saint Thomas there is in practice no contradiction between contemplation and activity. There are characters and situations in which activity can even favor contemplation to some extent. How this checks with the questions in the II IIae, I don't know. But it is interesting. I have noticed myself, sometimes, that when your mind is utterly dead around the house and in church, you can go out to work and soon find God within you after you have been sweating a little in the sun. The sacrifice, the obedience, and the penance have brought Him there quite quickly. Just how much there may be of nature in this I don't know: but it is true that obedience and work clear your mind of preoccupations that make conscious union with God impossible: and preoccupations of that kind tend to accumulate when you are left to yourself and to your books.

I also find God quite easily sometimes after an hour or half an hour of intense intellectual work. This too gets rid of my other preoccupations and clears the surface of my inner mirror without my knowing it. But both these experiences of contemplation are of a low and elementary kind. Conceivably, to continue activity beyond this point would only hinder progress to a higher and deeper union—something more fundamental and more real, though perhaps less "felt."

August 8

Merely to set down some of the communicable meanings that can be found in a passage of Scripture is not to exhaust the true meaning or value of that passage. Every word that comes from the mouth of God is nourishment that feeds the soul with eternal life. *Non in solo pane vivit homo sed in omni verbo quod procedit de ore Dei.* Whether Scripture tells of David hiding from Saul in the mountains and Saul's men surrounding his hiding place like a crown; or whether it tells about Jesus raising up the son of the widow of Naim; or the prescriptions for the evening sacrifice of incense; or sings the hymn of Deborah; or tells us that Heli the priest of Silo thought Anna was drunk, when she moved her lips in prayer; whether it tells us in the *Canticle* that the Spouse has gone down to see if the vineyards are in flower; or shows us the new Jerusalem coming down from God adorned as a bride; or rebukes the incestuous Corinthian; or leads Paul to the river in Macedonia where the women gathered and the Holy Spirit opened the heart of Lydia, the seller of dye, to hear the Gospel—everywhere these are doors and windows opened into the same eternity and the most powerful communication of Scripture is the *insitum verbum,* the secret and inexpressible seed of contemplation planted in the depths of our soul and awakening it with an immediate and inexpressible contact with the Living Word, that we may adore Him in Spirit and in Truth. . . .

By the reading of Scripture I am so renewed that all nature seems renewed around me and with me. The sky seems to be a pure, a cooler blue, the trees a deeper green, light is sharper on the outlines of the forest and the hills and the whole world is charged with the glory of God and I feel fire and music in the earth under my feet.

The blessings of my Cistercian vocation are poured out on me in Scripture and I live again in the lineage of Bernard and I see that if I had been deeper in Scripture all my past temptations to run to some other Order would have more quickly lost their meaning, for contemplation is found in faith, not in geography: you can dig for it in Scripture, but you will never find it by crossing the seas.

August 10 SAINT LAWRENCE
Sapientia scribae in tempore vacuitatis et qui minoratur actu sapientiam percipiet (Eccli., 38:25).

I was very interested in this verse and in everything that followed. Our Douay version translates it: "The wisdom of the scribe cometh by his time of leisure and he that is less in action shall receive wisdom."

The following verses give wonderful descriptions of farmers— "his whole talk is about the offspring of bulls"; blacksmiths— "sitting by the anvil and considering the iron work. The vapour of the fire wasteth his flesh and he fighteth with the heat of the furnace." "The noise of the hammer is always in his ears"; silversmiths, potters—"Everyone is wise in his own art," "Without these a city is not built." Yet "they shall not go up into the assembly." "They shall not be found where parables are spoken." "But they shall strengthen the state of the world and their prayer shall be in the work of their craft, and searching the law of the Most High." *Deprecatio illorum in operatione artis.* This (says Knabenbauer) means that they pray that their work will turn out successfully and they do not have a higher end— but it seems to me one could also take it to mean that their work is a prayer.

August 12
No matter how simple discourse may be, it is never simple enough. No matter how simple thought may be, it is never

simple enough. No matter how simple love may be, it is never simple enough. The only thing left is the simplicity of the soul in God, or, better, the simplicity of God.

August 16

Steaming hot day, the first in the Octave of Our Lady's Assumption. For the first time it occurred to me to wonder who Saint Hyacinth might be, with the ladylike name. I haven't time to look him up.

The rejection of Christ. *His own received Him not.*

The most terrible thing about the rejection of Jesus was that He was rejected by the holy and He was rejected because He was God!

The Pharisees rejected God because He was not a Pharisee.

The Pharisees would have nothing to do with God because God turned out to be not made in their own image.

"I am come in the name of my Father and you receive me not: if another shall come in his own name, him you will receive" (John 5:43).

What is implied by the expression, "in the name of my Father"? Jesus came to us having nothing of His own. Not merely did He have nowhere to rest His head, not only was He poor on earth, but He explains that the very fact of His divine generation means that He has absolutely nothing of Himself and yet He is everything. In this same chapter Jesus defended Himself against the charges of violating the Sabbath by explaining that He lived in the very heart of the Sabbath which is the interior life of God where "the Father works and I work." "The Son cannot do anything of Himself but what He seeth the Father doing." The condition on which divine life is given to men is that they accept it from Him Who has received everything that He has, and therefore does not come in His own name. The Father has given all judgment to the Son and they who do not receive the Son by believing in Him Who has nothing of His own, are by that very fact judged. And the

Father wills that the Son, Who has nothing of His own, should be honored as the Father is honored because without this honor given to the Son, the Father cannot be honored as He really is. The test of our worship and adoration of God is in our reception of Him Who cannot come to us in His own name.

Those who live for themselves, who live "for their own name," cannot believe in such a God because He contradicts everything they really believe in and live for. They will not go to Him that they may have life, because He does not receive glory from men. *Claritatem ab hominibus non accipio.*

How can you believe who receive glory one from another? And the glory which is from God alone you seek not!

This explains the meaning of the word vainglory—*vana gloria* —ultimately it implies the love of non-existence, because it is the love of what is not and cannot be.

And this is at the root of the rejection of Christ—we do not really believe in Him because we want to believe only in ourselves, and we want to fabricate a basis for that belief by making other men praise us.

August 17

The sixth chapter of Saint John's Gospel was written for me. When Jesus worked the miracle of the loaves and fishes, on the hillside outside Tiberias, when He escaped into the mountain Himself alone, walked on water to find the disciples, and afterward first told the people of the mystery of the Eucharist, He saw all His priests and He saw—or sees—me sitting here, writing this, His priest, crushed that I do not understand the greatness of the Mass and happy because I do not have to—for, in any case, it is impossible.

"I am the bread of life."

"That if any man eat of it he may not die."

To say Mass better each day will be to say it more simply each day, each day with one less crease in your brow and one less anxiety in your head, and one less shadow of fear in your heart. To arrive at this no doubt one may have to say Mass for ten years in the valley of the shadow of death, but for my part I don't see why a priest couldn't say Mass from the beginning with simplicity and joy and go on saying it with more and more simplicity and joy each day. *Servite Domino in laetitia!* One reason why we are less fervent than we ought to be is that we cripple our own spirit by taking ourselves too seriously. We expect too much from ourselves when we ought to expect everything from God on Whom we utterly depend.

"Except you eat the flesh of the Son of Man and drink His blood you shall not have life in you!" What is easier than to eat and drink? What is simpler than this greatest sacrifice?

"As the living Father hath sent me and I live by the Father so he that eateth me the same shall live by me."

Also this chapter contains the community-solitude problem (v. 15ff.) stated almost violently. Jesus made no compromise with a merely worldly society. Confronted with kingship His answer was not even a word—it was rejection and solitude. But He emerged from this solitude to teach of a "society" that was to be one flesh and one bloodstream with Himself, a mystical union of all men in His Body, where solitude and the common life are realized perfectly both together at the same time.

I am consoled to realize how often Jesus was abrupt in His words and movements. He never bothered to be diplomatic. Yet He was never impatient or impulsive. He did things without hesitation because He was the Truth. *Et sic est omnis qui natus est ex spiritu.*

August 19

Fillion, a Scripture scholar whom I am appointed to read, encourages young priests to study Hebrew, Greek, Aramaic, Itala, Arabic, Syriac, Assyrian, Ethiopian, Coptic, Armenian, Persian, Slavonic, Gothic, and the three main Egyptian dialects, namely Salidic (spoken at Thebes), Fayoumic (spoken at the oasis of Fayoum), and Memphitic (spoken at Memphis). Besides being grounded in oriental archeology and ethnography, the young priest should also possess a smattering of botany, zoology, geology, and have more than a nodding acquaintance with the Tal-mud. Also he says one ought to read a few Yiddish novels, by way of recreation.

When you have mastered all this you will be able to elucidate the ivy passage in Jonas, for instance, and you will come to the conclusion that Jonas in Nineveh sat down under a castor oil plant (ivy) and became attached to its shade.

On the whole, I think Saint Teresa's interpretation of Jonas's ivy is more interesting, and she didn't know one word of Egyptian either.

Yet on the other hand, at Mass this morning, I was momen-tarily distracted with a mild fit of compunction over the Little Flower's statement that if she were a priest she would learn Hebrew and Greek in order to read the revealed word of God in the original languages.

From Fillion, *The Study of the Bible*, p. 220:

"One day Cardinal Foulon, Archbishop of Lyons, said to me: 'Why is the cat, that charming animal, not mentioned in the Bible?' (Is it so charming after all?—Fillion's comment.)

"I answered: 'Your Eminence, it is mentioned in the Book of Baruch or to be more exact in the letter of Jeremias at the end of that book; the prophet shows it walking over the heads and bodies of the Babylonian idols.' "

So I rush to the Book of Baruch (6:20-21) and find:

"Their faces are black with the smoke that is made in the house. Owls and swallows and other birds fly upon their bodies and upon their heads, and cats in like manner."

It is the first time I have read the sixth chapter of Baruch and it is a wonderful chapter, written by Jeremias to the Jews going to Babylon, into captivity, to preserve them against temptations to idolatry.

"For as a scarecrow in a garden of cucumbers keepeth nothing, so are their gods of wood and of silver, laid over with gold. They are not better than a white thorn in a garden upon which every bird sitteth. . . ."

August 22   OCTAVE OF THE ASSUMPTION

Father Macarius and three others all started out for South Carolina during the Night Office yesterday morning (after saying
Mass at 2 A.M. in the infirmary chapel) and today they say Mass
—the first Cistercian Mass—at the Mepkin Plantation which is to
be the new monastery of the Immaculate Heart. The deeds were
signed and the affair was made public (with many errors) in the
newspapers and we expect the foundation to be made after the
General Chapter and after the annual retreat which begins this
year a month early, on November 1st.

Anyway, I was very happy saying the Mass of the Octave day
this morning at Saint Robert's altar—with a little side chapel all
to myself. The really hot weather stopped all of a sudden the
evening before Saint Bernard's day but prickly heat tends to be
especially sharp when you are cooling off.

On Saint Bernard's day—I sat up on the hill behind Nally's, not
wanting to walk far into the woods, because the more time you
spend walking the less you have for really deep prayer. So I
looked at the great big sweep of country and that far line of
hills that is steeped in spiritual associations for me, and at the
abbey and the church sitting in the carpet of fields like a rel-
iquary, and containing all that is most precious in the world, the
Body of Christ, and His Divinity, the Living God.

How true it is that our knowledge and sense and experience of
God is sometimes so much sharper and cleaner when we are un-
comfortable and hot and physically cramped and suffering than
when we are cool and at rest. So, though I am always recollected
and in God's presence in the woods, and at peace and happy with
Him, I am in more obscurity sometimes than when in the hot
choir: for instance kneeling before the Blessed Sacrament on a
day of recollection with the sweat pouring down my ribs.
Usually in church my mind is paralyzed with distractions, especially during the evening meditation. Yet how often in the last
three minutes of that meditation, my mind will suddenly be
swept clean of images and my heart will sink into deep rest in

God and I will be free for that little moment of rest and joy He allows me.

The Abbé Fillion has written a book that is in some ways strange. However, it is very good—especially for someone like myself— to read, under obedience, a book that I would not otherwise have touched with a ten-foot pole. And now although I still think some of his notions are funny, I have conceived a real affection for Fillion because his book has brought so many graces with it.

Whether or not this particular sentence contains a grace, I do not know, but here it is: it has struck me and made me pause. It is something I had never really thought of. I don't know whether it means something to me or not:

"Every priest ought to be as familiar with the geography of the sacred books as that of his own country, and with the plan of the city of Jerusalem as that of his own town or the place where he lives" (p. 225).

Since I have a vow of stability, geography has more or less ceased to interest me—except when I think we are going to start a new foundation somewhere.

All I know about Palestine now is what I hear from our monastery of El Athroun, which seems to have been finally evacuated. So many people in the world think it is ridiculous for Catholics to worry about the Holy Places.

But it seems to me that a Christian who would have no interest in the Holy Sepulchre or Gethsemani or Bethlehem or Nazareth or the Sea of Galilee or Capharnaum or Naim or Jacob's well . . . what kind of a Christian would he be? Yet all I know about Jerusalem is what the Jesuits tell us when they preach our annual retreat or what we get from Archbishop Goodier in the refectory.

August 25 FEAST OF SAINT LOUIS

This morning after two hours of peaceful meditation and Night Office I went to vest for Mass, completely unmindful of the indignities that were to be imposed on me for my feast day. I had thought of all that yesterday, and made a few rudimentary efforts to steel myself for the ordeal but, by the divine permission, that was all forgotten. As a result, I was overwhelmed by the lace alb and by the vestments which I cannot describe as I am not sufficiently familiar with the language of dressmakers. It was the evident intention of my brethren that I should say the Mass of Saint Louis in oriental splendor.

I wormed my way into these horrible decorations and proceeded to the altar palpitating with anxiety. There were, as far as I remember, at least three carpets in Saint Robert's chapel and since you cannot possibly get three carpets in that small space in any other way, they were piled one on top of the other. Being of different sizes you could see the elements of the ones underneath sticking out on all sides. I tried to begin Mass with my eyes shut, ignoring the gilt bookstand covered with little bits of red and green glass and the huge chocolate frames of the altar cards. It did not work. I went through the Mass in unrelieved misery. After the Gloria I said *Dominus vobiscum* and then wondered if I had said the Gloria, hoped that I had and made for the Book, said the Collects in a daze.

At the Offertory I got a closer look at the base of the chalice, which was a labyrinth of the most intricate carving and it suddenly occurred to me that I was really saying Mass in a bazaar in Cairo. So I accepted the bitter humiliation in union with the humiliations of Saint Louis's imprisonment by the paynims, thanked God that no one was physically present at my Mass to see me in my atrocious finery and went on with interior peace but not without superficial anguish. Finally I flopped down on the kneelers in front of Our Lady of Victories when it was all over. Some thirty-five minutes went by and I staggered out of Church dimly aware that perhaps, after all, I had been subjected to some great but painfully incomprehensible manifestation of grace.

August 26

My pious Abbé Fillion suggests that when we are stumped and cannot find out the meaning of a passage of Scripture we ought to pray to the "sacred author," that is, to whoever it was that served as God's instrument in writing the book. The suggestion appeals to me, for I have a great, though confused, affection for the writers of the Bible. I feel closer to them than to almost any other writers I know of. Isaias, Moses, David, Matthew, Mark, Luke, and John are all part of my life. They are always about me. They look over my shoulder, earnest men, belonging to the façade of a medieval cathedral. I feel that they are very concerned about me and that they want me to understand what God told them to write down and that they have always surrounded me with solicitous prayers and that they will always love me and protect me.

They are more a part of my world than most of the people actually living in the world. I "see" them sometimes more really than I see the monks I live with. I know well the burnt faces of the Prophets and the Evangelists, transformed by the white-hot dangerous presence of inspiration, for they looked at God as into a furnace and the Seraphim flew down and purified their lips with fire. And I read their books with joy and with holy fear, *cum tremore divino,* and their words become a part of me. They are solemn and dreadful and holy men, humbled by the revelation they wrote down. They are my Fathers. They are the "burnt men" in the last line of *The Seven Storey Mountain.* I am more and more possessed by their vision of God's Kingdom, and I wonder at the futility of seeking anything else on earth but the truth revealed in them and in tradition—the Church's treasure, to which she holds all the keys.

I also have great reverence and love for the Patriarchs of the Old Testament—Abraham, Isaac, Jacob—and for the Prophets— Samuel, Elias, Eliseus. When I walk in the cemetery in the cool evening when the sun is going down—there is almost no sunlight left now in the interval after supper—I think of Isaac, meditating in the fields at evening and of Rebecca coming to marry him from a far country riding on a rich camel, sailing across the desert like a queen in a great ship.

August 27

My soul is united to the soul of Christ in the priestly character impressed upon me and in the Mass His soul and my soul act together as closely and as inseparably as two rays of light shining together. That is why I am not aware of a foreign "Stranger Presence." Rather it seems to me as if, without ceasing to be who I am, I had become Somebody else—as if I had been raised to a higher and much simpler and cleaner level of being.

August 30

Last Sunday was the Feast of Our Lady's Most Pure Heart—whose Mass I love well, and the whole day was beautiful. Beautiful, I mean, for me, although the weather was cloudy and it rained in the morning. After Chapter I was on the kitchen-refectory squad and spent one hour going around the one hundred and ninety-two places counting out four thin cookies for each Trappist and handing out various very small bon-bons and some stuff that pretended to be candied orange. I was very happy doing all this, not because of the candy, which nauseates me, but because of God and Our Lady, and the Feast Day.

In the afternoon I went out to the old horsebarn with the Book of Proverbs and indeed with the whole Bible, and I was wandering around in the hay loft, where there is a big gap in the roof, and one of the rotting floorboards gave way under me and I nearly fell through.

Afterwards I sat and looked out at the hills and the gray clouds and couldn't read anything. When the flies got too bad, I wandered across the bare pasture and sat by the enclosure wall, perched on the edge of a ruined bathtub that has been placed there for the horses to drink out of. A pipe comes through the wall and plenty of water flows into the bathtub from a spring somewhere in the woods, and I couldn't read there, either. I just listened to the clean water flowing and looked at the wreckage of the horsebarn on top of the bare knoll in front of me, and remained drugged with happiness and with prayer.

Presently the two mares and the two colts came over to see me and to take a drink. The colts looked like children with their big grave eyes, very humble, very stupid and they were tamer than I expected. They came over and nudged me with their soft muzzles and I talked to them for a bit and then Father Nabor who was hiding behind some sumacs a hundred paces away came out to see what was the matter.

Later on I saw other interesting things—for instance a dead possum in a trap and a gold, butter-and-egg butterfly wavering on the dead possum's back. There are many Rhode Island reds over in the southwest corner of the enclosure this year. When I was on retreat for ordination to the priesthood I did half a day's work on the roosts we were building for them then.

August 31

Morning after morning I try to study the sixth chapter of Saint John and it is too great. I cannot study it. I simply sit still and try to breathe.

There is a small black lizard with a blue, metallic tail, scampering up the yellow wall of the church next to the niche where the Little Flower, with a confidential and rather pathetic look in her eye, offers me a rose. I am glad of the distraction because now I can breathe again and think a little.

It does no good to use big words to talk about Christ. Since I seem to be incapable of talking about Him in the language of a child, I have reached the point where I can scarcely talk about Him at all. All my words fill me with shame.

You cannot say, of a chapter in the Gospel, "This is terrific." It is indecent to call the Bible wonderful. It would be indecent too to say "My mother is a wonderful person." And so you cannot praise Christ the way you would praise a mere human being. You have to fall on your face and cry out for mercy: the only way you can talk about God is to "confess"—*confessio Laudis*—either that or else confession of your shame. If Christ is merely interesting to you, or merely admirable—what will become of your miserable soul?

That is why I am more and more thankful for the Office and for the Psalms. Their praise of Him is perfect as well as neutral, and God gives it to me to utter as more my own than any language I could think up for myself.

Domine Dominus noster! quam admirabile est nomen tuum in universa terra!

When I have the whole Church crying out with me, there is some chance of finding peace, in the feeling that God is somehow, after all, receiving praise from my lips.

PART FIVE

The Whale and the Ivy

Ordination is only the beginning of a journey, not its end. The beginning was easy and pleasant. But when summer was over the serious business of being a priest began. I am glad that I have put something about it down on paper, even though what I have put down may not be clear to anyone but myself. As far as I know, nothing special has ever been written about what the priesthood means in a contemplative monastery.

A young priest in the active ministry has a stern task ahead of him, but it is easy to understand. The way may be steep, but at least it is relatively clear. Also, there are plenty of books on the subject. It is a well-beaten track. It brings him face to face with all kinds of practical and human difficulties. He has a tremendous amount of work to do. He discovers many things he never expected, in his contact with people and with other priests. Some of these things are encouraging and some are not. In any case, he immediately begins to grow and to develop and within a few months he is no longer the callow and perhaps self-complacent seminarian he was until now. He has begun to learn humility and mercy in the school of labor and of sorrow.

Whatever may be the place in the Church to which a priest is called, he is bound to be purified by fire. That fire is the fire of divine charity, in which his soul must become one with the soul of Jesus Christ. The character of Christ's priesthood, stamped upon the depths of his being at ordination, needs to work itself out into his whole life. Christ the priest, Christ offered to the Father on the Cross, must appear in the priest's whole life, must manifest Himself in the priest's actions. The furnace of purification for the priest in the active ministry is charity for other men.

The contemplative, as a rule, has no ministry. The fire by which he is purified is the fire of God, in solitude. He lives his Mass on a level too deep for conscious analysis.

When the summer of my ordination ended, I found myself face to face with a mystery that was beginning to manifest itself in the depths of my soul and to move me with terror. Do not ask me what it was. I might apologize for it and call it "suffering." The word is not adequate because it suggests physical pain. That is not at all what I mean. It is true that something had begun to affect my health; but whatever happened to my health was only, it seems to me, an effect of this unthinkable thing that had developed in the depths of my being. And again: I have no way of explaining what it was. It was a sort of slow, submarine earthquake which produced strange commotions on the visible, psychological surface of my life. I was summoned to battle with joy and with fear, knowing in every case that the sense of battle was misleading, that my apparent antagonist was only an illusion, and that the whole commotion was simply the effect of something that had already erupted, without my knowing it, in the hidden volcano.

From this moment on, the journal became a patchy affair. Sometimes I wrote page upon page, and then tore everything up. Sometimes I went for weeks without being able to write anything at all. Finally, in April, 1950, I gave it all up, as I thought, for good.

Nevertheless, in the depth of this abysmal testing and disintegration of my spirit, in December, 1950, I suddenly discovered completely new moral resources, a spring of new life, a peace and a happiness that I had never known before and which subsisted in the face of nameless, interior terror. In this journal, I have described the peace, not the terror: and I believe that I have

done well, because as time went on, the peace grew and the ter-
ror vanished. It was the peace that was real, and the terror that
was an illusion.

And now, for the first time, I began to know what it means
to be alone. Before becoming a priest I had made a great fuss
about solitude and had been rather a nuisance to my superiors
and directors in my aspirations for a solitary life. Now, after my
ordination, I discovered that the essence of a solitary vocation is
that it is a vocation to fear, to helplessness, to isolation in the
invisible God. Having found this, I now began for the first
time in my life to taste a happiness that was so complete and so
profound that I no longer needed to reflect upon it. There was
no longer any need to remind myself that I was happy—a vain
expedient to prolong a transient joy—for this happiness was real
and permanent and even in a sense eternal. It penetrated to the
depths below consciousness, and in all storms, in all fears, in the
deepest darkness, it was always unchangeably there.

Meanwhile, my outward life was changing too. In November,
1949, after Gethsemani made her third foundation in South
Carolina, I began to give some conferences to the novices. Then
I was to give classes on Patristic theology to the scholastics.
This work, which I liked, occupied much of my time. It did
nothing to reduce the pressure of my other work, which had by
now become completely jammed and was a source of nervous
strain.

Most of the spring of 1950, I was ill with influenza. It started
before Lent and kept coming back. By the middle of Lent the
epidemic was so bad that we were dispensed from the Lenten
fast. Most of the community had the 'flu at one time or another;
many of them were in bed. I had it in various degrees practically
all the time, but did not have to remain very long in bed. The
enormous community of over two hundred monks was still de-
pending on a little ten-room infirmary half of whose rooms had
to be reserved for those who, whether they had the 'flu or not,
were too old and feeble to stay anywhere else. The others, who
could more or less take care of themselves, camped where they
could find a quiet corner.

In the spring of 1950, on top of all this, I became involved in the work that was being done in our abbey by Professor Lefevre, from the Schola Cantorum in Paris, and which led to the recording of our chant in the spring of the year. I myself had nothing to do with the gramophone records, Laudate Dominum, *except to write a commentary; I did not sing, nor did I speak the translated text of the chant, as many may have been led to believe. But I did enough practicing with the schola in the spring to reduce the time available for my other work.*

This morning, under a cobalt blue sky, summer having abruptly ended, I am beginning the Book of Job. It is not warm enough to sit for long in the shade of the cedars. The woods are crisply outlined in the sun and the clamor of distant crows is sharp in the air that no longer sizzles with locusts.

And Job moves me deeply. This year more than ever it has a special poignancy.

I now know that all my own poems about the world's suffering have been inadequate: they have not solved anything, they have only camouflaged the problem. And it seems to me that the urge to write a real poem about suffering and sin is only another temptation because, after all, I do not really understand.

Sometimes I feel that I would like to stop writing, precisely as a gesture of defiance. In any case, I hope to stop publishing for a time, for I believe it has now become impossible for me to stop writing altogether. Perhaps I shall continue writing on my deathbed, and even take some asbestos paper with me in order to go on writing in purgatory. Except that I hope Our Lady will arrange some miraculous victory over my sins that will make purgatory unnecessary.

And yet it seems to me that writing, far from being an obstacle to spiritual perfection in my own life, has become one of the conditions on which my perfection will depend. If I am to be a saint—and there is nothing else that I can think of desiring to be—it seems that I must get there by writing books in a Trappist monastery. If I am to be a saint, I have not only to be a monk, which is what all monks must do to become saints, but I must also put down on paper what I have become. It may sound simple, but it is not an easy vocation.

To be as good a monk as I can, and to remain myself, and to write about it: to put myself down on paper, in such a situation, with the most complete simplicity and integrity, masking nothing, confusing no issues: this is very hard, because I am all mixed up in illusions and attachments. These, too, will have to be put down. But without exaggeration, repetition, useless emphasis. No need for breast-beating and lamentation before the eyes of anyone but You, O God, who see the depths of my fatuity. To be frank without being boring. It is a kind of crucifixion. Not a very dramatic or painful one. But it requires so much honesty that it is beyond my nature. It must come somehow from the Holy Ghost.

One of the results of all this could well be a complete and holy transparency: living, praying, and writing in the light of the Holy Spirit, losing myself entirely by becoming public property just as Jesus is public property in the Mass. Perhaps this is an important aspect of my priesthood—my living of my Mass: to become as plain as a Host in the hands of everybody. Perhaps it is this, after all, that is to be my way into solitude. One of the strangest ways so far devised, but it is the way of the Word of God.

Yet after all, this only teaches me that nothing vital about myself can ever be public property!

September 3

It is alarming to find out how much one's theology fits the theology of Job's friends! The form of the drama of Job demands that the reader identify himself with Job. Actually most of us are more like Eliphaz or Baldad. We are hardly much closer to God than they were. And, after all, at least one of them was a mystic. Eliphaz started out with a modest enough explanation of Job's suffering, based on mystical experience. I am startled to find that this is the interpretation I myself made of Job eight years ago. It is the explanation I gave to Bob Lax's sister, Gladio, and to Mary Davis, before I came to the monastery.

Numquid homo, Dei comparatione, justificabitur, aut factore suo purior erit vir? "Shall man be justified in comparison with God, or shall a man be more pure than his maker?" And the same strain is taken up by Baldad in xxv, 4. Then, too, *Beatus homo qui corripitur a Deo* (v, 17), (iv, 17), "Blessed is the man whom God correcteth," is written on the heart of every Trappist in the first months of his novitiate.

God's purity, says Eliphaz, who knows from experience, causes us anguish and suffering when we come in contact with Him. But it is for our good that He thus purifies us. We should be humble and patient. Which reminds me that Job is a proverbial model of patience when he was anything but patient: at least so his friends thought. But that is only one of the paradoxes of Job. His tempestuous impatience is really a higher form of patience. It is a kind of adoration.

Really, the problem of Job is not so much to find out who has the right answer to the question of suffering. All their answers are more or less correct. But what Job himself demands, and justly, is the *Divine* answer not to the problem of suffering in general but to his own personal suffering. In the end, the answer that God gives to Job is simply a concrete statement of what Eliphaz had said in the abstract: "Shall man be compared to God?"

Job wanted the answer and he got it. God Himself was his answer. In the presence of God, Job acknowledged his sufferings to be just and God reproved all the arguments of Job's friends, because they were all insufficient.

Thus the Book of Job does not solve the problem of suffering, in the abstract. It shows us that one man, Job, received a concrete answer to the problem, and that answer was found in God Himself. If we are to have Job's answer, we must have Job's vision of God. Otherwise, our arguments are only modifications of the arguments of Job's friends. I hasten to say that those arguments should be sufficient for most of us. But they probably would not have been sufficient for Job.

Then there is the fact that Job is a type of Christ. And what argument of men can convince Christ that He ought to be put to death for us? Jesus did not die to prove any argument of ours. His death was not measured by any human standard of justice. The Pharisees who reviled Him and told Him to come down from the Cross were Job's friends speaking now no longer as personages in a drama, but in their own name and in that of fallen man.

September 10

Once before I read the Book of Job and got the feeling that I was going to begin living it, as well as reading it. That has happened again.

September 13

I find consoling lines here and there in Dom Chapman's *Spiritual Letters*. For instance: "Humility in oneself is not attractive, though it is attractive in others." I do not know if what is in me is humility. But it is certainly not attractive. Anguish and fear. Nobody likes to be afraid.

There are different kinds of fear. One of the most terrible is the sensation that you are likely to become, at any moment, the protagonist in a Graham Greene novel: the man who tries to be virtuous and who is, in a certain sense, holy, and yet who is overwhelmed by sin as if there were a kind of fatality about it.

One sentence of Job is always with me: "Even though He kill me, yet will I trust in Him." *Sufficit tibi, Paule, gratia mea.*

Two more sentences from Dom Chapman:
"Pray as you can and do not try to pray as you can't.
Take yourself as you find yourself: start from that."

September 14

FEAST OF THE EXALTATION OF THE HOLY CROSS
There has been a legal change of seasons, and the monastic fast has begun today. It is cool again, and the leaves of the sycamores are already beginning to turn yellow and brown. We brought down our mattresses and blankets from our dormitory cells and

spread them out in the bright September sun. My mind is full of Saint Francis on Mount Alvernia.

A moment ago, someone was playing the harmonium in the novitiate. Our psalms sound very wistful and strange on a harmonium: plaintive, sentimental and thin, as if they were filled with an immense nostalgia for the heaven of the books of meditations. It reminded me of the night Father Alberic died, three years ago. I watched by the body in the middle of the night, and then went back to the dormitory and could not get to sleep, even when I stayed to catch up my two hours while the others went down to church for the Night Office. Finally they sang Matins and Lauds of the Dead, for Father Alberic, and I could hear the garbled music coming into the dormitory through the back of the organ pipes—that great, big, dusty closet full of muffled chords! The poignancy of that music was very affecting. It seemed to sum up all the sufferings of the long life that was now over. Poor little gray Father Alberic, writing the history of the Order on scraps of paper up in the infirmary! All the relief, all the mystery, all the unexpected joy of his meeting with God could be guessed at in those strange harmonies. And so, this morning, the sound of this harmonium in the novitiate (it has begun to play again) chimes in with the last days of a two weeks' battle, and I feel a wistful and chastened sobriety filling my heart, as if I were one of the eight human survivors of the deluge, watching the world come back to view from the summit of Mount Ararat!

In the tempest, I have discovered once again, but this time with a peculiarly piercing sharpness, that I cannot possess created things, I cannot touch them, I cannot get into them. They are not my end, I cannot find any rest in them. We who are supposed to be Christians know that well enough, abstractly. Or rather, we say we believe it. Actually we have to discover it over and over again. We have to experience this truth, with deeper and deeper intensity, as we go on in life. We renounce the pursuit of creatures as ends on certain sacramental occasions. And we return, bit by bit, to our familiarity with them, living as if we had in this world a lasting city. . . .

But creatures remain untouchable, inviolable. If God wants you to suffer a little, He allows you to learn just how inviolable they are. As soon as you try to possess their goodness for its own sake, all that is sweet in them becomes bitter to you, all that is beautiful, ugly. Everything you love sickens you. And at the same time your need to love something, somebody, increases a hundred times over. And God, Who is the only one who can be loved for His own sake alone, remains invisible and unimaginable and untouchable, beyond everything else that exists.

You flowers and trees, you hills and streams, you fields, flocks and wild birds, you books, you poems, and you people, I am unutterably alone in the midst of you. The irrational hunger that sometimes gets into the depths of my will, tries to swing my deepest self away from God and direct it to your love. I try to touch you with the deep fire that is in the center of my heart, but I cannot touch you without defiling both you and myself, and I am abashed, solitary and helpless, surrounded by a beauty that can never belong to me.

But this sadness generates within me an unspeakable reverence for the holiness of created things, for they are pure and perfect and they belong to God and they are mirrors of His beauty. He is mirrored in all things like sunlight in clean water: but if I try to drink the light that is in the water I only shatter the reflection.

And so I live alone and chaste in the midst of the holy beauty of all created things, knowing that nothing I can see or hear or touch will ever belong to me, ashamed of my absurd need to give myself away to any one of them or to all of them. The silly, hopeless passion to give myself away to any beauty eats out my heart. It is an unworthy desire, but I cannot avoid it. It is in the hearts of us all, and we have to bear with it, suffer its demands with patience, until we die and go to heaven where all things will belong to us in their highest causes.

September 15

If I were more immersed in the Rule of Saint Benedict, I would be a better writer.

If I were more absorbed in the Presence of God, I would be a better writer and would write much less.

There are now over two hundred in the community.

September 17

Nisi granum frumenti . . . unless the grain of wheat, falling into the ground, die, itself remaineth alone. The words are much more poignant in their context. Some gentiles had asked Philip if they might speak to Jesus. This is Our Lord's answer. They cannot come to Him through Philip and Andrew, they cannot even come to Him if they talk to Him, because words will not unite them with Him. They can only come to Him if He dies for them.

Itself remaineth alone. Saint John emphasizes more and more the loneliness, the moral isolation, of Christ before His Passion. He is alone from the beginning because He is God and all the rest are men. He is alone because nobody can understand Him. Already in the sixth chapter a whole crowd of disciples has abandoned Him because His doctrine of the Eucharist is so far beyond them. He is isolated by the increasing hatred of the Pharisees, who form a stronger and stronger front against Him, forcing others to separate themselves from Him. He is isolated by His own greatness, which elevates Him further and further above His enemies. Now He is alone among men who either hate Him or do not know how to love Him, because they are unable to know Him as He really is. Yet there are some who want to come to the true knowledge and love of Him. If they want to be with Him, He must pass through death and take them with Him into life.

I am alone in the world with a different loneliness from that of Christ. He was alone because He was everything. I am alone because I am nothing. I am alone in my insufficiency—dependent, helpless, contingent, and never quite sure that I am really leaning on Him upon whom I depend.

Yet to trust in Him means to die, because to trust perfectly in Him you have to give up all trust in anything else. And I am afraid of that death. The only thing I can do about it is to make my fear become part of the death I must die, to live perfectly in Him.

Our souls are baptized in His death. Our souls have passed from death to life. Yesterday at the Communion of the Conventual Mass, my faculties were also baptized in His death, for a short time. Without any work on my own part, and in spite of myself—for I was dull and distracted—I suddenly found myself completely recollected and sunk in Him and protected on all sides by His Presence so that my imagination became incapable of going anywhere and doing anything and my memory was completely sated by darkness. Comfortably locked away in recollection and peace I had the feeling that I couldn't get out if I tried. I was so numb that all the business of movements in choir slowed down to a dream and this went on until after Sext. The dream ebbed out of me when I walked off to our books. The same thing came back at None and Vespers, but not at Compline, and not today either. It was a great and merciful relief because it washed away much of the strain and sorrow of all the interior fighting I have been doing and still have to do.

September 21

The word "poignant" is taking a very prominent place in my vocabulary these days! That is because there is some power that keeps seizing my heart in its fist and wringing cries out of me (I mean the quiet kind that make themselves heard by twisting within you) and beating me this way and that until I am scarcely able to reel. Day and night I am bullied by the most suspicious of joys. I spend my time wrestling with emotions that seem to be now passion, now anguish, and now the highest religious exaltation.

Fortunately I have much intellectual work, and the books are my best shock-absorbers. But the absorption is not complete, it is only sublimated. The emotion is transferred to a spiritual plane. Every article in *La Vie Spirituelle*, every line of Job or Tobias seems to send me sky high, and I don't come down again for an hour. It is a terrific nuisance.

This morning, consecrating the Precious Blood, I became so

overwhelmed that I had doubts (I hope they were negative doubts) whether I had actually said all the words properly and whether the consecration were valid.

But occasionally I get a little rest. Yesterday, for instance, I was able to relax practically all day in a blessed aridity in which things were, once again, mercifully insipid and distasteful. What a relief to be indifferent to things, after having been pushed around by a crowd of different intoxications, some of which seem to be intensely holy and some of which do not even bother to wear a disguise.

It is not much fun to live the spiritual life with the spiritual equipment of an artist.

Yesterday afternoon, in the cornfield, I began to feel rather savage about the whole business. I suppose this irritation was the sign that the dry period was reaching its climax and was about to go over again into the awful battle with joy. My soul was cringing and doubling up and subconsciously getting ready for the next tidal wave. At the moment all I had left in my heart was an abyss of self-hatred—waiting for the next appalling sea.

We have a new machine that rushes through the cornfield, raffishly seizing the corn and reducing it instantly to finely minced particles, which it then sprays into a truck that travels along beside it. This apparatus charges through the field doing all the work and the rest of us simply have to cut a few stalks that have blown down and are lying too low for the monster to snatch with its knives. Things have changed greatly in the six years since I was a novice. But since there is much more work, we can do with a few machines.

October 7

Spiritual joy depends on the cross. Unless we deny ourselves, we will find ourselves in everything and that is misery. As soon as we begin to deny ourselves, out of love for God, we begin to find God, at least obscurely. Since God is our joy, our joy is proportioned to our self-denial, for the love of God. I say: our self-denial for the love of God, because there are people who deny themselves for love of themselves.

It is not complicated, to lead the spiritual life. But it is difficult. We are blind, and subject to a thousand illusions. We must expect to be making mistakes almost all the time. We must be content to fall repeatedly and to begin again to try to deny ourselves, for the love of God.

It is when we are angry at our own mistakes that we tend most of all to deny ourselves for love of ourselves. We want to shake off the hateful thing that has humbled us. In our rush to escape the humiliation of our own mistakes, we run head first into the opposite error, seeking comfort and compensation. And so we spend our lives running back and forth from one attachment to another.

If that is all our self-denial amounts to, our mistakes will never help us.

The thing to do when you have made a mistake is not to give up doing what you were doing and start something altogether new, but to start over again with the thing you began badly and try, for the love of God, to do it well.

November 16

Today, on the eleventh anniversary of my Baptism, I began teaching theology—an introductory conference, lasting an hour and a half. On Monday I began a series of orientation classes for the novices.

The colony left for South Carolina Monday morning. It was very quiet, because they got out while we were chanting the Night Office, at about half past three. During the morning meditation we could see the non-priests going to Communion at Saint Joseph's altar. Twenty-nine left, in all.

A priest is here with a "Pilgrim Statue" of Our Lady of Fatima. It is one of those super-pretty statues, but I like it, without apology, not for art's sake but for Our Lady's sake. Father Gervase tapped it all over with his knuckles to see if it was wood or plaster and it sounded (to my relief) like wood. I asked Our Lady for the grace of interior solitude and spiritual virginity. There is nothing to live for but God, and I am still full of the orchestras that drown His Voice.

November 24   FEAST OF SAINT JOHN OF THE CROSS
The other day I read how Ezechiel saw the glory of God—those
wheels, those wings, those fires flashing and those living creatures
running to and fro—go back to Jerusalem from Babylon.

I think I shall ask permission to write to a Hindu who wrote me
a letter about Patanjali's yoga, and who is in Simla. I shall ask
him to send us some books. A chemist who has been helping us
with some paint jobs turned out to have been a postulant in a
Zen Buddhist monastery in Hawaii and he spoke to the community about it in Chapter.

It was raining and there was a wind. I went out to the wagon
shed. You could still see the hills in the distance, not too much
rain for that—many black clouds, low and torn, like smoke from
a disaster, flying angrily over the wide open ruin of the old
horsebarn, where I now love to walk alone. On sunny days it
does not have this Castle of Otranto look about it. Today, first
I was full of a melody that might have been related to something
in Stravinsky's "Firebird" which I have nevertheless forgotten.
This was mostly my own and I sang it to God, along with
angels. Then the melody went away and I sat on a stone.

November 25   SAINT CATHERINE
In the refectory we are reading Exodus and I have discovered
Saint Gregory of Nyssa's *De Vita Moysis*. I will probably try to
talk about it in the Mystical Theology class. Having trouble
organizing material. I have no textbook to follow—except I will
take Gilson on Saint Bernard when I get the preliminaries out of
the way. I feel much better mapping out my own approach—
from Scripture and the Fathers, Mysticism and Dogma together.

No man's land. The half-light of the cloud. Father Bruno describing a Carthusian monk somewhere uses the expression "sacred exhaustion." It amuses me, but I see the point. I experience
it from head to foot. This from the special number of *Etudes*

Carmelitaines on Joy which Monsignor Sheen gave us during the retreat he preached here and which I read each day behind the horsebarn. Very good.

December 3

Kenneth Patchen's "For losing her love all would I profane" struck me with great force and after a moment I realized that for me (perhaps not for him) it simply echoes Saint John of the Cross's "*Por toda la hermosura nunca yo me perdere*—For all the beauty in the world never will I lose myself."

I remember the misty afternoon (late October) when I was out in the woods behind Nally's, walking uphill in the bare washed-out place where the oak trees were cut down and the stumps and roots are black in the wreckage of shale. I read Saint John's poem over and over again and tried to get it right into the marrow of my bones. And so I sit bewildered by the dialectic of those two similar yet contrary poems, equally good. Kenneth Patchen is an admirable poet. According to Laughlin, he is very sick. Naomi Burton came here today.

December 4

SECOND SUNDAY IN ADVENT.

DAY OF RECOLLECTION

Last Sunday morning Father George died, after Reverend Father had announced that he would give him Extreme Unction in the afternoon. Father William, who is always in the infirmary, anointed him quickly just before he died, and Reverend Father told us about it over the refectory microphone at the end of dinner.

I am hebdomadary, sang Mass this morning at the temporary altar in the front of the presbytery (the new marble one shines in the gloom behind it but the steps leading up to it are not finished).

After Sext, I went out for a moment to see Naomi at the gate. She came out from Louisville smartly and soberly dressed in a costume I am sure would be approved in any ecclesiastical circles.

Behind the horsebarn after dinner I made my thanksgiving. The little clouds were beautiful. The sun on the grass was beautiful. Even the ground seemed alive.

Walking along the fence of the new vineyard after Benediction, I looked at the dim full moon and the bare brown woods on the far side of the bottoms where our neighbor built that little wooden house last summer. It is the only house we can see in that direction or, in fact, in any other. But what I wanted to say was that I don't think I like to walk in the fields with clothes smelling of incense.

December 6

Tomorrow is the Vigil of the Immaculate Conception. I am busy most of the time preparing classes—Orientation, Mystical Theology. I am still trying to lay foundations for all of them—and I make notes on a lot of things that I will probably never talk to them about. There is supposed to be a Seminar group coming to the vault after Benediction on Sundays and Feasts to talk about special points. That means mostly Saint John of the Cross, as far as I am concerned. I am going through the *Spiritual Canticle* again in Spanish out behind the horsebarn in a little corner behind the cedars where I can sit among the blackberry bushes out of the wind. It is still warm enough to sit out there even in summer clothes. I feel like learning snatches of Saint John's Spanish by heart—just snatches. It is inviting and easy. Phrases cling to you without your making half an effort to grasp them.

This evening, before Vespers, low gray clouds, very dark, all the woods and bottoms looked grim, but there was a brushfire along the road that skirts the ridge of Mount Olivet and you could see the jagged bloody wound of flame eating its way among the trees, with blue smoke pouring out over the road and the pasture. It was a strange and beautiful background for the Sorrowful Mysteries of the Rosary. I walked along the edge of the dead vineyard and there was a strong wind that blew our summer cowl against the barbed wire and it got torn.

December 7

VIGIL OF THE IMMACULATE CONCEPTION

One of the many nice things about being hebdomadary is that you get the scriptorium all to yourself during a good part of the wonderful interval after the Night Office. All the other priests are saying Mass and the young professed are going to Communion. I listen to the clock tick. Downstairs the thermostat has just stopped humming. God is in this room. So much so that it is difficult to read or write. Nevertheless I'll get busy on Isaias which is Your word, O my God, and may Your fire grow in me and may I find You in Your beautiful fire. It is very quiet, O my God, Your moon shines on our hills. Your moonlight shines in my wide open soul when everything is silent. *Adolezco peno y muero.*

December 9

Here is a passage in Rilke's *Journal* that I like immensely. It ought to be true of me, but I talk too much—keep the contacts open:

What's the use of telling anyone that I am changing? If I am changing then surely I am no longer the person I was and if I am something else than heretofore, then it is clear that I have no acquaintances. And to strange people, to people who do not know me, I cannot possibly write.

Is the last sentence true of me? No! I write for a hundred thousand people who do not know me, but I am not writing this for them.

Tomorrow it will be eight years since I came to Gethsemani. I somehow feel less clean than I did then when I thought I was throwing my civil identity away.

Last night in the little cloister a disheveled young layman with a lot of black hair who looked as though he might be one of the neighbors, burst in through the door out of the dark, came up to me as if he knew he ought not to do it, and stretched out his hand to shake hands with me. Then he rushed out the door, pleased but guilty. He seemed to be wearing two raincoats. I had never seen him before. I wondered if he were some stranger who had done this on a bet. But today I saw him in choir with the laybrothers, so he is a postulant. (Later he left.)

(Evening.) It is snowing now. First snow of the winter. Most of us are wearing summer clothes all winter since the church is now heated.

Today after dinner I got Father Placid, the Cellarer, to discuss amicably and in sign language the possibility of putting more bookshelves in the vault and throwing out the closetfuls of the vestments we wear on the big feasts for Pontifical High Mass. At present I have the *Vie Spirituelle* lying all over the floor. Also I got him to remove two hideous small statues of plaster saints which I found there when I first came. I had tried to stuff them out of sight but the only place that would contain them had a glass door to it, so you could still see their faces, congealed in expressions of the most fatuous piety. Father Placid took one saint in each hand, holding them by their heads, and walked off to the guest house, convinced that the retreatants would love them. And I suppose they will. My guess is that the saints were Saint John Eudes and Saint Vincent de Paul but I never had the courage to look and see if their names were on them. Poor saints! Pray for us, holy saints! May God have mercy on us.

Emotion does a man great injury in this monastic life. You have to be serious and detached and calm all the time. Faith is the antidote: cleansing yourself of impressions and feelings and the absurd movements of a half-blind understanding by a clear penetration into the heart of darkness where God is found.

December 10

I am abashed by the real solitude of Rilke which I admire, knowing however it is not for me because I am not like that. But his is a solitude I understand objectively, perhaps not by connaturality at all but it moves me tremendously. You see, to begin with, he did not *want* it or go looking for it. It found him. Tremendous how he finds himself in the solitude of Christ (David) in the psalms, all of a sudden, there, on page 53 of Malte Laurids Brigge. (Who is the French poet that he quotes there?)

Anyway, here is something Rilke himself wrote down. It will make one page of mine look good!

For a while yet I can write all this down and express it. But there will come a day when my hand will be far from me and when I bid it write it will write words I do not mean. The time of that other interpretation will dawn when not one word will remain upon another and all meaning will dissolve like clouds and fall down like rain. Despite my fear I am yet like one standing before something great . . . This time I shall be written. I am the impression that will change.

No, one does not envy the fear that is another man's private vocation. But I am abashed by that fear and by Rilke and Kafka who are solitaries without, for all that, being my brothers—not my close brothers like the calm and patient and long-suffering men in cowls who live and pray with me here in this busy family.

I guess it is the right fictional element that makes this solitude in Rilke's book just intangible: real, but not quite my own. Same too with Kafka.

December 13   SAINT LUCY

Eight years since I walked into the novitiate behind Father Robert, with the fat boy from Buffalo. Father Joel and I were making signs about it tonight.

I am deacon this week. As soon as I stand in front of the open book at the Gospel-stand to sing the Gospel, the memory of the time I passed out in the middle of the Gospel last July comes over me and I can't breathe and my legs turn into jelly and it is all I can do to look at the book and keep an ordered series of noises coming out of me. This morning I thought I was going to collapse for sure. A big wave of darkness came up from inside me somewhere, but I shook my head and it went away for a bit. Hope I can finish out the week with its three Ember days.

Reverend Father is making me sleep late—until 3 A.M.—tomor-row and the rest of the week.

I am throwing myself too much into this class-work. That is one thing that is wearing me down. There is no need to try to sweep them off their feet by sheer intensity. "It is pride only—sit still."

December 15

The other night I woke up at midnight and began to worry over whether I would be able to get through the Gospel at High Mass. By Chapter the next morning I was so worn out thinking about it and making all kinds of resolutions that I had to ask Father to let me off being deacon for the rest of the week. Father Savinian took over. Dom Gildas, who is celebrant, up-braided me in sign language. But it was a great relief. I felt much lighter. I am under pressure, through my own fault. The Gospel business can be tackled sometime when, by God's grace, I am a little more in the clear.

Nevertheless, working in the woods in the afternoon, I felt lonely and small and humiliated—chopping down dead trees with a feeling that perhaps I was not even a real person any more.

Apart from that, it was nice working in the woods. The day was very gray and gloomy. We were on Mount Olivet clearing out cedars that had been killed by the brush fires. Through the trees I could see the next-door farm, the one where the Font-gombault monks once were. And I could see the knobs from a new and interesting angle and the Introit of the Christmas Morn-ing Mass kept going around and around in my mind because we had practiced it, all together in choir, right after Chapter. So that contributed to keeping me alive.

Otherwise—feeling of fear, dejection, non-existence. Yet it gives me a kind of satisfaction to realize that it is not by contact with any other creature that I can recover the sense that I am real. Solitude means being lonely not in a way that pleases you but in a way that frightens and empties you to the extent that it means being exiled even from yourself.

I must have mixed inks in our well for the ink is turning pale green.

                                                        December 17

"*Vacio, hambriento, solo, llagado y doliente de amor, suspenso en el aire*" ("Empty, famished, alone, wounded and suffering with love, suspended in the air!").

Walking back from the barns in the warm sun on the muddy road between the orchard and the vegetable garden with the *Spiritual Canticle* under my arm, and saying those wonderful words! I found a fine place to read and pray, on the top floor of that barn building where the rabbits used to be. Up under the roof is a place reached by various ladders. Some stovepipes and old buckets are there and many of the little boxes in which the novices gather strawberries in the early summer time. There is a chair and there is a beautiful small rectangular window which faces south over the valley—the outside orchard, Saint Joseph's field, the distant line of hills. It is the quietest and most hidden and most isolated place I have found in the whole enclosure—but not necessarily the warmest. However, it was good yesterday with the sun coming in the window: "*Vacio, hambriento, solo, llagado y doliente de amor, suspenso en el aire.*" Almost all activity makes me ill, but as soon as I am alone and silent again I sink into deep peace, recollection, and happiness.

I have been elevated to a position on the monastery fire department. We are just organizing one. A man was here from Louisville today. Broad, muscular and calm. He told us that fire fighting was serious business, and that our equipment was hopeless, and that in the city they would lock people up for being as careless as we are about fire hazards. After that there was a lot of conversation about fire creeping up on you inside the walls and under the floor.

I heard somebody practicing the Graduals of the big feasts that are to come—Christmas, Saint Stephen, Saint John, and somehow I thought of all the old monasteries of the Order and of the life our Fathers led. All this has become part of my body of Christmas associations. And I am happy—perfectly happy to be a Cistercian —not a Carmelite or Carthusian or Camaldolese but a Cistercian and sit in the top of a barn with more beautiful stove-pipes and strawberry boxes and lovelier old junk than a Carthusian ever saw, all alone and *suspenso en el aire*.

December 20   VIGIL OF SAINT THOMAS

Rilke's Notebooks have so much power in them that they make me wonder why no one writes like that in monasteries. Not that there have not been better books written in monasteries, and books more serene. But monks do not seem to be able to write so well—and it is as if our professional spirituality sometimes veiled our contact with the naked realities inside us. It is a common failing of monks to lose themselves in a collective, professional personality—to let themselves be cast in a mold. Yet this mold does not seem to do away with what is useless or even unpleasant about some personalities. We cling to our eccentricities and our selfishness, but we do so in a way that is no longer interesting because it is after all mechanical and vulgar.

I have fallen into the great indignity I have written against—I am a contemplative who is ready to collapse from overwork. This, I think, is a sin and the punishment of sin but now I have got to turn it to good use and be a saint by it, somehow.

Teaching wears me out. Like Ezechias I am in a big hurry to show all my treasures to the Babylonians. Not that the novices and the young monks are Babylonians in their own right—but relatively to me and my treasures they might just as well be. And yet what can I show them, or what can I share with them? There is so little one can communicate. I talk my head off and they seem to be listening to somebody who wasn't there, to stories I never told them. They have received messages I never intended them to hear. While I talk they sit there—perhaps imagining they like what I say—and all the while they are building up myths of their own upon a few fragments of words that came

out of me. I am astonished at their constructions. But in the end
I think I am astonished that I am able to say anything at all that
passes from me to some other mind except God's.

The terrible thing is the indignity of thinking such an en-
deavor is really important. The other day while the new high
altar was being consecrated I found myself being stripped of one
illusion after another. There I stood and sat with my eyes closed
and wondered why I read so much, why I write so much, why
I talk so much, and why I get so excited about the things that
only affect the surface of my life—I came here eight years ago
and already knew better when I arrived. But for eight years I
have obeyed the other law in my members and so I am worn out
with activity—exhausting myself with proclaiming that the thing
to do is rest. *In omnibus requiem quaesivi* . . .

December 22

Yesterday, the Feast of Saint Thomas, was, as I think, an important day. It was warm and overclouded and windy but tranquil. I had a kind of sense that the day was building up to some
kind of deep decision. A wordless decision, a giving of the depths
and substance of myself. There is a conversion of the deep will
to God that cannot be effected in words—barely in a gesture or
ceremony. There is a conversion of the deep will and a gift of
my substance that is too mysterious for liturgy, and too private.
It is something to be done in a lucid secrecy that implies first of
all the denial of communication to others except perhaps as a
neutral thing.

I shall remember the time and place of this liberty and this
neutrality which cannot be written down. These clouds low on
the horizon, the outcrops of hard yellow rock in the road, the
open gate, the perspective of fence-posts leading up the rise to
the sky, and the big cedars tumbled and tousled by the wind.
Standing on rock. Present. The reality of the present and of
solitude divorced from past and future. To be collected and
gathered up in clarity and silence and to belong to God and to
be nobody else's business. I wish I could recover the liberty of

that interior decision which was very simple and which seems to me to have been a kind of blank check and a promise.

To belong to God I have to belong to myself. I have to be alone —at least interiorly alone. This means the constant renewal of a decision. I cannot belong to people. None of me belongs to anybody but God. Absolute loneliness of the imagination, the memory, the will. My love for everybody is equal, neutral and clean. No exclusiveness. Simple and free as the sky because I love everybody and am possessed by nobody, not held, not bound. In order to be not remembered or even wanted I have to be a person that nobody knows. They can have Thomas Merton. He's dead. Father Louis—he's half dead too. For my part my name is that sky, those fence-posts, and those cedar trees. I shall not even reflect on who I am and I shall not say my identity is nobody's business because that implies a truculence I don't intend. It has no meaning.

Now my whole life is this—to keep unencumbered. The wind owns the fields where I walk and I own nothing and am owned by nothing and I shall never even be forgotten because no one will ever discover me. This is to me a source of immense confidence. My Mass this morning was transfigured by this independence.

They are pulling down the horsebarn. The Traxcavator was tethered to it, in the rain, after dinner. The barn was already half in ruins. And house upon house shall fall. The roof was down in a hoisted heap spreading its red old wings clumsily over the wreckage of the stables. The other half of the barn was tied to the monster and ready to fall. The stone pillars were already crooked and awry. When I was at work I could hear the engine roar but did not hear the fall of the old building.

I seek no face, I treasure no experience, no memory. Anything I write down here is only for personal guidance because of my constant gravitation away from solitude. It will remind me how to go home. Not to be like the man who looked in the glass and straightway forgot what manner of man he was: yet I shall not remember myself in such a way that I remember the person I am not.

As I re-discover solitude, prayer in choir becomes difficult again. But the other day—Tuesday at the Night Office—Psalm 54 had tremendous meaning for me. I felt as if I were chanting something I myself had written. It is more my own than any of my own poems:

Cor meum conturbatum est in me, et formido mortis cedidit super me.
Timor et tremor venerunt super me, et contexerunt me tenebrae:
Et dixi: quis dabit mihi pennas sicut columbae et volabo, et requiescam?
Ecce, elongavi fugiens, et mansi in solitudine.
*Expectabo eum, qui salvum me fecit a pusillanimitate spiritus, et tempestate.**

It is fear that is driving me into solitude. Love has put drops of terror in my veins and they grow cold in me, suddenly, and make me faint with fear because my heart and my imagination wander away from God into their own private idolatry. It is my iniquity that makes me physically faint and turn to jelly because of the contradiction between my nature and my God. I am exhausted by fear. So that yesterday, for example, I thought I would fall with the ciborium, distributing Communion to the brothers. But last night in the middle of the night I was awake for an hour and a half and the last line I have quoted there was verified. All five lines are truer of my life than anything I have ever written, and this gives me great confidence in the liturgy. This is the secret of the psalms. Our identity is hidden in them.

*"My heart is troubled within me: and the fear of death is fallen upon me.
Fear and trembling are come upon me: and darkness hath covered me.
And I said: who will give me wings like a dove, and I will fly and be at rest?
Lo, I have gone far off, flying away; and I abode in the wilderness.
I waited for Him that hath saved me from pusillanimity of spirit and a storm."

In them we find ourselves, and God. In these fragments he has revealed not only Himself to us but ourselves in Him. *Mittit crystallum suum sicut buccellas.*

December 23

Saint Augustine, of Adam in Eden: *"vivebat fruens Deo, ex quo bono erat bonus."**

It is very quiet now in the vault where I pause in my work on the *City of God.* I am supposed to be doing a preface for Random House. The work feeds me, strengthens me, knits my powers together in peace and tranquillity. The light of God shines to me more serenely through the wide open windows of Augustine than through any other theologian. Augustine is the calmest and clearest light.

Now I listen to the watch ticking on the table. It loses time, but nobody cares. A train whistled out in the valley a moment ago, but now everything is very silent except for the faint clanking of ropes against the metal flagpole in the garden, as they move in the wind.

Sunlight on the table. *Bolletino Bibliografico Internazionale* (a book catalogue), Gardeil, *La Structure de l'Ame,* on interlibrary loan from the Catholic University. Frater Primo, all smiles, is shooting the second volume on microfilm and I will soon let him take the first. I liked the passage where Gardeil thought it necessary to defend himself against the charge of having become an Augustinian. The whole first volume is on Augustine. Cayré's book (*La Contemplation Augustinienne*) is here too. Kenneth Patchen's *Dark Kingdom.* Henry Suso in French. *Le Paradis Blanc* (with pictures of La Val Sainte, the Swiss Charterhouse), Saint John of the Cross, red and green false leather, in Spanish, Tauler, De Lubac, Berlière, *Renascence,* Dom Jean LeClercq on Saint Bernard, *Etudes Carmelitaines,* Dom Anselme Stolz, and Daniélou on Origen, John of Saint Thomas in Raïssa Maritain's translation, Jacques Maritain's *Quatres Essais sur l'Esprit dans sa Condition Charnelle,* and a College Handbook of

*"He lived in the joy of God, and by the power of this good he was himself good."

Composition lent to me by the Infirmarian, which I ought to consult some day.

Angelico's *Annunciation* on a postcard Clare Luce sent from Florence, and Giotto's *Flight into Egypt* on a Christmas card from the Poor Clares in New Mexico. The sun shines in a very happy room this morning, in which a monk is where he belongs, in silence, with angels, his hand and eye moved by the living God in deep tranquillity. The watch ticks: but perhaps there is after all no such thing as time.

(*Lux mundi Dominus cum potestate venit.*)
. . . *in anima tota tranquillitas.*
Nihil omnino triste, nihil erat inaniter laetum
. . . *nulla ex cupiditate vel timore accidebat bonae voluntatis offensio*
  gaudium verum perpetuabatur ex Deo in quem flagrabat caritas de
  *corde puro . . .**

De Civitate Dei, xiv, 26
P<small>L</small> 41.434

(Late afternoon.) The quiet of the afternoon is filled with an altogether different tonality. The sun has moved altogether around and the room is darker. It is serious. The hour is more weary. I take time out to pray, and I look at the Angelico picture, feeling like the end of Advent, which is today. *Ecce completa sunt omnia quae dicta sunt per angelum de Virgine Maria*—that was the antiphon after the Benedictus this morning. For a few minutes I stayed silent and didn't move and listened to the watch and wondered if perhaps I might not understand something of the work Our Lady is preparing.

It is an hour of tremendous expectation.

I remember my weariness, my fears, my lack of understanding, my dimness, my sin of over-activity. What is she preparing: have I offended her? What is coming up? She loves me. I reject

*"The Lord, the Light of the World, cometh with power."
. . . . in his soul was all tranquillity.
There was nothing at all of sadness in him, nothing of empty joy. . . .
Nothing of cupidity or fear stood in the way of his good will as an obstacle, but his true joy was ever renewed out of the depths of God for Whom he burned with charity in his pure heart . . ."

emotion about it. Her love is too serious for any emotion of which I might be capable. Her love shapes worlds, shapes history, forms an Apocalypse in me and around me: gives birth to the City of God. I am drawn back again into liturgy by a sense of my great need. I look at the serene, severe porch where Angelico's angel speaks to her. Angelico knew how to paint her. She is thin, immensely noble, and she does not rise to meet the angel. Mother, make me as sincere as the picture. All the way down into my soul, sincere, sincere. Let me have no thought that could not kneel before you in that picture. No image. No shadow. I believe you. I am silent. I will act like the picture. *Ecce completa sunt:* it is the end of Advent and the afternoon is vivid with expectancy.

Perhaps I have found an answer to this mysterious thing. Is it a certain strange presence of Our Lady, who is here before Jesus is here? That would be the solution suggested in Daniélou's article in *Dieu Vivant* 10.

She is here, and she has filled the room with something that is uniquely her own, too clean for me to appreciate. She is here, with the tone of her expectancy. There is nothing wrong in writing it, for it is she who makes me write it down.

December 24 CHRISTMAS EVE
*Constantes estote, videbitis auxilium Domini super vos.**

Daniélou quoted something from Abbé Monchanin—an unpublished document on the sweet and terrible virgins adored in India—dealers of death and of pleasure or of asceticism and wisdom.

But Our Lady's virginity—contained the Word of God, the Virginity of God.

She kept all His words in her heart which was therefore immaculate and was established in virginity by marriage to God.

She comes bringing solitude and society, life and death, war and peace, that peace may come out of war and that my solitude may place me somewhere in the history of my society. It is clear to me that solitude is my vocation, not as a flight from the world

*"Persevere, and you shall see the help of God descend upon you."

but as my place in the world, because for me to find solitude is only to separate myself from all the forces that destroy me and destroy history, in order to be united with the Life and Peace that build the City of God in history and rescue the children of God from hell.

Christ is to be born. He is the hermit Who is the center of history. He has made His solitude the Heart of society—Cross and *Agape*. Sacrifice and recovery, death and love. Virginity is therefore both terrible and necessary. Without it I do not live. Without it no fruitfulness. Tomorrow I am born of a virgin in order to die of virginity and draw all things to Christ.

The best thing for me is a lucid silence that does not even imagine it speaks to anybody. A silence in which I see no interlocutor, frame no message for anyone, formulate no word either for man or paper. There will still be plenty to say when the time comes to write, and what is written will be simpler and more fruitful.

December 27 FEAST OF SAINT JOHN
Yesterday Father Cellarer lent me the jeep. I did not ask for it, he just lent it to me out of the goodness of his heart, so that I would be able to go out to the woods on the other side of the knobs. I had never driven a car before. Once or twice at Saint Bonaventure's I took lessons. Father Roman tried to teach me to drive a little broken-down Chevvie he had there. Yesterday I took the jeep and started off gaily all by myself to the woods. It had been raining heavily. All the roads were deep in mud. It took me some time to discover the front-wheel drive. I skidded into ditches and got out again, I went through creeks, I got stuck in the mud, I bumped into trees and once, when I was on the main road, I stalled trying to get out of the front-wheel drive and ended up sideways in the middle of the road with a car coming down the hill straight at me. Thank heaven I am still alive. At the moment I didn't seem to care if I lived or died. I drove the jeep madly into the forest in a rosy fog of confusion and delight. We romped over trestles and I sang "O Mary I love

you," went splashing through puddles a foot deep, rushed madly into the underbrush and backed out again.

Finally I got the thing back to the monastery covered with mud from stem to stern. I stood in choir at Vespers, dizzy with the thought: "I have been driving a jeep."

Father Cellarer just made me a sign that I must never, never, under any circumstances, take the jeep out again.

This morning at the beginning of Matutinal Mass, Reverend Father passed a note around the choir that Brother Owen was dead. He had a heart attack in the dormitory last night and they took him to the hospital this morning about three. He died a half hour after arriving there. He was about seventy-six years old but had not been in the monastery much longer than I. He was a novice when I came and I remember he was very ill in the infirmary in Lent 1942 when I was up there. He was a good, quiet, holy brother.

December 30

Tomorrow is Saint Sylvester's and another year is over. I wish I knew what I had done to justify my existence this year—besides collecting royalties with which the monastery supports General Motors by buying new trucks. There is only one thing—and that is better than anything else I have done in my life. For six months I have been saying Mass. That one fact is teaching me to live in such a way that I do not care whether I live or die.

Yet there is a sinful way of being prepared to die; to live in the midst of life, at the source of life, and to feel in your heart that cold taste for death that is almost ready to refuse life—the dead rot of acedia that eats out your substance with discouragement and fear!

I wonder if there are not hundreds of people in monasteries with that most pitiable of sicknesses. It makes you wish you could get something respectable, with a real pain attached to it, like cancer, or a tumor on the brain.

I like the Augustinian themes in Parain's *Mort de Jean Madec*
yet I would not know whether it was a good book. To me it is
a good book. The only other novel I have read in the eight years
I have been here is Greene's *Heart of the Matter* and I read only
half of that. Then I read bits of *The Loved One* and a few pages
of *Brideshead Revisited*.

I like Kenneth Patchen's *Dark Kingdom* but it does not do
anything beyond interesting the surface of my mind. It does not
make a deep impression and it cannot because it is only poetry.
The only books that move me deeply are the Bible, Saint John
of the Cross, *The Cloud of Unknowing*, and a few others like
that: Tauler, Saint Augustine, parts of Saint Bernard, Saint Gregory of Nyssa.

> Let us run by patience to the fight proposed to us,
> Looking on Jesus the author and finisher of faith who, having joy
> set before Him endured the cross, despising the shame and now
> sitteth on the right hand of the throne of God.
> For think diligently upon Him that endured such opposition from
> against Himself that you be not wearied, fainting in your minds.
> For you have not yet resisted unto blood, striving against sin
> . . . Persevere under discipline for God dealeth with you as with
> sons . . .
> But if you be without chastisements, whereof all are made partakers,
> then you are bastards and not sons.
>
> *Hebrews* c.12

I spent the whole day, morning and afternoon work, trying
to re-establish the appearance of order in the vault. It took all
that time to clean up the piles of ragged envelopes full of notes
and manuscripts, the accumulated books and copies of *La Vie
Spirituelle*. I even had one *Life* and two *Atlantic Monthlies*
stuffed under one of the closets. The *Life* was the one with
Waugh's article on the Church in America and the *Atlantic* was
an issue with two of my poems in it. I hadn't looked at them,
though, because I hadn't had time and because almost everything
with a picture or an advertisement suggesting secular life makes

me ill to look at. The whole business finally made a nice bonfire. Turned in some twenty books to the library, sent off a lot of old galley proofs to Sister Thérèse and Father Connolly to save myself the trouble of burning them, and finally the place began to look neat. I like to feel that there is something almost ascetic about those two clean tables. I wonder how long it will last. I am hoping that I can start the new year with more discipline in my work and in everything—once again trying to tighten up and simplify things and work more slowly and more thoroughly.

Evelyn Waugh got T. F. Burns of Hollis and Carter to send me a copy of Fowler's *Modern English Usage* as an incentive to clean up my prose style, if I can be said to possess a prose style. I am resolving to use it. That is one of my New Year's resolutions, along with a return to the Stations of the Cross daily and regularly after Chapter—or sometime—at least once a day.

I want to say that my three Masses on Christmas morning were three of the best things that have ever happened in my life. I took plenty of time—perhaps too much time, not realizing that Father Pius was waiting to say his three Masses after me at the same (Sacred Heart) altar.

Before we got up at 5:30, in the lovely sleep that follows Lauds of Christmas morning, I had been dreaming of my Masses. I dreamt I was driving to a new foundation we were to make on the Pacific coast, somewhere in the Northwest. And I was going to say my three Masses in three different churches in three different towns on the way and each one would be a big step nearer to some inexpressible happiness in union with God. The way I felt about where I was going, in the dream, makes me think of a few dreams I had about going away to be a Carthusian—which is all over now.

January 2 [1950]

The contemplative life becomes awfully thin and drab if you go for several days at a time without thinking explicitly of the Passion of Christ. I do not mean, necessarily, meditating, but at least attending with love and humility to Christ on the Cross. For His Cross is the source of all our life and without it prayer dries up and everything goes dead.

A saint is not so much a man who realizes that he possesses virtues and sanctity as one who is overwhelmed by the sanctity of God. God is holiness. And therefore things are holy in proportion as they share what He is. All creatures are holy insofar as they share in His being, but men are called to be holy in a far superior way—by somehow sharing His transcendence and rising above the level of everything that is not God.

January 3

In the natural order, perhaps solitaries are made by severe mothers.

There is a beautiful passage on manual labor in *La Mort de Jean Madec*. It tells me one reason why I like the book so much; I am secretly reading it as a new and more interesting edition of the Cistercian *Spiritual Directory*.

Solitude is not found so much by looking outside the boundaries of your dwelling, as by staying within. Solitude is not something you must hope for in the future. Rather, it is a deepening of the present, and unless you look for it in the present you will never find it.

The fact that the Holy Father has proclaimed this a Holy Year means that he has turned it over to Our Lady and that she will make her influence felt in many ways that will make us glad and, with her near us, we will run in the ways of God's commandments. I had not planned to speak of her yet to the novices in orientation. But I was talking about grace and it would be foolish to talk of grace without talking of her. Instantly the love of her filled the room. Wide-eyed attention. You could feel the quiet. There was a different sense of peace—deeper than before; the peace of children who are at home and satisfied. And I feel as if I had contracted a new spiritual relationship with them all—novices yesterday, young professed today. It is as if we had all discovered something new to love in one another, something more innocent and perfect than any of us had seen before.

January 4 OCTAVE OF THE HOLY INNOCENTS
The tide of feasts has ebbed. We are left with all our graces and without any celebration—a comfortable condition. Now we go forward into the new age walking in simplicity. Our hearts are dilated with faith and obedience. The Innocents have saluted us. Last night at the Magnificat when we sang their antiphon *O Quam Gloriosum* (O how glorious is the Kingdom in which the Innocents rejoice with Christ), I envied them. I would have wept, but I am as dry as a stone. Thank heaven for it. Tears are not for our choir.

There has been no sun in the sky since New Year's but the dark days have been magnificent. The sky has been covered with wonderful black clouds, the horizon has been curtained with sheets of traveling rain. The landscape has been splendidly serious. I love the strength of our woods, in this bleak weather. And it *is* bleak weather. Yet there is a warmth in it like the presence of God in aridity of spirit, when He comes closer to us than in consolation.

On Sunday, that is on New Year's Day, I took one of the two torn raincoats that hang in the grand parlor for the use of the monks, and went out into the woods. Although I had not at first determined to do so, I found myself climbing the steepest of the knobs, which also turned out to be the highest—the pyramid that stands behind the head of the lake, and is second in line when you begin to count from the southwest. Bare woods and driving rain. There was a strong wind. When I reached the top I found there was something terrible about the landscape. But it was marvelous. The completely unfamiliar aspect of the forest beyond our rampart unnerved me. It was as though I were in another country. I saw the steep, savage hills, covered with black woods and half buried in the storm that was coming at me from the southwest. And ridges traveled away from this center in unexpected directions. I said, "Now you are indeed alone. Be prepared to fight the devil." But it was not the time of combat. I started down the hill again feeling that perhaps after all I had climbed it uselessly.

Halfway down, and in a place of comparative shelter, just before the pine trees begin, I found a bower God had prepared for me like Jonas's ivy. It had been designed especially for this moment. There was a tree stump, in an even place. It was dry and a small cedar arched over it, like a green tent, forming an alcove. There I sat in silence and loved the wind in the forest and listened for a good while to God.

After that I quickly found my way into the gully that leads through the heart of the hills to Hanekamp's house. Hanekamp is the hermit who comes down to Mass in the secular church. He used to be a monk here. I saw him Christmas eve, kneeling at the communion rail in his black beard and he reminded me—quite unreasonably—of Bob Lax. He does not really look like Lax at all. I came home walking along the shelves of shale that form the bed of the creek. Our woods are beautiful. The peace of the woods almost always steals over me when I am at prayer in the monastery.

January 7

I wanted to write down an incident that happened New Year's eve, in the afternoon. I was sitting by the ruins of the old horse-barn, looking down at the bleak pasture, the cedars, the enclosure wall, the woods and then that little heavenly vista of far hills in the southeast. It was gray. Hunters were in the outside orchard. I saw them going into the woods. White pants and brown pants. They were not very serious hunters because they were talking all the time; their talk echoed all through the wood. Their dog was far ahead of them, barking and barking. Soon they just stopped in the middle of the wood and talked. But the dog ranged from one end of the wood to the other, barking. It was easy to see that the whole hunt was a lie. The dog was after nothing. Neither were the hunters.

Suddenly White Pants climbed up on the enclosure wall. He stood on top of it, with his gun. It was all an act: "Well, I am standing on the wall. I am preparing to shoot all the rabbits as they go by. My dog will rout them out and they will all come running past this point in the wall in an orderly procession. From my point of vantage I will easily be able to pick them off, one by one." The whole universe knew that as soon as he fired the gun he would fall off the wall backwards inside the enclosure, perhaps into the dirty old bathtub full of rain water and spring water and green weeds which is placed there as a horsetrough. Then he would have to become a monk.

Meanwhile I was in an equivocal position. I began to wonder if perhaps I was expected to resent the presence of White Pants on top of the enclosure wall. Was I supposed to act like a responsible member of society, stand up, wave my arms and shout "Hey!" and make guttural sounds signifying, "Get down off the wall!" Naturally he knew I could not *talk* to him. But we came to an understanding. I allowed him to gather, by my immobility, that I was invisible. I permitted him, however, to deduce from the fact that I looked in his direction, that I entertained toward him and the universe he represented an abstract, disembodied, and purely official good will. So there we stayed. He sat on top of the wall, hunting, and I sat on a board reading, meditating on eternal truths, or what you will. I believe I must have had some book or other with me, just as he quite clearly had a gun. Both were simply factors in a disguise. I don't know who he was. I am not quite sure I knew who I was. In neither case did it matter.

Soon the dog came inside the enclosure, through a hole under the wall, and ran about barking and wagging his tail with mongrel optimism. Then the three colts ran from the other end of the pasture to investigate the dog. White Pants spoke to his companion, "Call that dog." Then he picked himself up and walked off stiffly, eastward, along the top of the wall. I do not know what became of him. If I had watched I might have ascertained.

Not a shot was fired. I did not turn a page of the book I may or may not have had with me. Not a drop of rain fell. Not a bird sang. Ours is a comfortable world, without either science or wisdom.

The dialectic between silence and utterance. We have to keep silence for two reasons: for the sake of God and for the sake of speech. These two reasons are really one; because the ultimate reason for speaking is to confess our faith in God and to declare His glory.

In practice, a priest lives in silence—or should have much silence in his life—for the sake of his Mass. The Canon of the Mass should emerge from that silence with infinite power and significance. Mass is the most important thing we have to say. The Office is a preparation for that utterance. Everybody in the universe is tongue-tied, except the priest, who is able to speak for them all. Speaking for the people, he also speaks to God. He unites men and God in a few simple sentences that are the words of God. To be exact, he brings mankind face to face with God in the words of consecration in which he pronounces the Word that is uttered by the Father—he causes the Word to be present in time, in a special state—incarnate and sacrificed.

We should realize very clearly when to speak and when to keep silent. It is important to speak seven times a day, in praising God. It is above all important to confess Him before men at Mass. Here we must speak and know what we are saying and realize at least some of its implications. Here everything in us, body and soul, must speak and announce our faith and utter the glory of God. Here speech is more important than life and death. Yet it does not have to be loud on earth—only heard in heaven, and somehow signified in time. It must be simply and essentially public.

But it is terribly important to keep silence. When? Almost all the rest of the day. It is essential that priests learn how to silence all their routine declarations of truths that they have not yet troubled to think about. If we said only what we really meant we would say very little. Yet we have to preach God too. Exactly. Preaching the word of God implies silence. If preaching is not born of silence, it is a waste of time.

There are many declarations made only because we think other people are expecting us to make them. The silence of God should teach us when to speak and when not to speak. But we cannot bear the thought of that silence, lest it cost us the trust and the respect of men. *Dabitur vobis in illa hora quid loquamini.*

January 9

There is a hunger for humiliation that is nothing else but a hunger for admiration turned inside out. It is a sincere desire to be despised, and it is, perhaps, a desire cherished by those who might be saints. But is it not a desire to be admired by angels? And is it not a desire to be admired by angels *only?* And is it not a desire to despise what men admire? And do we not often despise what men admire in revenge for having to do without it? And is it not even more humiliating to be admired for what men admire than to be despised for what the angels admire?

January 11

For the first time in my life I am finding you, O solitude. I can count on the fingers of one hand the few short moments of purity, of neutrality, in which I have found you. Now I know I am coming to the day in which I will be free of words: their master rather than their servant, able to live without them if need be. For I still need to go out into this no-man's land of language that does not quite join me to other men and which throws a veil over my own solitude. By words I mean all the merely human expressions that bind men to one another. I also mean the half helpless and half wise looks by which they seek one another's thoughts. But I do not abdicate all language. For there is the word of God. This I proclaim and I live to proclaim it. I live to utter the Mass—the Canon that implicitly contains all words, all revelation and teaches everything. One day I thought I heard thunder all around me when I was saying it, but that was fancy. It is in the Canon and at the words of Consecration that all solitudes come to a single focus. There the City of God is gathered together in that one Word spoken in silence. The speech of God is silence. His Word is solitude. Him will I never deny, by His grace! We are travelers from the half-world of language into solitude and infinity. We are strangers. Paper, I have not in you a lasting city. Yet there is a return from solitude, to make manifest His Name to them who have not known it. Then to re-enter solitude and dwell in silence.

January 12

It is in deep solitude that I find the gentleness with which I can truly love my brothers. The more solitary I am, the more affection I have for them. It is pure affection, and filled with reverence for the solitude of others. Solitude and silence teach me to love my brothers for what they are, not for what they say. Now it is no longer a question of dishonoring them by accepting their fictions, believing in their image of themselves which their weakness obliges them to compose, in the wan work of communication. Yet there will, it is true, always remain a dialectic between the words of men and their being. This will tell something about them we would not have realized if the words had not been there.

"Blaise est toujours saisi d'une sorte d'épouvante qui dégénère ensuite en pitié lorsqu'il s'aperçoit à nouveau que l'art est tant nécessaire aux hommes" (Jean Madec, p. 273).*

La Mort de Jean Madec is a magnificent tract against angelism.

It is a tract on transcendence and immanence. It says that God is above all, and yet in all. I thought the theme of purity of heart was in it. Now I find it is indeed the heart of the book. *"Madec, le seul homme pur, . . . Madec* n'aurait pas eu besoin de la guerre pour être malheureux. *Madec n'avait jamais eu besoin de vouloir qu'il y eût la guerre pour ravoir le silence. Il y était depuis toujours.* (280) *C'est en lui seul que tout pouvait renaître."*†

The solution of the problem of language in I Cor. 13: "If I should speak with the tongues of men and angels . . ."

---

*"Blaise is always seized with a kind of panic which afterwards degenerates into pity when he realizes anew that art is so necessary for men."

†"Madec never would have needed a war to make him desire to recover silence. He had always been in silence. It was in him only that everything could come back to life."

Solitude is not merely a negative relationship. It is not merely the absence of people. True solitude is a participation in the solitariness of God—Who is in all things. His solitude is not a local absence but a metaphysical transcendence. His solitude is His Being. For us, solitude is not a matter of being something *more* than other men, except by accident; for those who cannot be alone cannot find their true being and they are always something less than themselves. For us solitude means withdrawal from an artificial and fictional level of being which men, divided by original sin, have fabricated in order to keep peace with concupiscence and death. But by that very fact the solitary finds himself on the level of a more perfect spiritual society—the city of those who have become real enough to confess and glorify God (that is: life), in the teeth of death. Solitude and society are formed and perfected in the Sacrifice of the Mass.

January 18
FEAST OF SAINT PETER'S CHAIR AT ROME

Last Saturday—the Feast of Saint Hilary—I signed a long-term contract with Harcourt, Brace for four books: Saint Ailred, Saint Bernard, The Ascent to Truth, and a book on the Mass. I prayed hard over it for three days, especially at the Conventual Mass of the day itself which was a Votive Mass of Our Lady and it is all her business.

I did not expect this legal act to have the effects it did. I put the thing in the mail, completely reconciled to my position and determined to waste no more time turning around and around like a dog before lying down in the corner that has been prepared for me by Providence. That probably means the final renouncement forever of any dream of a hermitage. God will prepare for me His own hermitage for my last days, and meanwhile my work is my hermitage because it is *writing* that helps me most of all to be a solitary and a contemplative here at Gethsemani.

But the real reason why the signing of this contract left me in peace, with no more desire to rationalize my fate, was the fact that all my days are now completely ordered to God's work in prayer and teaching and writing. I have no time to be anything but a contemplative or a teacher of the contemplative life. And because I still know so little of my subject I can no longer afford to waste time dramatizing my approach to it in mental movies or interior controversies. There is nothing left for me but to live fully and completely in the present, praying when I pray, and writing and praying when I write, and worrying about nothing but the will and the glory of God, finding these as best I can in the sacrament of the present moment.

January 20   EVE OF SAINT AGNES

O small Saint Agnes dressed in gold
With fire in rainbows round about your face,
Sing with the seven martyrs in my Canon.

Come home, come home O centuries
Whose soundless islands ring me from within,
Whose saints come down this winter morning's iris
To wait upon our prayers with hyacinths.

I speak your name with wine upon my lips
Drowned in the singing of your lovely catacomb
My feet upon forget-me-nots.
I sink this little frigate in the Blood of Peace

And put my pall upon the cup
Working our peace, our mystery, who must
Run down and find you, saint, by Saint John's stairs.

No lines, no globes,
No compasses, no staring fires
No candle's cup to swing upon my night's dark ocean
No signs, no signals claim us.

There the pretended horns of time grow dim.
The cities cry like peacocks in their sleep.

I speak your name with blood upon my wrist
With blood upon my breast
O small Saint Agnes dressed in martyrdom
With fire and water waving in your hair.

January 21 SAINT AGNES

I mean to write down the words of responsories that made a deep impression on me at the Night Office. Meanwhile I probably will not get time.

Saint Bernard's Serm. 110 *De Diversis* which I stumbled on just now by accident when I set out to look for the Sermon for the Fourth Sunday in November, has some interesting ideas on speech and silence.

He laments the poverty of man. We are so indigent we even need words. (Consequence: the more words we need, the greater our poverty.) We need them not only to communicate with others, but also to communicate with ourselves. For we are not ourselves. We are divided, exiled from ourselves. We have to talk to the self from which we are separated. *Nempe cor meum dereliquit me et necesse habeo ad meipsum nempe ad me alterum loqui.* Here too, our indigence is proportioned to our division. *Atque id interim tanto amplius quanto minus sum adhuc reversus ad cor . . . unitus mihi ipsi.* (Corollary—if I become silent *without* finding myself—damnation; atheism. Like Madec's father.) But the solution (as Brice Parain says) is *charity.* When we shall all unite in one perfect man (The Mystical Christ). *Opportune igitur linguae interibunt.* Then there will be no further need of tongues.

January 27

Nam gloria nostra haec est quod in simplicitate cordis et in sinceritate Dei et non in sapientia carnali sed in gratia Dei conversati sumus in hoc mundo (II Cor. 1; 12).*

The more I read Saint Bernard and the Cistercian Fathers the more I like them. There was a time when I was tempted not to like Saint Bernard at all (when the *Sermons in Cantica* were read in the refectory, during my novitiate, I was irritated by the breasts of the Spouse). I think that now, after eight years and

---

*"For our glory is this, the testimony of our conscience, that in simplicity of heart and sincerity of God and not in carnal wisdom but in the grace of God we have conversed in this world."

more, I am really beginning to discover the depth of Saint Bernard. This is because I have realized that the foundation of his whole doctrine, which is expressed, as clearly as anywhere, in Letter 18, is that God is Truth and Christ is Truth Incarnate and that Salvation and sanctity for us means being true to ourselves and true to Christ and true to God. It is only when this emphasis on truth is forgotten that Saint Bernard begins to seem sentimental.

Today, in a moment of trial, I rediscovered Jesus; or perhaps discovered Him for the first time. But then in a monastery you are always discovering Jesus for the first time. Anyway I came closer than ever to fully realizing how true it is that our relations with Christ are something utterly beyond the level of imagination and emotion.

His eyes, which are the eyes of Truth, are fixed upon my heart. Where His glance falls, there is peace; for the light of His Face, which is the Truth, produces truth wherever it shines. *Aequitatem vidit vultus ejus.* There too is joy; *adimplebis me laetitia cum vultu tuo. Signatum est super nos lumen vultus tui; dedisti laetitiam in corde meo.* And again *oculi tui videant aequitates.* And he says to those He loves—*firmabo super te oculos meos.** His eyes are always on us in choir and everywhere and in all times. No grace comes to us from heaven except He looks upon our hearts. And what is more—He looks at us from within our own hearts, for we and He are one.

February 5   SEPTUAGESIMA

Beautiful hard frost. The sun was coming up and throwing soft mother-of-pearl highlights on the frozen pastures of Olivet. And the birds were singing. And I thought of the lessons from Genesis in the Night Office, on the creation of the world. Really I think the thought of creation in the Septuagesima liturgy is overlooked. We should see this day as the beginning of the Easter season, not as a sort of "feast of original sin." It is the first chap-

---

*"His face has beheld equity . . . Thou wilt fill me with joy with Thy face. The light of thy face is sealed upon us; thou hast given joy into my heart . . . may thy eyes behold justice . . . I will fix my eyes upon thee."

ter in the Church's Theology of the Redemption. It begins sensibly by telling us of the joy for which we were created by God—the joy which Jesus died to restore to us.

I spoke on joy in Chapter—Day of Recollection conference.

It helps me to speak, although I hate speaking. My classes help me very much too. I have learned more theology in three months of teaching than in four years of studying. But talking also helps my prayer—at least in the sense that it inviscerates the mysteries of faith more deeply into my soul. It is very important to live your faith by confessing it, and one of the best ways to confess it is to preach it.

I think the chief reason why we have so little joy is that we take ourselves too seriously. Joy can only be real if it is based on truth, and since the fall of Adam all man's life is shot through with falsehood and illusion. That is why Saint Bernard is right in leading us back to joy by the love of truth. His starting point is the truth of our own insignificance in comparison with God. To penetrate the truth of how utterly unimportant we are is the only thing that can set us free to enjoy true happiness. This morning, before speaking, I felt very strongly the limitations imposed on me by my absurd desire to speak well as if it somehow *mattered*, as if something *important* depended on it! Instead of simply desiring to speak as best I could in order to please God.

February 7 SAINT ROMUALD

Today in orientation class I shall try to make all the scholastics happy by showing them two wonderful photographs of the Abbey of Saint Martin-du-Canigou where Saint Romuald was a hermit—or near which he was a hermit.

Reading Genesis again I am fascinated by mysterious discoveries. What was this fountain that sprang up in the center of the earth and watered it all before man was made and before there was even any rain? (2:6).

Importance of the notion of "Generations" in Genesis. The transmission of the totality of life from a common Father to a whole race. All life goes back to God the Father and Creator of all; but the great Patriarchs contained in themselves the pattern of their race's destiny. All this is fulfilled in the "Seed of Abraham," Christ, the New Adam, in Whom we all live to God, in the Holy Ghost. He brings back all things to God. *In ipso condita sunt universa et in ipso omnia constant.** In Him all things came forth from God.

February 10 SAINT SCHOLASTICA

I went to the garden house attic, as usual, after dinner. Climbed up the ladder, observing all the hoes and shovels lying on the floor. I made my way through the litter of old stove-pipes and broken strawberry boxes to the chair by the window. On the chair is a sack, stained with either paint, creosote, or the blood of something slaughtered. I opened the small window (a pane fell out one day when I let it slam; I can still see the fragments of glass on the red roof of the shed below).

Today it was wonderful. Clouds, sky overcast, but tall streamers of sunlight coming down in a fan over the bare hills.

Suddenly I became aware of great excitement. The pasture was full of birds—starlings. There was an eagle flying over the woods. The crows were all frightened, and were soaring, very high, keeping out of the way. Even more distant still were the buzzards, flying and circling, observing everything from a distance. And the starlings filled every large and small tree, and shone in the light and sang. The eagle attacked a tree full of starlings but before he was near them the whole cloud of them left the tree and avoided him and he came nowhere near them. Then he went away and they all alighted on the ground. They were there moving about and singing for about five minutes. Then, like lightning, it happened. I saw a scare go into the cloud of birds, and they opened their wings and began to rise off the ground and, in that split second, from behind the house and from over my roof a hawk came down like a bullet, and shot straight into the middle of the starlings just as they were getting off the ground. They rose into the air and there was a slight scuffle on the ground as the hawk got his talons into the one bird he had nailed.

*"In Him all things are made and in Him all exist."

It was a terrible and yet beautiful thing, that lightning flight, straight as an arrow, that killed the slowest starling.

Then every tree, every field was cleared. I do not know where all the starlings went. Florida, maybe. The crows were still in sight, but over their wood. Their guttural cursing had nothing more to do with this affair. The vultures, lovers of dead things, circled over the bottoms where perhaps there was something dead. The hawk, all alone, in the pasture, possessed his prey. He did not fly away with it like a thief. He stayed in the field like a king with the killed bird, and nothing else came near him. He took his time.

I tried to pray, afterward. But the hawk was eating the bird. And I thought of that flight, coming down like a bullet from the sky behind me and over my roof, the sure aim with which he hit this one bird, as though he had picked it out a mile away. For a moment I envied the lords of the Middle Ages who had their falcons and I thought of the Arabs with their fast horses, hawking on the desert's edge, and I also understood the terrible fact that some men love war. But in the end, I think that hawk is to be studied by saints and contemplatives; because he knows his business. I wish I knew my business as well as he does his.

I wonder if my admiration for you gives me an affinity for you, artist! I wonder if there will ever be something connatural between us, between your flight and my heart stirred in hiding, to serve Christ, as you, soldier, serve your nature. And God's love a thousand times more terrible! Now I am going back to the attic and the shovels and the broken window and the trains in the valley and the prayer of Jesus.

February 11   OUR LADY OF LOURDES

I have just finished a week of Masses at Our Lady of Victories, where the scholastics receive Communion, and where I always make my thanksgiving and where John Paul received his first Communion. I once might have thought that it would disturb my own prayer to have to leave the altar and give Communion to others. As if this function made my union with Jesus less perfect because less recollected. I now see what an error that is. I feel as if my Communion were somehow less perfect when I cannot turn and give the Body of Christ to some of my brothers also. There is something a little cold and rigid about Sunday Masses for that reason. The servers all go to Communion at Matutinal Mass. And you are left stranded with no one to share your Mass with you visibly and tangibly. But there is much more exterior beauty and warmth, humanly speaking and spiritually also, when ten or twelve monks approach the altar at the *Agnus Dei* and receive the kiss of peace and kneel there waiting for God to come to them from your hands. There is an inexpressibly sweet and deep joy in giving Communion to your brothers, whom you know and love so well and so completely after years with them in the monastery. I can think of no private satisfaction that could surpass or even approach this sharing.

Father Abbot no longer lets me say Mass in the secular Church. The reasons are obvious. But it used to be a great joy for me to give Communion to a dozen strangers. You feel a profound interest in these faces, these overcoats, the old ones and the young ones. You wonder what their troubles are, their joys and their sorrows. You love them and you want them to be happy and it is very very good to be able to give them Christ, their freedom, and pray that they may go away to be great saints if they are not that already.

February 12 SEXAGESIMA

Can one say that by love the soul receives the very "form" of God? In Saint Bernard's language this form, this divine likeness, is the identity we were made for. Thus we can say "*caritas haec visio, haec similitudo est.*"*By love we are at once made like to God and (in mystical love, pure love) we already "see" Him (darkly), that is we have experience of Him as He is in Himself. Thus by loving we know God in God and through God for in love the Three Divine Persons are made known to us, sealing our souls not with a static likeness but with the impression of their infinite Life. Our souls are sealed with the character of God as

*"Charity is this vision and this likeness."

the air is full of sunshine. Glory to God in the highest, who has sealed us with His holiness, sealed us all together, brothers, in His Christ. Amen. Amen.

February 14

Abraham and Lot could not live together because they had too many possessions. The whole world was hardly big enough for both of them with all their tents and all their flocks and all their fighting shepherds. The language the Vulgate uses for this situation is *"erat substantia eorum multa et nequibant habitare communiter."* They could not live in common. They could not live the common life. Their possessions made it impossible for them to live as brothers unless they lived apart (Genesis, 3:8-9). Their riches imposed upon them an imperfect solitude. Lot retired to the Paradise that surrounded Sodom—and this was marked for destruction because of great sins. Genesis is the history of the breaking up of the human race, originally one man in Adam. But in this dispersal, the seed of unity is saved.

February 16

We do not appreciate the writing of a Saint Bernard or an Ailred of Rievaulx because the Scripture references mean little or nothing to us. And since all that they write is apt to be a tissue of Scripture passages, we miss the point altogether. We must first possess something of their knowledge of Scripture and have the same *pictures* in our imagination—and something of the same associations. Ailred's first Palm Sunday Sermon is full of meaning, but only on condition that you see Jeremias' two baskets of figs and know their import, and see the ark of the Covenant coming through the divided Jordan carried by the Levites and followed by Josue's army—and have in your mind at the same time the expectation of Christ's final triumph and entry into Jerusalem with all the elect; and the expectation of being one of them. Your heart must burn with the love and faith that sees all Scripture and all history pointing to this last event which is the fulfillment of everything. Otherwise you do not understand.

February 21 FORTY HOURS

This is the third day of the Forty Hours. I have been rather dry and a bit scared. Also I have had the 'flu. Last night at collation the Servant of the Refectory astonished me by bringing me a saucer of badly scrambled eggs (pale white) with a sign that Father Prior had sent them to me. The first time such an astonishing favor has befallen me in my eight years in the monastery. Last night in the dormitory I kept waking up when the novices came in and out after changing guard before the Blessed Sacrament. Between these awakenings I dreamt in relays of a curious ascetical problem.

I dreamt that Reverend Father was to take a party of religious to Haiti, not for a new foundation but just for a trip. In fact I think they were to give a concert in the Cathedral of Port au Prince. I had asked permission, on impulse, to go with them; not to sing, but just to see Haiti. The permission had been granted. And now the substance of the dream was this: I kept debating in my mind whether God wanted me to take back my request and just stay at home. I dreamt of many factors in the problem and finally asked Reverend Father what I should do and he said he wished I would make up my mind once and for all. But the thing was still not settled. I was coming to the conclusion that I would not go, when it turned out that all the others had (probably) already left. At this point I found myself in the Chapter Room, where there was a line of barber chairs and the monks were getting shaves and haircuts in grand style. Then the two o'clock bell rang and ended the dream.

February 22 ASH WEDNESDAY

Gray skies. It rained in the night. The lights all went out at ten to two and we said Matins and the Office of the Dead and Lauds and Prime with many candles. The 'flu has not left me and my head is full of glue and I can't breathe and I am worried that my neighbors in choir may finally become completely exasperated at my snorting. And yet Ash Wednesday is full of joy. In a minute we will sing None and go barefoot to get ashes on our heads to remember, with great relief, that we are dust. The source of all sorrow is the illusion that of ourselves we are anything but dust. God is all our joy and in Him our dust can become splendor. The great sorrow of mankind is turned to joy by the love of Christ, and the secret of happiness is no longer to see any sorrow except in the light of Christ's victory over sorrow. And then all sorrow contributes somehow to our happiness. Thus I sit here in the corner of the upstairs Scriptorium and look out the window at the bare trees in the préau and the gray guest house wall and at my own little happy corner of the sky.

February 23

I came out of choir yesterday morning after the distribution of ashes and put on our shoes and socks in the cloister and walked off to work with a keen desire to read some very obscure, very disciplined poetry—something like William Empson. Of course I was much too busy. But this unexpected hunger still strikes me as having been clean and even somehow appropriate to Lent. Only at the end of work did I get a minute, and I came away from the vault with *Four Quartets* and read the magnificent opening to "Little Gidding" which, though not obscure, exactly suited my mood.

February 25

The wind buffets the side of the building bringing perhaps more rain and more influenza. I had a second dose of influenza after Ash Wednesday. As a professor I take the frustulum, along with my students. I had to find another Lenten penance so after the frustulum I am studying moral theology for a few minutes every day. It is four years since I had my course in Moral. I have forgotten everything that Caius and Titius ever did. I no longer know the ins and outs of Bertha's marriages. And I never learned the comic rhyme that helps the young confessor to call to mind the ecclesiastical censures he cannot absolve unless he gets around them by means of Canon 2254.

MONDAY OF THE FIRST WEEK IN LENT

The song of my Beloved beside the stream. The birds descanting in their clerestories. His skies have sanctified my eyes, His woods are clearer than the King's palace. But the air and I will never tell our secret.

The first Sunday of Lent, as I now know, is a great feast. Christ has sanctified the desert and in the desert I discovered it. The woods have all become young in the discipline of spring: but it is the discipline of expectancy only. Which one cut more keenly? The February sunlight, or the air? There are no buds. Buds are not guessed at or thought of, this early in Lent. But the wilderness shines with promise. The land is dressed in simplicity and strength. Everything foretells the coming of the holy spring. I had never before spoken so freely or so intimately with woods, hills, birds, water, and sky. On this great day, however, they understood their position and they remained mute in the presence of the Beloved. Only His light was obvious and eloquent. My brother and sister, the light and water. The stump and the stone. The tables of rock. The blue, naked sky. Tractor tracks, a little waterfall. And Mediterranean solitude. I thought of Italy after my Beloved had spoken and was gone.

The difference between the moral life and the mystical life is discovered in the presence of contradiction. When we move ourselves as men, morally, *humano modo* we end up by hanging on one horn of the dilemma and hoping for the best. But when we are moved by God, mystically, we seem to solve the dilemma in ease and mystery, by choosing at the same time both horns of the dilemma and no horn at all and always being perfectly right. For instance in choir: orders are to keep up the pitch and make a pause of two beats at the median of the psalm verse: but the cantors drop the pitch and rush through the median with one beat. Moral activity: either (a) follow the cantor with a pure intention or (b) shut up and concentrate on praying, also with a pure intention. Mystical activity: the dilemma suddenly ceases to matter. You both follow the cantor and pray and find God and suddenly if God wills the contradiction disappears, and some attempt begins to be made to keep the rules the legislators have broken.

March 1

I enter into this gay, windy month with my mind full of the Book of Josue. Its battle scenes are like the Bayeux tapestry. The books of the Old Testament become to us as signs of the zodiac and Josue (somewhere near the spring equinox) stands at the opposite side of heaven from Job (where all the sky is sailing down to darkness). Here is a book for spring. The sap is rising in the trees and the children of God are winning all their battles. And it is Lent, when Josue (our Christ) calls the five captive kings cowering from their cave and makes his officers put their feet upon their necks. Then the five kings go to the gibbet. That is what Jesus makes us do to the five senses in Lent. Josue is a conqueror and even a poet. He lifted up his head in the heat of battle and sang a two-line poem to the sun and moon and they both stood still. For the sun did not go down toward Gabaon nor the moon to the valley of Ajalon. Even so, Christ has delayed the day of Judgment giving us time to do penance, until the number of the elect be filled and His enemies be all cast down into the lake of fire.

So Josue is my favorite epic. I like it better than *The Iliad*, infinitely better than Virgil or the *Song of Roland*. It is a clean book, full of asceticism. The field is swept of all enemies. Only one small band of them remains: the Gabaonites with their old shoes and their mended wineskins and their dry bread, who pretended to have come from a distant land to make a treaty, knowing the children of God had been told to clear the Promised Land of all its natives. And all the while their town was just over the hill.

God leans over Canaan and spreads His hand over the mountain and sends forth His armies to work His work, to plant the seed of His promise and blessings in a safe land overflowing with plenty. And the armies of Israel fight with their faces and their eyes questioning the brilliant and cloudless heavens. (Look, outside the window the sky is beginning to be very blue and the sun is dazzling on the white side of the Church! I love this corner of the upstairs Scriptorium, where God has prepared me a bower under the iron mezzanine, face to face with sermons which no one ever reads.)

God is delighted with the victories of Josue because they are the victories of obedience and therefore this is a Benedictine book. But the whole Pentateuch too is Benedictine.

Saint Bernard (who entered Citeaux with a whole family of Josues) says that God cannot truly take pleasure in our acts unless He is their cause. And if He is their cause He must also be their end. *Insipida namque Deo et insulsa quodammodo nostra obedientia seu etiam patientia est nisi omnium quae vel agimus vel patimur ipse sit causa.** We know if He is the cause of our actions when we know the end for which we perform them. And the purer the love with which we seek His glory the more completely does He live and act in us. This purity is the sign of His action. By our bright armed virginity that suffers no compromise with idols, we glorify Him by the victories of Josue and march into the mountains of contemplation. This is the Promised Land.

March 3

The Christian life—and especially the contemplative life—is a continual discovery of Christ in new and unexpected places. And these discoveries are sometimes most profitable when you find Him in something you had tended to overlook and even despise. Then the awakening is purer and its effect more keen, because He was so close at hand, and you neglected Him. I am ashamed that it has taken me so long to discover Him in moral theology. I thought moral theology was just a set of rules by which one learned to keep imperfect Christians and sinners from getting mad at the Church and walking out altogether—as if they needed to know how much they could get away with and still remain

---

*"Our obedience and even our patience are tasteless and without savor to God unless He be the cause of all our actions and of our acceptance of suffering."

Christians. That may perhaps be the way moral is applied in practice sometimes—but my attitude had something a little impious about it. In assuming that moral theology was almost necessarily an apparatus devised for pharisees, I myself have been a pharisee, and more than that, a fool as well. Saint Teresa had much more sense because she had much more humility. Because we are all sinners, moral theology applies to us all, not as a system of sanctions or restrictions but as a *means* to find Christ in God's commandments and in His sacraments.

What would be the use of ascetical and mystical theology for a priest who was slovenly and careless and unintelligent in the reception and administration of the Sacraments? I am studying the Sacrament of Penance and find to my shame that I have had far too little appreciation of it, precisely because I had looked at it only from an ascetic point of view without a real foundation in moral.

March 5

My Lent is all influenza and chant and moral theology. Got rid of the 'flu last Sunday and received it back again last Friday. It is going in waves through the community. In choir and in Chapter we are swept by periodic storms of nose-blowing that drown all words and all thought. And I am trying to teach the novices to desire mystical prayer and the mystical life and they write me notes saying, "We do not understand, but it is not your fault. What books should be read?"

Chant. Professor LeFevre came from Paris to teach us chant. He made his debut on my birthday, January 31. On that day he gave a lecture in the Chapter room full of illuminating remarks about the relation of Gregorian chant to Gnostic, Hebrew, and Greek music. Ever since then we have been practicing furiously every day: voice training in Chapter every morning for fifteen minutes or more after Lauds and Prime. Special classes in the interval after dinner. Schola practice at the beginning of the afternoon work. No more time for anything. Professor LeFevre fills the air with lamentations declaring that we think only of quantity and know nothing of quality, and it is true: the old business of solving all problems by energy. Hard work and good will are not enough: taste and intelligence and a certain sensitiveness to musical *values* are what we lack most of all.

He directs the *Salve* standing on a little stool near the presbytery step while one of the brother oblates points a flashlight at him. This throws a dim target of light on his stomach, which is a distraction to everybody.

Two and three and four years ago when I complained bitterly that there was no time in my life for contemplation, all these demands on our time and energy would probably have upset me considerably. For now it is actually a fact, and not a fancy, that we get very little time to ourselves. But it no longer upsets me, and I find that I am not tempted to waste time in complaining. That shows that I must have learned something since ordination. So now, the time I would have lost in complaining is spent in something more like union with God.

March 7   SAINT THOMAS AQUINAS
The feast of the Angelic Doctor falls this year on the Tuesday of the second week of Lent. This means a curious coincidence in the liturgy: the Gospel of the feast speaks of the true Teachers, the salt of the earth, who "do and teach" and whose *works* shine before men, and the Gospel of the feria speaks of the false teachers who have sat in the chair of Moses and have not done the works of Moses, that is they have not kept the laws they talked about. Yet they have done works that have been dazzling in the eyes of men—and have done them *in order to shine* before men, to have the first places in the synagogues and to be called Rabbi. The theme of both the feast and the feria is summed up in the line "*Unus est Magister vester, Christus.*"* It is Jesus who teaches us in and through Saint Thomas Aquinas, and in Saint Bonaventure and Saint Augustine and in all the other doctors of the Church. We have no other Father and no other Doctor than Christ. It is Jesus who manifests Himself to us through the words of the Fathers and the theologians. The false doctors preach their own sanctity, and the holiness of Christ is not seen

* "One is your Master—Christ!"

or heard in them. But the true preach the sanctity of Christ, and He shines through them. He it is whose Truth has made them holy.

March 8

There are lovely things in the little new *Kyriale* that has come over from France. Since I haven't yet had time to read the *monitum* I do not know where this *Kyriale* comes from or what it is all about. All I know is that the Carmelite nuns in Cherbourg are responsible for the peculiar lettering. The *Kyriale* itself, of course, is ours. I am sure this Celtic sounding *Kyrie* we sang yesterday for the first time, on Saint Thomas's day, was never in our old books. The same Mass has a haunting *Sanctus* and the *Agnus Dei* is rather poignant. This morning we were practicing a *Kyrie* for Paschal time which is one of the freshest and most beautiful things I have ever seen. I could easily believe that it was dictated by angels (as so many of Saint Dunstan's antiphons are supposed to have been. I am sure that angels did dictate that sixth tone "*Gaudent in Coelis*" which we sing for Saints John and Paul—John Paul's feast day). This Easter *Kyrie* has all the cleanness, not only of spring, but of the new leaven of Christ's Resurrection. It has the pure savor of another life, the savor of heaven, of the Risen Savior walking the earth with men in His new Kingdom. My whole being longs for Easter, to drink this wine new with Christ in His Father's Kingdom, and to know that Christ our Pasch is slain and that our life is in heaven and hear the Spirit crying out in my heart (as He cried out at Mass this morning) that we are the Sons of God and God is our Father.

March 9

Before dawn. Red Mars hangs like a tiny artificial fruit from the topmost branch of a bare tree in our *préau*.

Today: commemoration of the forty martyrs who were left naked on the ice to freeze to death in Armenia. They helped me once at Saint Bonaventure in tribulation. It is cold here, too. Fingers numb, during Mass at Our Lady of Lourdes altar, in the back sacristy, at the extreme end of the heat line, where the steam does not quite come.

Yesterday, out in the beginning of a snowstorm, dipped into the spiritual notes of Charles de Foucauld and was moved by their intensity. He speaks to God in a clear and vibrant voice, simple words, sentences of fire. This voice rings in the ears of your heart after you have put the book away and turned to others less saintly, even though they may be religious voices too. M. LeFevre saw I had the book and told me how, some twenty-five years ago, it made him weep and had driven him to the Seminary. From which, as he said, by the grace of God, he eventually emerged again into the world. I forget whether he has ten children or twelve.

March 10

God gives Himself to those who give themselves to Him. The way does not matter much, as long as it is the way He has chosen for us. I find that I can get just as close to God by studying the dry problems of moral theology as by reading the most burning pages of the mystics. For it is God's will that I, as a priest, should know my moral theology. Duty does not have to be dull. Love can make it beautiful and fill it with life. As long as we draw lines of division between duty and pleasure in the world of the spirit we will remain far from God and from His joy.

March 12   THIRD SUNDAY IN LENT

On this gray morning when the birds sing in the rain, I proclaim that there is a sad note to our spring. We lift our eyes to you in heaven, O God of eternity, wishing we were poorer men, more silent men, more mortified. Lord, give us liberty from all the things that are in this world, from the preoccupations of earth and of time, that we may be called to cleanness, where the saints are, the gold and silver saints before your throne.

March 14

Dawn. I looked out the window again and this time Mars is much lower down in the branches of the tree. In ten days the planet will hide behind the Church. Yesterday, Saint Gregory's day, was in some ways terrible. All our time went west. Not one decent interval, barely ten minutes here and there to read or to pray. We learned an Ambrosian *Gloria* and *Sanctus* and so on for the feast. Special schola work in the afternoon. No time to prepare classes, let alone write. No Lenten reading. The dentist Dr. Simons came from Cincinnati and I spent three quarters of an hour in the chair watching the buzzards circling in the gray sky over the old sheep barn while he drilled a wisdom tooth. At night my head was full of chant and my mouth tasted of silver nitrate and the tooth was sore and for some time I did not sleep.

March 15

In the Mass in which all prayer is perfect, we talk to everybody. Sometimes we speak to the Blessed Trinity (*Suscipe Sancta Trinitas*), sometimes to the Father (*Elevatis oculis ad Te Deum Patrem* . . .), sometimes to Jesus the Word, sometimes to the Holy Ghost (*Veni Sanctificator*), sometimes to the saints in heaven, and sometimes to the people around us, and sometimes even to ourselves, musing in the presence of God: *Quid retribuam Domino . . . calicem salutaris accipiam*. If we don't talk to the angels (until the prayers after Mass) at least we talk to God about the angels who are present as His ministers and play an active part in the Sacrifice. And we talk to Him of the saints and of the holy souls in Purgatory and of the Pope and the Bishop and of all our friends. Nothing could be less private than the Mass. And yet it is also a perfect solitude.

March 16   MID LENT

This morning I directed the schola and the whole choir at the Conventual Mass. It was the first time I had ever tried anything like cheironomy and at first I was scared. But it went well enough. Cheironomy is not difficult as long as you don't bother to follow any set rule. I shall never forget this Mass as long as I live. For three nights I have sung it in my sleep. "*Salus populi ego sum dicit Dominus* . . ."* The movements of my hand may

*"I am the salvation of my People, saith the Lord!"

or may not have had something to do with the neumes in the book. Anyway my right arm was active. I hoped that what I was doing was also artistic. But I do not have the presumption to imagine that it was Gregorian. Yesterday at practice, Professor LeFevre said: "If the monks of Solesme saw you they would have a fit." Secretly however I am very pleased, and sometimes when I am by myself I direct some snatch of chant I know by heart, trying to make my hand tumble like a seagull in the wind, following the imagined music like a leaf in November, sailing earthward through the branches of the trees.

I was in the Cellarer's new offices. The little house is very pleasant, with venetian blinds and two small rooms paneled with cedar, which smells overpowering. There is a nook for the cheese salesman, and a door leads into a fair-sized warehouse, then there is a small garage to hide the jeep in, and a larger place where trucks can drive in and unload the riches of Araby and Ophir.

Having once directed the schola I have been dispensed from any more special practice, and have returned to the rank and file in order to have time to prepare my classes and get something done on those four books I am supposed to be writing.

But my chief joy is to escape to the attic of the garden house and the little broken window that looks out over the valley. There in the silence I love the green grass. The tortured gestures of the apple trees have become part of my prayer. I look at the shining water under the willows and listen to the sweet songs of all the living things that are in our woods and fields. So much do I love this solitude that when I walk out along the road to the old barns that stand alone, far from the new buildings, delight begins to overpower me from head to foot and peace smiles even in the marrow of my bones.

March 17

The people of Israel were afraid to come too close to God. They wanted Moses to protect them and stand between them and God, lest God come down too close to them, and lest His fire consume them. They wanted men to reign over them, rather than God. But Gedeon said to them: "I shall not rule you, neither shall my sons, but the Lord God shall rule you" (Judges, 8: 23). And when Samuel was old and the people demanded a king God said to him: "It is not you they have rejected, but me." For a king would make treaties with other kings, and treaties meant compromise with the gods of other kings. But our God is a God with whom no idol can enter into contract because there is no communion between light and darkness, between the temple of God and idols, between Pure Being and the fictions of men. For Israel, unlike all other people, was made to have no ruler and no king but God. In the end, on Good Friday, the Rulers of Israel cried out: "We have no king but Caesar."

It is Saint Patrick's day. Frater Esdras, the monastery electrician, has hung up a green streamer and a picture of Saint Patrick in the library doorway; and yet he is not Irish but Dutch. The sun is out, and during the processions, reciting the Penitential Psalms, I was praying for two nineteen-year-old boys who are being electrocuted as murderers somewhere today. Word came in asking us to pray for them. *Percussus sum ut foenum et aruit cor meum* . . . We are praying for another one who is in prison for life.

March 18

This morning at Mass, read the long history of Susanna and came out of it at the end half carried away with exultation at the triumph of Daniel for "innocent blood was spared in that day." But at Tierce and Sext—from which we have just come— I was haunted by the mercy of Jesus to the woman taken in adultery. That is the day's Gospel and the counterpart to Susanna in the Old Testament Lesson.

My soul is trying to awaken and discover again the beauty of penance. I am ashamed of having made so many confessions of my faults, in the monastery, with so little sorrow and so feeble a hope of doing better. I want to say, over and over again, that

I am sorry. I do not know how I can go on living unless I convince You, Jesus, that I am really sorry. The psalms say this better than I ever could. I am sorry that it has taken me so long to begin to discover the psalms. I am sorry that I have not lived in them. Their words are full of the living waters of those true tears with which You taught the Samaritan your mercy. (She did not weep with her eyes—or if she did the Gospel does not tell us: but her simplicity and frankness were her compunction. Her penance was above all a matter of admiration: "I have found a man who told me everything I have ever done. Can He be the Christ?")

I am sorry for having let myself become so stupid and so torpid, thinking more of myself than of what I owe to Your Love—and I owe You everything. Forgive me for paying so little attention. Without compunction and deep sorrow, contemplation is likely to be nothing more than a kind of idolatry. How can I love You if I do not know who I am and who You are? And how can I know this without sorrow? Jesus, I no longer want to have anything to do with love that forgets that it was born in sorrow, and therefore forgets to be grateful. Otherwise I will only go on lying to You: and I want to be done with all insincerity for ever and for ever.

Every day I mean to pray, especially in choir, for all the priests in the world who hear confessions and for all their penitents. I ask that everywhere this Sacrament may be administered and received in truth and justice and prudence and mercy and sorrow, and that priests and penitents may better know what they are doing and that they be filled with a great love and reverence for what they do. I ask that everywhere men may discover in themselves a great admiration for this Sacrament and may love it with their whole being, giving themselves entirely with contrite hearts to the mercy and truth of God, that His love may re-make them in His own likeness—that is, that He may make them true.

The Pharisees accused the woman in adultery and when Jesus bent down to write with His finger in the dust, perhaps he meant to show them by this mystery, that the judgments of men are words written in the dust, and that only God's judgments are true and just. *Judicia Domini recta justificata in semetipsa. Rectum judicium judicate* . . . They judged according to appearances. And because they did so they tried to judge the Uncreated Truth by the light of their own principles. For Christ is the Truth, and they had accused the adulteress not out of love for Truth but out of hatred for Truth. He is Justice, and they were trying to judge and destroy Him by a subversion of that technical justice which ceases to be just as soon as it ceases to express the Truth of Him in Whom Justice and Mercy are one. Daniel delivered Susanna by a judgment inspired by the Holy Spirit and Christ came down to the Temple from the Mount of Olives to deliver the adulteress with the grace of counsel. The Mount of Olives is the mount of chrism, of anointing, of inspiration and counsel and the gifts of the Holy Spirit. But the most striking thing of all about the Gospel is that in saving the adulteress Jesus was also saving Himself. Defending and delivering a sinner from the injustice of the legally "just" he was saving the Truth from defilement by the unholiness of the holy. For these ascetics were so holy that they hated Mercy and thus their holiness was sin. The test of their sin was this: when Truth came to them as a Person, not as an abstraction, they rejected Him. The abstraction they clung to was then no more than a fiction because it had in it nothing of Him Whom they had decided to kill.

March 21   FEAST OF SAINT BENEDICT
Contemplative prayer is the recognition that we are the Sons of God, an experience of Who He is, and of His love for us, flowing from the operation of that love in us. Contemplative prayer is the voice of the Spirit crying out in us, "Abba, Pater." In all valid prayer it is the Holy Ghost who prays in us: but in the graces of contemplation He makes us *realize* at least obscurely that it is He who is praying in us with a love too deep and too secret for us to comprehend. And we exult in the union of our voice with His voice, and our soul springs up to the

Father, through the Son, having become one flame with the Flame of their Spirit. The Holy Ghost is the soul of the Church and it is to His presence in us that is attributed the sanctity of each one of the elect. He prays in us now as the Soul of the Church and now as the life of our own soul—but the distinction is only real in the external order of things. Interiorly, whether our prayer be private or public it is the same Spirit praying in us: He is really touching different strings of the same instrument.

Down there in the wooded hollow full of cedars I hear a great outcry of bluejays, and yonder is one of the snipes that are always flying and ducking around Saint Joseph's hill. In all this I am reassured by the sweet constant melody of my red cardinals, who sing their less worldly tunes with no regard for any other sound on earth. And now the jays have stopped. Their tribulation rarely lasts very long.

A third plague of 'flu has hit the community. This time it is a bad one. The choir is half empty. There were so few in their stalls on the Abbot's side this night, at Vigils, that the psalms of the second nocturn were being given out by scholastics in simple vows. There are too many ill for the infirmary. They lie and cough in the dormitories. Food is brought to them. They cannot touch it, for the most part. And Father Abbot this morning was forced to lift the fast. There was mixt this morning after Chapter.

Then the sanctuary is all torn up, ready to be rebuilt, according to the Ritual, with the *gradus altaris* in the proper place —we hope! The carpenters began work yesterday. I find by the grace of God that carpenters no longer disturb me when I pray in church. But now I am under the sky, away from all the noise. The birds are all silent now except for some quiet bluebirds. The frogs have begun singing their pleasure in all the waters and in the warm green places where the sunshine is wonderful. Praise Christ, all you living creatures. For Him you and I were created. With every breath we love Him. My psalms fulfill your dim, unconscious song, O brothers in this wood.

I am sitting on a pile of lumber by the ruins of the old horse-barn. There is a beautiful blue haze in the sky beyond the enclosure wall, eastward and over the brow of the hill. There is going to be a new garden there, and I see the furrows Frater Nehemias has been plowing with the John Deere tractor. I guess I will stop and read Origen.

March 22

Toward the fall of night the ghosts in the community come down and stagger through the cloister on some vague business, before returning to their cells. We, who are nearly as badly off as they, make them signs to ask if they are well and they reply with haggard smiles that they are better. But I have the 'flu again myself. I do not have it badly enough to be in bed. I am sick enough to fall asleep over a very good Lenten book (Saint Teresa, Vol. II) and I cannot breathe in choir and I rated a shot of penicillin this morning.

This morning in Chapter Reverend Father told us that the Abbey of Our Lady of the Valley burned down last night. The monks all escaped and no one was hurt but the whole monastery, except for the novitiate, was destroyed with all their books and everything. The fire started about ten-thirty last night (on the Feast of Saint Benedict) in that old fire-trap of a guest house. The monks and novices are scattered around in various religious communities in the neighboring towns.

March 25   THE ANNUNCIATION

Yesterday evening I went down with a slight fever. The infirmary is full. In the dormitory, there is a lot of noise, to which I contribute by my unsuccessful efforts to breathe.

The terrible thing about sickness is that you tend to think you are sick. Your thoughts are narrowed down to your own little rag of a body. And you take care of her. My God, forgive me. I take care of myself too well to be a good Cistercian. True, Father Zeno is glad. He doesn't have to worry about me much. Since the infirmary is full he gave me a cot in the room where I work and left me there. He came in this morning and I said I had been out in the sun. He was satisfied and went away. Reverend Father encourages me to go out in the sun behind the garden house, where I am alone. There I sat, this morning, in that Bermuda carriage. (A carriage fits my most decent ideas of comfort. I feel human in a modest carriage, with beautiful wheels.) And there, bewildered, with Father François de Saint Marie's book about the Rule of Carmel in my hand, I wondered if I ought to try to begin my Cistercian life over again from the beginning. O my God, what does it mean to love You? What does it mean, to believe in You? What does it mean that You have brought us all here? Is it after all good for me to be sitting in a carriage? Yes. I think it is good for me to sit there and bad for me to think about my sitting there rather than thinking about God. It is good to go to the Minor Mass where I am now going, to pray for love which is the health of the soul, wherefore my soul also is sick for lack of love.

The liturgy of Passion Sunday has never impressed me so much before. I have been talking to the orientation classes about attention and vigilance in the life of prayer, and so for the first time I noticed how important is this theme of vigilance in the Passion Liturgy. *Hodie si vocem ejus audieritis* . . . Today if you shall hear His voice harden not your hearts. And that terrifying Gospel: "Everyone that is of God hears the words of God . . ." The Pharisees had so hardened their hearts that when the Messiah came they accused Him of "having a devil." They who were the custodians of the Law and the interpreters of the Word of God crucified the Word of God in the name of His own Law. It was the ones who had most thoroughly searched the Scriptures who were unable to recognize Him whom the Scriptures promised. And it happened that the twenty-eighth chapter of Deuteronomy was read in the refectory today. I wonder when I ever heard anything so moving as those curses, in the light of today's Office. "But if thou dost refuse to listen to Him . . ." *Hodie si vocem ejus audieritis!* And yet the Scribes and Pharisees, and the Doctors of the Law, thought they were listening. Perhaps the one thing that made it impossible for them to hear the voice of God when He spoke to them, was their conviction that they were the only ones capable of hearing it! "Thou hast hidden these things from the wise and prudent and revealed them to little ones." So to listen to God means, first of all, to recognize our helplessness, our stupidity, our blindness and our ignorance. How can we ever hear Him if we think of ourselves as experts in religion?

March 28

This is a most peculiar disease. It pretends to leave you, but it only pretends. Actually it is only drawing back to take a good spring at you and claw you all over again. I thought at first that I was doing very well. The day after going to bed I was back in choir. I offered to sing on the schola to replace Frater Amos who was beginning to be ill, and then, after two days, I found myself worse off than before. This afternoon I finally stayed in bed for good. Why should it be a penance to stay in bed? I scarcely know. It is quiet, and pleasant, and you can pray. And yet it almost takes ropes to keep me there. For instance, I am not there now. But I shall take up the breviary and say Matins and reflect with sorrow that it is hard to become a saint by taking care of your health, but that there just doesn't seem to be any point in dragging this thing out indefinitely either. So in the end the best thing is to do what the Infirmarian wants me to do, take a real rest, and get ready, by God's grace, to get back quickly into the community life.

April 2   PALM SUNDAY

Father Zeno has plied me with penicillin from every angle. I even have penicillin chewing gum, which I chewed this morning while washing dishes as it was my Sunday to be in the kitchen after mixt. With the new sanctuary more than half finished, Palm Sunday was beautiful. But after dinner I went to bed and stayed there. I still have a cough that tries to turn me inside out.

After Vespers (I said Vespers sitting up on the cot) I at last rediscovered a moment of true solitude in the midst of the false, dead solitude of sickness in which silence is poured away in sleep or wasted in the soul's immersion in its own corruptible flesh.

April 5 GOOD FRIDAY

Yesterday, Holy Thursday, it was not altogether easy to get up at two o'clock. Half the night carpenters had been hammering in the church trying to finish the new sanctuary floor before Holy Thursday and I lay and listened to the echoing hammers and to the coughing of my neighbors in the dormitory. Also I had the sorest throat I can remember ever having had.

So when the bell rang—by the time the bell rang I had actually had a few hours of what could truthfully be called sleep—I lay and debated within myself, wondering if I ought to stay in bed. But I got up and peeled off the sweaty clothes I had been sleeping in and got into something dry and staggered off to choir and, when the office began, instead of feeling worse I began to feel better. I was deacon at the High Mass, and when we were vesting and the choir was chanting None, I felt pretty tired but it was nice in the clean new sanctuary. The spaciousness of it is rather calming. I could hardly produce a sound, while singing the Gospel. But I sang it slowly with no desire to be appreciated by anyone but Our Lord. And perhaps He was the only One who heard me. After that I was very happy. It was the first time I had stood at the clean new marble altar in any capacity and I now know that the whole sanctuary, which is supposed to be built according to our ancient usages, is more or less what it ought to be except the temporary steps immediately leading to the altar make it rather difficult to give Communion: we were crowded and I thought I might tumble off the step with the paten in my hand.

Today I was back again by the garden house and in the mute solitude that is indifferent to verbal communication. The sun was warm and all the living creatures sang.

April 8 HOLY SATURDAY

Early morning. The darkness is thinning and expects the sun. Birds begin to sing. No Mass. But everything is waiting for the Resurrection.

At the end of the Night Office, when the whole choir sank into the darkness of death and chanted without the faintest light, I thought of the darkness as a luxury, simplifying and unifying everything, hiding all the accidents that make one monk different from another monk and submerging all distractions in deep obscurity. Thus we are all one in the death of Christ. The darkness that descends upon us at the end of Lauds hears us sing the *Benedictus*, the canticle of thanksgiving for the Light who is to be sent. Now He is sent. He has come. He has descended into the far end of night, gathered our Fathers the Patriarchs and Prophets to Himself in Limbo. Now we will all be manifest. We will see one another with white garments, with palm branches in our hands. The darkness is like a font from which we shall ascend washed and illumined, to see one another now no longer separate but one in the Risen Christ.

For we must see one another. Christ must be manifest in glory. His soul is now charged with the glory of victory, demanding a Body, and not only His own physical Body but the whole Mystical Body of the elect. Lord, how can You be so patient? How can You deny the desire of Your soul for all these centuries? His soul has desired us in the night of death in which He has sought us and found us and united us to Himself. All history has become like the Blessed Mother, in whose womb is formed the Mystical Christ and the last day will be Christmas and Easter and the Ascension: all Liturgy will be explained and enacted in one word and Liturgy will be the world's judgment.

April 9 EASTER SUNDAY

The grace of Easter is a great silence, an immense tranquillity and a clean taste in your soul. It is the taste of heaven, but not the heaven of some wild exaltation. The Easter vision is not riot and drunkenness of spirit but a discovery of order above all order—a discovery of God and of all things in Him. This is a wine without intoxication, a joy that has no poison hidden in it. It is life without death. Tasting it for a moment, we are briefly able to see and live all things according to their truth; and to possess them in their substance hidden in God, beyond all sense. Desire clings vainly to the vesture and accident of things, but charity possesses them in the simple depths of God.

If Mass could only be, every morning, what it is on Easter morning! If the prayers could always be so clear, if the Risen Christ would always shine in my heart and all around me and before me in His Easter simplicity! For His simplicity is our feast, this is the unleavened bread which is manna and the bread of heaven, this Easter cleanness, this freedom, this sincerity. O my God, what can I do to convince You that I long for Your Truth and Your simplicity, to share in Your infinite sincerity which is the mirror of Your True Being, and is Your Second Person! Only the little ones can see Him. He is too simple for any created intelligence to fathom. Sometimes we taste some reflection splashed from the clean Light that is the Life of all things: Baptism; First Mass; Easter Morning. Give us always this bread of heaven. Slake us always with this water that we may not thirst forever.

April 12 EASTER WEDNESDAY

This afternoon we were out planting trees in the woods. There is no work I can think of that would be more favorable for contemplation than this. The woods have been sadly cut. There is no real timber left there since Dom Frederic sold all our white oak to the distillery. When the brothers bought that chain-saw three or four years ago they went off on an orgy of cutting, and felled trees on steep hillsides and in gullies without stopping to consider where a horse and wagon could get close enough to haul them away. So now we spent the afternoon putting pine seedlings into the ground. Most of the monks were working south of the lake but the Cellarer got me and we went off into that deep valley behind the lake, which is the quietest and most isolated corner of our forest, and we planted on a shoulder of hill where the trees were very thin and where, several Sundays ago, I entertained for five minutes the reprehensible dream of building a hermitage.

For the first time I have come to understand why all the Graduals sung in the Masses of Easter week are basically the same. Easter week is the extension of the Christian eighth day, the Lord's day which is a Sabbath beyond and above our Sabbaths because it really belongs outside time. Sunday is less the first day of the week than the eighth day in a seven-day week: which is to say that Sunday is the "day" of eternity. And so this octave signifies the eternal "day" of heaven and every day hears the return of the same melody and phrases from the same psalms of the Hallel which Jesus and His disciples sang at the Last Supper, at His passage out of the world, just as all the Jews chanted them in memory of the passage of the Chosen People through the Red Sea and out of Egypt—and just as we will chant them in eternity. *"Confitemini Domino quoniam bonus, quoniam in aeternum misericordia ejus. Dicat NUNC Israel quoniam bonus . . ."** because this is the NOW of heaven.

April 14

The mystery of speech and silence is resolved in the Acts of the Apostles. Pentecost is the solution. The problem of language is the problem of sin. The problem of silence is also a problem of love. How can a man really know whether to write or not, whether to speak or not, whether his words and his silence are for good or for evil, for life or for death, unless he understands the two divisions of tongues—the division of Babel, when men were scattered in their speech because of pride, and the division of Pentecost when the Holy Ghost sent out men of one dialect to speak all the languages of the earth and bring all men to unity: that they may be one, Father, Thou in Me and I in Them that they may be one in us!

The Acts of the Apostles is a book full of speech. It begins

"*Give praise to the Lord for He is good, for His mercy endureth forever. Let Israel NOW say that He is good . . ."

with tongues of fire. The apostles and disciples come downstairs and tumble into the street like an avalanche, talking in every language and the world thinks they are drunk but before the sun has set they have baptised three thousand souls out of Babel into the One Body of Christ. At Pentecost we sing of how they spoke. The antiphon *"loquebantur"* even now displays its sunlit cadences in my heart. The false Jerusalem, the old one that was a figure and had died, could not prohibit them from speaking (Acts, 4). But the more they loved one another and loved God, the more they declared His word. And He manifested Himself through them. That is the only possible reason for speaking—but it justifies speaking without end, as long as the speech grows up from silence and brings your soul to silence once again.

April 16 SATURDAY IN ALBIS

All week I have been thinking of the inestimable greatness and dignity of faith. Faith is higher and more perfect than all knowledge that is accessible to us on earth. The only really valuable mystical experience is a deepening and intensification of faith and love by the gifts of the Holy Ghost—an intensification that only simplifies our faith and makes it more clear by purifying it of every created image and species. So that the purest experience of all begins with the realization of how far faith transcends experience. All that can be thought of and desired as an experience, this side of the simplicity of faith, is worthless compared with faith. And the greater it seems to be the more worthless it is. Our only true greatness is in the humility of living faith and the simpler and purer our faith is, the closer it brings us to God, Who is infinitely great. That is why everyone who humbleth himself shall be exalted and everyone who exalteth himself, in the appetite for great lights and extraordinary experiences and feelings and mystical consolations, shall be humbled. Because the richer he desires to be in these things the poorer he will be in the sight of God, in whose eyes all greatness is as nothing.

April 18

The task of a priest is to spiritualize the world. He raises his consecrated hands and the grace of Christ's resurrection goes out from him to enlighten the souls of the elect and of them that sit in darkness and in the shadow of death. Through his blessing material creation is raised up and sanctified and dedicated to the glory of God. The priest prepares the coming of Christ by shedding upon the whole world the invisible light that enlightens every man that comes into the world. Through the priest, the glory of Christ seeps out into creation until all things are saturated in prayer.

PART SIX

The Sign of Jonas

The last part of this journal covers a longer period than any of the others—a period in which many more things happened and in which I had less time to write. The peace I had found, the solitude of the winter of 1950, deepened and developed in me beyond measure. They continue to do so, and they inspire me with no further explanation of themselves, since no explanation of them is necessary. Nor, perhaps, is it desirable.

In September of 1950 I was sent to the hospital in Louisville for examination. In October I came home with orders to rest. I was back again in the hospital in November for treatment. In December when I returned to the monastery in better health, my impotence as a writer suddenly disappeared and in three months I finished The Ascent to Truth *which for two years I had been trying, without success, to begin.*

In May, 1951, after the regular Visitation of the monastery, the students at Gethsemani were grouped together in a regular "scholasticate" and I became their Father Master. This meant receiving them for private spiritual direction, giving them conferences on the interior life, and generally watching over their development as they prepare for solemn vows and for ordination.

The following month, in June, I went in to Louisville to become an American citizen.

October 9 [1950]

Two colored bricklayers from South Carolina are working on the guest house building with the rest of Mr. Ray's crew. The laybrothers are building their new novitiate. The two colored bricklayers from South Carolina are the two best-dressed bricklayers I ever saw. Especially one of them called Moses, who works in a soft felt hat and what appears to be a gabardine suit. The other is more informal—he wears a baseball cap and a windbreaker. They are very high-priced bricklayers. Today they came in from work with newspapers, and sat down out of the rain on some potato sacks under the cellar entry by the secular kitchen; as they opened their papers I thought I will never again be mad at people for reading the newspapers. (The mystical body of those who read the newspapers.) For half a second I wondered if I were missing something, not because of the news, but because of the happy calm of the two bricklayers sitting on the potato sacks.

October 10

There are times when ten pages of some book fall under your eye just at the moment when your very life, it seems, depends on your reading those ten pages. You recognize in them immediately the answer to all your most pressing questions. They open a new road. The first ten pages of Pierre Emmanuel's *"Qui est cet homme?"* (chapter 1) are that for me. They tell me clearly what I was trying to get obscurely last month out of Ecclesiastes. His is the message of Ecclesiastes. He is the enemy of my angelism. He has given me the word *discontinuity* and has reminded me of what I already found out about isolation being different from solitude.

Discontinuity = chaos = animality, even though you pretend to think like a pure spirit.

After the first ten pages of the book I could not read another line.

October 21

When I was in the hospital in Louisville last month, Benediction, Rosary, litanies in chapel with the sisters and nurses, made a big impression on me: sense of the religious vitality in these devotions which are frowned on as "unliturgical." Felt that the Holy Spirit was really there—sense that this was the Church at prayer, even though not liturgy—not official public prayer. Seemed to me that something of Catholicism was lacking at Gethsemani on this account—yet we can't have all these things. They are not for us—except in private. I would never do without the rosary.

Ideas of authority and freedom in *Mediator Dei*:

Mass—this is stressed—is "unconstrained and voluntary homage to God."

Jesus the deliverer—first paragraph.

Later—a quote from Saint Ambrose on the Psalms: The Psalms—voice of Christ—confession of faith "signifying deep attachment to authority—the joy of freedom."

The Church (Christ) is our liberator. Submission to her authority is *freedom*.

Catholicity is freedom—*no* limitation on the spirit. Authority prohibits what limits and restricts the spirit of men. Hence— errors condemned in *Mediator Dei*—narrowness of exaggerated archaism in liturgy. The Church protects freedom of spirit in devotions—protects mental prayer, contemplation, etc. Holy Spirit must be permitted to "breathe where He will" in spiritual exercises and retreats (※179 translation). Churches are not to be locked up outside time of public liturgical services. Freedom protected by the guarantee of unity in spiritual life—against the

error of those who had begun to create a division between public
and private prayer, "morality and contemplation."

Must not interpret *Mediator Dei* as a defense of mere individualism. Individualism is not freedom. *Sentire cum Ecclesia* is
freedom. Catholicity. Individualism is another form of limitation—false freedom, separation from Christ.

November 3 FEAST OF SAINT MALACHY

Yesterday morning, All Souls Day, during my three Masses: I
was at the consecration of the third Mass and the choir was
chanting *Lauds*. I paused just before pronouncing the words
of consecration over the Host and these words of Psalm 87
came clearly to me from the choir: "*Sicut vulnerati dormientes
in sepulchris quorum non es memor amplius . . .*" (Like the
wounded sleeping in the tombs, whom Thou rememberest no
more!)

The darkness and depth of purgatory! Mercy of God seen in
contradiction: He has "forgotten" them and yet if He had not
remembered them He would not be there at my Mass; He
would not have us saying three Masses for the Poor Souls. Happiness, simplicity in this paradox. Because His "memory" of the
dead is infinitely deep it is necessary that we accuse Him, as if
we were Job, of having forgotten. They sleep in the bosom of
His forgetfulness which is deep mercy, as He bides His time,
doing all things well. The day will come when the dead will be
reborn. Meanwhile His punishment of them is like a womb.
The poverty of Christ has bought them. The resurrection of
Christ will shine in their flesh when Calvary has made them
altogether clean.

I am in the hospital again. This time I am on the first floor in the
priests' corridor which is a wild, amusing section of the world.
I believe many more men have died in the bed I sleep in than
in the one I had on third west.

There are other Trappists here.

A moment ago—Father Noah's voice booming all down the

corridor as he roars at Brother Fiacre (next door): "Do what the sister tells you! *Obey!* OBEY!!"

A Passionist scholastic stopped me yesterday in the corridor and we had a long discussion of various points in *Seeds of Contemplation*. He took me to see Father Campion, a Passionist priest who was in a head-on collision and is lying upstairs in an apparatus evidently designed by Salvador Dali.

November 5

It is Day of Recollection in the hospital.

First time in my life I have said Mass without a proper server. The brother who was serving me went home yesterday. Sister Imelda knelt behind a pillar and answered the prayers while I wondered what to do with the cruets.

Over the public address system they seemed to be paging "Sister Tenacious! Sister Tenacious!"

Bright sun, trees nearly bare. Behind the hospital, that line of low houses with sycamores and willows, the iron fence, the wooden garages. The field, the blue sky, would have interested Manet.

November 6

Behind the hospital: the willows were like silver this morning. Beautiful sky. Then came a junk wagon along the little road behind the wire fence at the far side of the field. First I heard its bells ringing. The wagon seemed to be all bells, like a Chinese temple. Then I saw the mule, the wagon of the Negro driver. The mule was flashing with brass disks. Brass and bells all over his harness. And then the wagon: the two front wheels seemed to be of different sizes. Yet the wagon was majestic. The two rear wheels were greater than the front. I think there was a wooden bucket suspended from the tail end of the wagon. The wagon was not piled high with junk. I was trying to think what kind of boat the wagon resembled. I am sorry for the ambiguity, but it had something of the lines of a Chinese junk. How can I explain the green, aged boards that made up this delicate cart? On top of it all sat the driver with his dog. Both

were immobile. They sailed forward amid their bells. The
dog pointed his nose straight forward like an arrow. The Negro
captain sat immured in a gray coat. He did not look to right or
left, and I would have approached with great respect what
seemed to be solid mysticism. But I stood a hundred yards off,
enchanted by the light on the mule's harness, enchanted by the
temple bells.

November 12

I was going to write something on November 10, but I ran out
of ink, and now suddenly it is November 12. Sunday. Quiet and
bright. The planes swim low over the hospital, making for the
airport.

Wednesday when it was neither quiet nor bright Doctor
Roser cut some three inches of bone and cartilage out of my
nose. Since it did not hurt I was unnecessarily jocose. Sister
Helen Elizabeth stood by saying the rosary. A student nurse
got sick. I sweated mightily. Sister put cold towels around my
neck and on my forehead. Doctor Roser sweated, but less mightily, and got no cold towels from anybody.

Impressions on arriving for a nose operation: It is nothing
like the movies. You find you are going to be operated on in
a very small room—a sort of closet that the architect forgot about
and which has a window. This small room is full of people
scrubbed and dressed in white. In this respect, it is like the
movies. Uniforms. Everything is sterile. I think the most interesting thing about it all is that you are surrounded by people,
mostly women, in white gauze masks and caps. This is delightful. I was waiting for the time when the masks would all come
off. Perhaps Doctor Roser would clap his hands twice and
cry, "It is finished!" And they would all unmask, some smiling,
some solemn, some tired. What actually happened was that
the nurse went away and got sick and Doctor Roser said, "Don't
go tell another nurse to get scrubbed up. He's got blood all over
everything anyway so we might as well break technique." This
turned out to be nicer after all. It made me feel very informal
—the end was in sight. A delightful sense of liberty came over

me, as if somehow "technique" had been a restriction on my own self-expression. It was then that I began to talk to Sister Helen Elizabeth about Elizabeth of the Trinity. It was the day before Elizabeth's "feast." Sister declared that she claimed no part in Elizabeth of the Trinity who was "too interior." I discussed the point briefly while Doctor Roser was chopping the last few bits of bone out of my left nostril. I did not commit the indignity of crossing my legs, or waving my arms in the air with grand gestures. However, I was capable of anything at that time. I even descended so low as to say, "Tell the nurse I will be praying for her." After this astonishing piece of pharisaism I was wheeled off to the elevator reclining on my left elbow like a guest at a Roman banquet.

Yesterday the other Trappist patients went home. I was here all alone and glad of it.

They are still trying to figure out my stomach and I had a slightly bad chest X-ray which the Doctor thinks calls for rest and penicillin. My own theory is this: the doctor is overworked and would like to have a vacation, but since he cannot, he is satisfying his instincts by making sure that *I* have one.

I have to go down to his clinic for treatments on the nose.

Louisville: miles and miles of one-story houses.

For years after I entered the monastery I had cherished the notion that Louisville was somehow a glamorous city. The glamour was all borrowed from Gethsemani. Louisville had registered in my memory as "wonderful" because it was the last outpost before the wilderness of the monastery. Now I know why Father Modestus can say Louisville is dead; he himself comes from St. Louis.

I feel, very dutifully, that Louisville is my city. Why? Well, it is the place I go to when I say "I am going to town." The fact that I practically never leave the monastery to go "in town" makes no difference whatever. Louisville (not Chicago, Cincinnati, Boston, Atlanta, or even Bardstown) is *town*.

There is no reason why a monk should not have a definite attitude toward the place which, in relation to his monastery, is "town." I do not think that being a monk means living on the moon.

November 19 SUNDAY

The Necessity of Silence

1. Exterior Silence—its special necessity in our world in which there is so much noise and inane speech. As *protest* and *reparation* against the "sin" of noise.

Babel. Silence not a virtue, noise not a sin. True. But the turmoil and confusion and constant noise of modern society are the expression of the *ambiance* of its greatest sins—its godlessness, its despair. A world of propaganda, of endless argument, vituperation, criticism, or simply of chatter, is a world without anything to live for. Advertising—radio, television, etc.

Catholics who associate themselves with that kind of noise, who enter into the Babel of tongues, become to some extent exiles from the city of God. (Mass becomes racket and confusion. Tension—babble. All prayer becomes exterior and interior noise —soulless and hasty repetition of rosary . . .)

Hence: though it is true that we must know how to bear with noise, to have interior life, *by exception* here and there in midst of confusion (Saint Thomas's principles for activity), yet to resign oneself to a situation in which a community is *constantly* overwhelmed with activity, noise of machines, etc., is an abuse.

What to do? Those who love God should attempt to preserve or create an atmosphere in which He can be found. Christians should have quiet homes. Throw out television, if necessary— not everybody, but those who take this sort of thing seriously. Radios useless. Stay away from the movies—I was going to say "as a penance" but it would seem to me to be rather a pleasure than a penance, to stay away from the movies. Maybe even form small agrarian communities in the country where there would be *no* radios etc.

Let those who can stand a little silence find other people who like silence, and create silence and peace for one another. Bring up their kids not to yell so much. Children are naturally quiet—

if they are left alone and not given the needle from the cradle upward, in order that they may develop into citizens of a state in which everybody yells and is yelled at.

Provide people with places where they can go to be *quiet*—relax minds and hearts in the presence of God—chapels in the country, or in town also. Reading rooms, hermitages. Retreat houses without a constant ballyhoo of noisy "exercises"—they even yell the stations of the Cross, and not too far from Gethsemani either.

For many it would mean great renunciation and discipline to give up these sources of noise: but they know that is what they need. Afraid to do it because their neighbors would think they were bats.

But at least *monasteries* should be silent!

2. The end—Interior Silence—of judgments, passions, desires.
        Saint Gregory the Great.
        Elizabeth of the Trinity.

Conclusion: When you gain this interior silence you can carry it around with you in the world, and pray everywhere. But just as interior asceticism cannot be acquired without concrete and exterior mortification, so it is absurd to talk about interior silence where there is no exterior silence.

I am surprised to find how much of the artist there is in doctors, for medicine is an art as well as a science and therefore its techniques demand a certain skill that is not abstract but born of a connatural intuition. Doctors adapt themselves to situations pretty much like poets or actors, although they would probably be incensed to hear me say so. They live their way intuitively into somebody else's symptoms and search for their secrets as much by the vital sympathy of art as by scientific intelligence. In any case, diseases do not exist all by themselves: they only present themselves concretely in patients. Therefore the physician's art is respectable because the physician treats not merely diseases but human beings.

The sisters eat dinner in a place on the ground floor of their wing that looks like the dining-room of an English seaside hotel.

I saw them this evening through the curtains as I went out walking, beyond the parking lot, in a dark interval between rainstorms.

November 29   VIGIL OF SAINT ANDREW

I came home to the monastery last Saturday, which was the feast of Saint Catherine. We were nearly killed driving to the monastery from the station. Coming down Saint Joseph's hill, just before turning in to the monastery, we pulled over on the curve to make room for a yellow truck coming the other way. As we pulled over we skidded on the ice. The car went spinning across the middle of the road like something you pay a dime to ride in at Coney Island. It looked as if the truck were going to hit us broadside on, but we had turned around before it reached us. We ended up in the ditch, but since we had spun completely around we were facing in the right direction. I had been praying the rosary all the way from the station—praying that the truck wouldn't hit us, praying to get out of the ditch. We got home, hastened across the snowy garden, and there was a colored retreatant standing by Our Lady's statue. He looked at me and said, "Father Merton?" but I made him a sign that I could not talk.

Talking was what exhausted me most in the hospital. I tried to do as little of it as possible. I spent a lot of time hiding in Room 122, a conference room which is never used for anything. It has a big table and a few chairs in it, and there, with Father Osborne's typewriter, I added something like twenty-five pages to *Bread in the Wilderness*. I had wired to Laughlin in New York for the manuscript.

Feast of the Presentation:

That morning was when I finished work on *Bread in the Wilderness*. I called up Gethsemani and asked Reverend Father if I could go to Carmel to say the Proper Mass of Saint John of the Cross, on Saint John's feast. So then I went to Carmel to get Reverend Mother's permission too. I rang the bell at the turn and said I came from Gethsemani and wanted to see Reverend

Mother. The sister, whose excitement I could not see, exclaimed in a faint, breathless voice, "O Father! Please give me your blessing!" Then I talked with Reverend Mother in what they call the Speak-room. I suppose the term is better than "parlor." The place is nothing like what anyone would think of as a "parlor." (In the South were parlors great salons where you could see everything reflected in the floor? Or did they have vast deep carpets? I would say the Good Shepherd Sisters on Bank Street really had a parlor. I have never forgotten the August day when I went there with Dom Gabriel.)

On Thanksgiving day I said the Community Mass at the hospital and gave them all Communion and in the evening I gave the Holy Hour in place of Father Osborne who went home to get a turkey dinner.

On the 24th, the feast of Saint John of the Cross, it suddenly got very cold. It had been snowing that night and there was snow on the ground. The streets were icy, and the parking lot was full of frozen cars. One of these was the car of the technician in the X-ray department who had arranged to drive me down to Carmel when he went off night duty.

A taxi, ordered by someone else who had already left, showed up at the hospital just when I needed it.

Everything was beautifully quiet. Only two ladies—extern sisters—were there, and were in on what was going on. They were the ones who told me where to find the vestments in the sacristy, who lit the candles, put them out, gave me breakfast. All the rest of the world was kept away by angels. Silence and sunlight everywhere outside. Bright snow on the slopes, among the sycamores, in the park. Silence everywhere inside the convent. It was like saying Mass in a hermitage on the top of a mountain.

The nuns behind the grille and behind the wall behind the altar were so silent I once wondered if they were there at all: I felt like Cassian at the Night Office of the desert fathers. No one even sneezed. The Carmelites are not like Trappists. We have great boots, and shoes as heavy as gun-boats. The Carmelites are silent, in slippers or sandals. No one was coughing though the house was cold. I would not have been completely happy saying that beautiful Mass in an overheated room. One nun answered the prayers behind the grille. She had a nice calm voice, took her time, and spoke the Latin words well.

To wash your hands in the sacristy there was a basin of warm water with a towel in the turn. I thought of something in Saint Theresa about rosewater. There was a faint scent somewhere—but maybe it came from the soap I did not need to use. And the Mass. *Anima mea desideravit te in nocte! Conversatio nostra est in coelis* . . . transformed from brightness to brightness as by the Spirit of the Lord!

December 3 ON RETREAT

Rain. It is cold. Everyone is getting colds, including Father Ignatius Smith, O.P., who is preaching to us. I bet his brother is a Police Captain. All retreats do me good. And this one too. Conferences simple, hard-boiled, and sometimes very loud. If his brother is not a cop, I'll settle for a football coach. But he does me good.

After having doctors and sisters telling me for three weeks to rest and take care of myself it is a relief to have someone roar at the whole community about idleness and timidity. "If you are worn out," he says, "you are just getting off to a good start."

Thursday, before the beginning of the retreat, I got off to a false start. I had to go to Louisville. I went into Saint Martin's Church, which might have been in Würzburg, but for the street outside, though the guardian angel in the sooty yard looked more like Dublin. Churches in cities are the most wonderful solitudes. No one was there. Emptiness, awful stained glass windows, rows and rows of empty pews. The place seemed enormously wide. There I sat facing a brigade of large and small statues, all of them quite tame. And the Tabernacle. And the silence. Big votive lights in front of Saint Anthony like ice-cream sodas. It must cost a dollar and a half to burn one. I began thinking about the Rule of Saint Benedict, solitude, poverty, starting a new order, twelve men in log cabins wearing the overalls of the country. That was what I referred to as the false start of my annual retreat.

I am haunted by the *Cautelas* of Saint John of the Cross. Especially the second against the flesh. Against solicitude for material things.

It is after first bell for Vespers, and through the window I cannot see the church, nor the rain, nor the storm, for my steam. Praised be Jesus for ever! Amen.

December 4

*Domus Jacob, venite, et ambulemus in lumine Domini.**

Moments of beauty in this day. Reading that line of Isaias was one of them. The cover of the new French translation of Saint John of the Cross. Sunlight and clear sky and wet grass behind the old wagon shed. Three young bulls in a pen where the chickens were, near that spring at the south end of the vegetable garden. Of the bulls I was afraid. But, to return to beauty—looking at the crucifix in the infirmary refectory. The crucifix on the yellow wall.

Domus Jacob, venite, ambulemus in lumine Domini.

December 6

After some beautiful pages on morning and on being awake, Thoreau writes in his *Walden* (p. 89):

I went to the woods because I wished *to live deliberately, to front only the essential facts of life, and see if I could not learn what it had to teach and not, when I came to die, discover that I had not lived.*

He adds mysteriously: "Nor did I wish to practice resignation unless it was quite necessary." I suppose he means he did not intend to be resigned to anything like a compromise with life.

December 8

Compare the basic asceticism in *Walden* with that of Saint John of the Cross—agreement on the fundamental idea, not of course on the means or technique, except to some extent. Ascesis of

*"House of Jacob, come and let us walk in the light of the Lord."

solitude. Simplification of life. The separation of reality from illusion.

"If we respected only what is inevitable, and has a right to be, music and poetry would resound along the streets" (p. 94).

The retreat is over. The retreat-master confessed at last that he had been a football coach and a boxing coach in the bargain. And a coach of something else besides, which I have forgotten. He is gone and we miss him—we always get attached to whosoever it is preaches to us for these eight days!

And he told us of Mike McCauliffe, the New York policeman, who was shot on First Avenue by an eighteen-year-old kid who was hopped up on heroin. He told us of the old rakes in the veterans' hospital and of the governor who walked about the grounds reading Greek poetry. He told us a lot of things. He told us to pray for the world. And when I went to speak to him he told me that the Dominicans were allowed and even encouraged to accumulate "books without number" so that I did not need to feel so bad about all the books in the vault.

Yesterday there was snow again and wind froze ribs on top of the drifts along the hillsides; sun shone through the copper grass that grew above the snow on Saint Joseph's hill, and it looked as if the snow was all on fire. There were jewels all over the junk the brothers dumped out there where the old horsebarn used to be. A bunch of old worn-out window-screens were lying about and they shone in the sun like crystal.

December 13   FEAST OF SAINT LUCY

The junk wagon I saw in Louisville comes back to me like the memory of something very precious once seen in the Orient. I saw it several times, and once I heard the bells on the mule without seeing anything. Once the driver had on a green sweater, and the dog was running behind the wagon. That was on a nice day. Then, on a bad day, in a storm of rain, the driver was riding bundled up in many old coats, under a huge gray canvas umbrella. There was no dog at all. The dog stayed home. Now having seen all this and remembered it, I dreamt last night that I saw the wagon once again. The bells of the mule were ringing. The brass disks glittered in the sun. The green boards held themselves together by miracle in their marvelous disorder. But now the junk man's wife was driving, the junk man walked behind.

I remember Gray Street, Louisville. A black carnival mask with broken elastic lying in the dirty snow in front of one of those ancient ornate houses. Gray Street must look nice in spring when the sun comes shining through the sycamores. If I were there in spring I would think of getting back as fast as I could to Gethsemani, where the spring is nicer.

In front of another house: a mounting block or step, or whatever you call those stone steps fashionable people used to get up on to mount a horse, or climb into a carriage. And on this step was written, as it were recently, by an amateur: *"Vive la France!"*

I passed two men on Fourth Street where the shops were gay for Christmas, and one man was saying to the other: ". . . so he drops his damn gun and reaches for a club." (I would put down the long story about the shooting up the road at Smith's corner, two miles from Gethsemani, but I haven't time.)

There is so much to say on this day about what I long to do and be.

In one mist of melting snow which overhangs Gethsemani and Louisville alike, I see the whole world like smoke and I am not part of it. There is nothing on this earth that does not give me a pain. Conversation in town, ambition in the cloister: I mean even ambition to do great things for God. That ambition is too much like the ambitions of the town.

I am aware of silence all around me in the country as of a world that is closed to men. They live in it and yet its door is closed to them. This silence, it is everywhere. It is the room Jesus told us to enter into when we pray.

December 15 SATURDAY

Curious experience—practicing the Christmas chant on a dark winter morning before dawn, and singing the Responsories that also come in the summer Office of Corpus Christi. *Verbum caro*

factum est*—flowers on the cloister pavement and the abbey full
of sun and the song of birds, the baldachin with nodding plumes,
and the procession where you sing to Christ with ineffable
pleasure, weary, with hot wax running down your candle and
across the back of your hand . . . No! now it is winter! But as
I write it is beautiful winter with bright sun on the bare trees and
on the white walls of our building.

Scripture—communion with God. Be careful. Geoffrey of
Auxerre's idea that Saint Bernard's interpretations were guided
by the same Spirit that inspired the prophets, has to be handled
with care. It sounds a lot like Luther. The modern Popes are
wiser. I read the controversy in *Dieu Vivant*. Claudel vs. Stein-
mann. Daniélou's summary gives the correct doctrine as far as I
can see. But the problem worries me. Everything inside me
revolts against an interpretation of the Old Testament that makes
it seem as if God never spoke to anyone but the Jews. Are not
the words of Isaias for me? Did his prophecies run out, and did
their message end when all the Jews came back from Babylon?

*Fear not, for I am with thee: turn not aside for I am thy God:
I have strengthened thee and have helped thee, and the right
hand of my just one hath upheld thee.* (Isaias, 41:10)

Who is God talking to? Israel. Who is Israel? Christ. I live, now
not I but Christ liveth in me. Who is God talking to? To me, to
this monk in Gethsemani.

> *February* 21 FEAST OF SAINT PETER'S
> CHAIR AT ANTIOCH [1951]

Today is the ninth anniversary of my reception of the habit of
novice, and it occurred to me that I should go on writing this
notebook which I had deliberately stopped again. There is nothing against it, since it is not a "Spiritual Journal."

This morning at Prime—at once I write something profes-
sionally and tediously spiritual—this morning at Prime I was

*"The Word was made flesh."

struck by the title the Trappist printer invented for Psalm 14, *De via ducente ad beatitudinem.** In the light of that light suddenly the whole psalm became full of light. It was as if I had never understood it before, as though (in fact I think I wrote this in *Bread in the Wilderness*), "there is more to this psalm than you might think."

The line that struck me most was "*qui loquitur veritatem in corde suo.*"† It could mean—the man who is completely true to the Word God utters within him, who is, by his simplicity, in perfect harmony with truth. That is our vocation—mine. I have to think about it more, but not on paper.

Someone sent a book with an excerpt in it from Gertrude Stein's *Toklas* which I had never read. But from the excerpt it seems to be one of the few sensible books written in our time. Perhaps I think that only because it is very well written.

I would have been more glad than I was to break rock with a sledge hammer yesterday if it had not upset me, but precisely for that reason I ought to be enough of a Trappist to be very glad. After nine years I am at last getting around to an appreciation of penance not merely in so far as it is "the spirit of an Order" but because it is pleasing to God and enables Him to take undisturbed possession of the soul. How secret penance has to be with the left hand not knowing what the right hand is doing, and the "Spiritual Journal" receiving no busy resolutions. It is the impurity of immature penance that brings distress, but deep and hidden suffering is joy. Part of this depth and this hiddenness comes from the fact that such suffering really *diminishes* you, reduces you to nothing, places you in darkness, and tells you you are nothing and that, as the *Imitation* says, "The old man is not dead." And yet, love can easily get rid of him—though not so much our love as Christ's, which becomes ours.

February 28

Studying the baby-talk citizenship textbook that is given out to help us aliens prepare for our naturalization. Suddenly realized

---

*"Of the road leading to blessedness."

†"Who speaks the truth in his heart."

that this business of citizenship raises a moral question. Impossible to take it as a mere formality. Either it means something or it doesn't. There is more to this than a problem of semantics. It is a question of justice and of charity. Why do half the people in America seem to think it is a moral weakness to admit that they owe America something—and perhaps everything? And that the country is worth loving?

March 3

March is Saint Benedict's month. Clearing thorn trees from the rocky shoulder over the middle bottom where the new road is being made, I got to be good friends with his relic yesterday. How weary I am of being a writer. How necessary it is for monks to work in the fields, in the rain, in the sun, in the mud, in the clay, in the wind: these are our spiritual directors and our novice-masters. They form our contemplation. They instill us with virtue. They make us as stable as the land we live in. You do not get that out of a typewriter. *Tunc vere monachi sunt si de labore manuum suarum vivunt sicut et Patres nostri et Apostoli.**

The sanity of Saint Benedict has something to do with the mystery of a monk becoming an American citizen. Yesterday I looked closely for the first time in ten years at the manuscript of the *Journal of My Escape from the Nazis,* which I wrote ten years ago at Saint Bonaventure's at the beginning of the war. Sister Thérèse borrowed it from Ed Rice and sent it on to me.

It was a very inhibited book, in spite of all the uninhibited explosives of an invented language which I still like. The action can never progress forward. In fact, there is no action in the book. A situation presents itself and the stream of the book—which after all has a stream—stops and forms a lake. It is sometimes quite a bright lake. But I can do nothing with it.

Sitting in the garden house I viewed the pale glare of sunlight in the roof of the distillery a mile away against the dark hills and

---

*"Then they are truly monks when they live by the labor of their hands as did our fathers and the Apostles" (Rule of St. Benedict).

I thought about the whole business. And although my thinking was a little incoherent—*motus orbicularis*, circling the subject with a laziness appropriate to the hour, which was 1:15 P.M.—nevertheless I came out of it more healthy than I went in, and descended the ladders more in one piece than I had climbed them.

One of the problems of the book was my personal relation to the world and to the last war. When I wrote it I thought I had a very supernatural solution. After nine years in a monastery I see that it was no solution at all. The false solution went like this: the whole world, of which the war is a characteristic expression, is evil. It has therefore to be first ridiculed, then spat upon, and at last formally rejected with a curse.

Actually, I have come to the monastery to find my place in the world, and if I fail to find this place in the world I will be wasting my time in the monastery.

It would be a grave sin for me to be on my knees in this monastery, flagellated, penanced, though not now as thin as I ought to be, and spend my time cursing the world without distinguishing what is good in it from what is bad.

Wars are evil but the people involved in them are good, and I can do nothing whatever for my own salvation or for the glory of God if I merely withdraw from the mess people are in and make an exhibition of myself and write a big book saying, "Look! I am different!" To do this is to die. Because any man who pretends to be either an angel or a statue must die the death. The immobility of that *Journal of My Escape* was a confession of my own nonentity, and this was the result of a psychological withdrawal.

On the other hand, if you let yourself be washed away with all the dirt on the surface of the stream you pile up somewhere in another kind of immobility, with the rest of the jetsam in the universe.

Coming to the monastery has been for me exactly the right kind of withdrawal. It has given me perspective. It has taught me how to live. And now I owe everyone else in the world a share in that life. My first duty is to start, for the first time, to live as a member of a human race which is no more (and no less) ridiculous than I am myself. And my first human act is the recognition of how much I owe everybody else.

Thus God has brought me to Kentucky where the people are, for the most part, singularly without inhibitions. This is the precise place He had chosen for my sanctification. Here I must revise all my own absurd plans, and take myself as I am, Gethsemani as it is, and America as it is—atomic bomb and all. It is utterly peculiar, but none the less true, that after all, one's nationality should come to have a meaning in the light of eternity. I have lived for thirty-six years without one. Nine years ago I was proud of the fact. I thought that to be a citizen of heaven all you had to do was throw away your earthly passport. But now I have discovered a mystery: that Miss Sue and all the other ladies in the office of the Deputy Clerk of the Louisville District Court are perhaps in some accidental way empowered to see that I am definitely admitted to the Kingdom of Heaven forever.

I am beginning to believe that perhaps the only, or at least the quickest way, I shall become a saint is by virtue of the desires of many good people in America that I should become one. Last night I dreamt I was telling several other monks, "I shall be a saint," and they did not seem to question me. Furthermore, I believed it myself. If I do become one—(I shall)—it will be because of the prayers of other people who, though they are better than I am, still want me to pray for them. Perhaps I am called upon to objectify the truth that America, for all its evil, is innocent and somehow ignorantly holy.

March 10 SATURDAY BEFORE PASSION SUNDAY Tenderness of the Epistle, austerity of the Gospel in this morning's Mass. Last night before Compline, out by the horsebarn, looking at the orchard and thinking about what Saint John of the Cross said about having in your heart the image of Christ crucified.

Confusion and fog pile up in your life, and then by the power of the Cross things once again are clear, and you know more about your wretchedness and you are grateful for another miracle.

It is good that I have been out to the common work more often, even though I nearly set the whole forest on fire yesterday burning brush out by Saint Gertrude's field on the slope nearest the lake.

Wind . . . flames springing up in the leaves across the creek like the spread of attachments in an unmortified soul!

So, *confortetur cor tuum et viriliter age!* Here are the things to be done:

Many lights are burning that ought to be put out.

Kindle no new fires. Live in the warmth of the sun.

April 6

Jean Cayrol has written a book about the dreams men had in the concentration camps. When first arrested they dreamt they had not been arrested but had escaped. Then, resigned to their arrest, they dreamt they were allowed to go home from time to time returning afterwards to their confinement. This in prison, before the camp itself.

In the concentration camp they had magnificent dreams of landscapes, of baroque architecture.

Color in their dreams. Blue dreams, green dreams, red dreams of salvation. A sailor dreamt he saw a diamond cross rising out of the sea.

I have walked alone on the road to the barns looking at the high clouds and thinking: "In war and in battle men look up sometimes and see such clouds as these." Cayrol tells of the *Appel* at Matthausen, men being beaten to jelly in the presence of a magnificent sunset on the Austrian alps.

The ones who were completely incommunicado were called *Nacht und Nebel* ("Night and Mist"), which might conceivably be the name of a perfume.

And I thought of Saint John of the Cross. His *Spiritual Canticle* was born of the imprisonment at Toledo! Confirmation of Cayrol's thesis in these two studies.

"Elles (ces Études) ont tenté d'expliquer comment naissaient dans un univers voué à l'échec et à la négation toutes les défenses surnaturelles de l'homme, comment elles se développent clandestinement et comment elles survivaient dans des prolongements multiples, difficilement séparables."

April 11

Feast of Saint Leo the Great. Preparing the Scripture course. Finished Leo XIII's *Providentissimus Deus* this morning. Keep dipping into Saint Thomas. Quiet, contemplative work. First time I have really made use of the opportunities the vault offers. For two years I have been a hermit and have not appreciated the fact, or lived as one. *Nunc coepi.* Father Barnabas Mary, the Passionist in Chicago, wrote to me about Father Charbel who lived as a hermit in Syria—he was a Maronite. Everyone forgot about him. He died. Fifty years later his body was discovered incorrupt and in a short time he worked over six hundred miracles. He is my new companion. My road has taken a new turning. It seems to me that I have been asleep for nine years— and that before that I was dead. I have never been a monk or a solitary. *Take up thy bed and walk!* Great help from the prayers of the Carmelites, the relics of Saint John of the Cross, Saint Theresa, and Saint Thomas Aquinas.

April 22

O April, we are coming to your end.

You, Father Charbel, hidden from men in glory, because of you perhaps, this journal is slowly coming to an end.

Because I will not tell them about the moon, about the cold hour beyond price, the mist in the early valley, the sun I did not know was rising behind me, or the sweet-smelling earth.

This morning was like the morning of that first poem, the retreat in the guest house, ten years ago. The barn—that is, the garden house, which from my room seemed to me beautiful and mysterious—had become the very mystery in which I was hidden. It was the same hour. Perhaps the years were no more. The tired man was on his tower among the little boxes. There was a quilt for covering plants in a garden. It smelled of rats. Also the chicken houses had been moved. The outward orchard is all down. The wry trees are gone. The earth is sown with new grass.

Famous but unknown, tired and powerful, a man without virtue and without prayer, impotent, hungry, at peace, unable to speak, looking at the valley: *Who is like unto God!*

God, my God, here is a traitor who loves You beyond speech! And yet I have no love. I have no moon, I have no valley.

I sat by the orchard heaters until I smelled all over of oil and flame. I saw the moon through the flame. Without heart, without brain, the senseless man has prayed for fire and apparently received none. Everywhere is beauty. Where are You, O my God? I was ashamed of singing on the road to the barn, but what else could I have done?

Alive and dead I climb the glorious barn. The mud of my feet going up is the mud of my hands going down. I will go down more wretched than I went up because more glorious. This barn cannot be known. It is Mount Lebanon, where Father Charbel Makhlouf saw the sun and moon.

I leaned my chin upon the windowsill and prayed to You, my Lover, in the following terms:

> "When the pie was opened
> The birds began to sing.
> Was not this a dainty dish
> To set before the King?"

My God, Who is like You? How can I compare the visits of your children with the silence that dwells on the hills? Yet I have made their hearts suffer by loving them. I have defiled many lives with my impertinence. We have all gone away and have begun over and over to pray, and I believe conversation is a punishment for false mysticism. How can we help ourselves? But I am once again made clean by frost and morning air, here in the presence of the moon.

As long as I do not pretend I suffer, as long as I do not trade in false coin, nor claim that I have already disappeared—my brothers' prayers can always mend me. The windows are open. Let the psalms fly in. Prime each morning makes me safe and free. The Day Hours sustain me with their economy, by night I am buried in Christ. At 3 A.M. I wear the old white vestment and say the Mass *de Beata*. Through the gaps in my own prayer come the psalms of the Night Office that I discovered in the woods yesterday afternoon.

There, there is the crooked tree, the moss with my unspoken words, those pines upon that cliff of shale, the valley living with the tunes of diesel trains. Nobody knows the exact place I speak of and why should I tell them? For every man is his own Jacob, wakes up at the foot of his own ladder. And thus he arises in his own unrecognizable house, his gate of heaven.

What happens after that? Do you put down "The rest is silence" and close the book and sell it to the public?

That would be a lie. For Jacob afterward married. His first wife, the fertile one, was ugly. He served fourteen years. He bred sheep. He fled from Rachel's father. His flocks drank from the well where Jesus later sat and spoke with my elder sister.

We too have all married over and over again, and yet we have no husband. But thank God for the hill, the sky, the morning sun, the manna on the ground which every morning renews our lives and makes us forever virgins.

May 7

Since Easter was early we are already on the threshold of Pentecost. Yesterday, in bright, blazing sun, we planted cabbage seedlings in the garden and over the wall I could hear them mowing hay in Saint Joseph's field where, probably, tomorrow we will all be loading wagons.

Last week was the week of the Visitation and the busiest I had ever spent in my life. Dom Louis le Pennuen, our Father Immediate, the new Abbot of Melleray, is young and likes work and does not know enough English to do without an interpreter. I was working for him most days from seven in the morning to six at night with time out only for dinner and the meridienne. Later on in the week when the interviews were over I was able to slip away for part of the Conventual Mass. He left the night before last (Sunday) after inviting me to dinner up in the guest house with Father Abbot and Father Prior.

June 13

It is sometime in June. At a rough guess, I think it is June 13 which may or may not be the feast of Saint Anthony of Padua. In any case every day is the same for me because I have become very different from what I used to be. The man who began this journal is dead, just as the man who finished *The Seven Storey Mountain* when this journal began was also dead, and what is more the man who was the central figure in *The Seven Storey Mountain* was dead over and over. And now that all these men are dead, it is sufficient for me to say so on paper and I think I will have ended up by forgetting them. Because writing down what *The Seven Storey Mountain* was about was sufficient to get it off my mind for good. Last week I corrected the proofs of the French translation of the book and it seemed completely alien. I might as well have been a proofreader working for a publisher and going over the galleys of somebody else's book. Consequently, *The Seven Storey Mountain* is the work of a man I never even heard of. And this journal is getting to be the production of somebody to whom I have never had the dishonor of an introduction.

*Ecce nova facio omnia!**

On Trinity Sunday I was named Master of the Scholastics. Dom Louis had asked for the formation of a regular scholasticate. Some of our large monasteries have them. They are absolutely necessary when the young professed are too numerous to remain for a long time in the novitiate. And they need a Spiritual Director as well as some sort of family life of their own. The problems of the young professed turn out to be perhaps the most crucial thing in their Cistercian formation.

The fact that I have suddenly ended up in this position clarifies

*"Behold I make all things new."

all the foolish pages of the journal I have written about my own problems as a scholastic. For now I know that the reason why I had to resist the temptation to become a Carthusian was in order to learn how to help all the other ones who would be one way or another tempted to leave the monastery. And when I read such a lot of Duns Scotus, it was in order to learn, after all, the importance of keeping to the straight line of Thomism and of keeping scholastics out of difficulties which are too great for a Cistercian to solve. Our life is not designed for theological controversy and Scotus is more than the Cistercian head can bear—at least until somebody distills his essence and gives it to us second-hand.*

As for the woods, on Whitmonday (just before we cut down the last grove of cedars where one could still hide inside the enclosure) I explored a wooded bluff outside the east wall which is sufficiently fenced-in to be considered an extension of the enclosure. With the full approval of Dom Louis, Reverend Father has given me this wood as a refuge for my scholastics. It is a pleasant place, and one can more quickly find solitude there than in the forest, which is further away. And so I find that now I spend more time praying and less time walking: and since the solitude is theirs rather than mine I have less time for self-admiration. My prayer is more confusing and more obscure. I disappear and know nothing (except a confused awareness that I and the woods exist but that I have a center which is outside the sphere of this existence). Two hours are the same as five minutes and the bell rings and I am too often late for Vespers. Meanwhile in the vault I bless my children and talk to them one by one and it is much more interesting than writing a book, besides being less fatiguing. Furthermore, since I am obliged to live the Rule in order to talk about it with any degree of authority, I go out to work as often as I can, and I now have blisters again the way I had them in the novitiate and I come home full of dirt and sweat and bathe and change and sit down under a tree behind the church where you can really pray.

*Since writing this, I think I have discovered a book which does this successfully: E. Gilson's *Jean Duns Scot.*

Thus I stand on the threshold of a new existence. The one who is going to be most fully formed by the new scholasticate is the Master of the Scholastics. It is as if I were beginning all over again to be a Cistercian: but this time I am doing it without asking myself the abstract questions which are the luxury and the torment of one's monastic adolescence. For now I am a grownup monk and have no time for anything but the essentials. The only essential is not an idea or an ideal: it is God Himself, Who cannot be found by weighing the present against the future or the past but only by sinking into the heart of the present as it is.

June 23

Yesterday morning, after saying a Votive Mass of the Seven Dolors and trying to make a thanksgiving in the back sacristy in the short interval that was left before Prime, I slipped out and shaved and got into a black suit and a Roman collar to go to Louisville and become an American citizen.

All week long I had been trying to think about it, but in the end I have come to the conclusion that I can't kid myself that it is as important a step as religious profession or taking the habit of novice and it is useless to try to act as if it were. However, I prayed over it, and Thursday evening, after supper, I was sitting out in the small calf pasture, on the north side of the vineyard, watching the blazing hot sunset over the wooded knobs, and it seemed to me that all that triumphant fire out there served as a sort of anticipated celebration. Within twenty-four hours there would be a sense in which I could definitely speak of all this as "my country." It was a bit disturbing to find that I was suddenly discovering America in 1951 when it was supposed to have been discovered for me by Christopher Columbus in 1492. And to think that I had lived in Kentucky all this time without ever questioning the fact that I belonged to the place and that it belonged to me! Perhaps that only proves that after all papers do not make a man a citizen of any country, earth or heaven.

Anyway, I drove to town with two family brothers. By the time we left the sun was glaring through an angry haze and everybody knew it was going to be hot including the men in undershirts and dungarees who were coming out with their mules to cultivate their plots of tobacco in all parts of Nelson county.

The ditches along the road were full of cornflowers and hollyhocks, and there were day lilies everywhere. Wild roses were climbing over the fences of the farms and were in bloom, and the trumpet vines were putting forth their dull red soundless horns. After I said the *Itinerarium* and Tierce and Sext, I sat back to memorize some of the things a citizen is supposed to know. I got them all out of a textbook that comes from the University of Kentucky and which we keep around here because almost every year now someone becomes a citizen. Last year it was Father Hermes, who came over from Ireland and maybe in a year or two it will be Father Savinian who also came over from Ireland.

I thought we were going to be late at the Federal Building, and according to the notification I was late indeed, but there was still plenty of time before the Court Session. The corridors were full of people, one of whom turned out to be a reporter. This is a peculiar world, in which the only man in a big crowd who has to worry about the reporters is a Trappist monk who has left the world.

My first sensation on entering the Court Room was one of spiritual discomfort at being in a place that was big enough to be a church but manifestly had no tabernacle. I had to stop myself from making a moderate bow to an imaginary crucifix, as if I were walking into the Chapter Room of a monastery. This bow would have seemed very mysterious to the bystanders, I am sure. The three big armchairs behind the Judge's bench failed, I fear, to remind me that all authority comes from God. The thought only occurred to me now, not yesterday, when it should have done so.

I looked for a chair in an out of the way place, but almost immediately they lined us up in some kind of official order, and I found myself sitting with the aisle on one side and a little red-haired lady on the other. When the Judge came in, the procedure began to be a lot of fun, because almost at once the examiner made each one stand up and say where he came from and what

he did. It was very amusing to sit there and find so much about
so many strangers—their names, their ages, the countries they
came from, and when they came from them, and why. It seems
to me that most of them were German girls who had married
soldiers now stationed at Fort Knox. But there were several Rus-
sians and there was a man with a fruit and vegetable business who
came from Mount Lebanon, which is what they now call Syria,
and there was a man from Finland and a little man called Romeo
who was from Italy and sold insurance and there was a girl from
Iceland and a tall red-haired man from Ontario who turned out
to be married to a relative of one of the doctors in Saint Joseph's
Infirmary. So when the atmosphere became more intimate I had
to stand up and explain why I had once belonged to the National
Students League. While I did so, a lot of eminently respectable
ladies who were quite obviously not immigrants turned around
and gave me the once-over. It was then that I realized that these
were members of the D.A.R. and my surmise turned out to be
quite correct, for when it was all over—our naturalization, I
mean—they stood up and started to make speeches and they gave
us American flags.

November 29

John the Baptist sends Andrew to Jesus, and Andrew gets Peter
and Peter tells Philip and Philip speaks to Nathanael, who does
not think that anything good can come out of Nazareth. But
Jesus says that Nathanael's suspicions are without guile. He
speaks to Nathanael about the fig tree. All at once the Kingdom
of God is formed in the world—*regnum Dei intra vos est.** The
angels are ascending and descending upon the Church, the Mystical Body of the Son of Man. Before Advent gets a chance to
start (at least this year's Advent) Christ appears among us—
Parousia. He cometh. He is already formed before our eyes in
His saints, even before the Church can begin to start from the
beginning, and draw Him forth from the types and mysteries of
the Old Testament. Before the cycle has begun, it has already
ended. The Vigil of Saint Andrew is a prelude to Pentecost, it

*"The Kingdom of God is in the midst of you."

contains Pentecost. The Body that is to be vivified with the Breath of God is already being formed from the slime of the earth.

Elias was a man like unto us. Andrew, Peter, James, and John were men like unto us. And like them we bring our infirmities to Christ in order that His strength may be glorified in the transformation of our weakness. Day after day the outward man crumbles and breaks down and the inward man, the Man of Heaven, is born and grows in wisdom and knowledge before the eyes of men—who cannot recognize him. Neither can we recognize ourselves in the image of Him which is formed in us because we do not yet have eyes with which to see Him. And yet we suspect His presence in the mystery which is not revealed to the wise and prudent. We feel His eyes upon us as we sit under the fig tree and our souls momentarily spring to life at the touch of His hidden finger. This flash of fire is our solitude; but it binds us to our brethren. It is the fire that has quickened the Mystical Body since Pentecost so that every Christian is at the same time a hermit and the whole Church, and we are all members one of another. It remains for us to recognize the mystery that your heart is my hermitage and that the only way I can enter into the desert is by bearing your burden and leaving you my own.

It is now six months since I have been Master of the Scholastics and have looked into their hearts and taken up their burdens upon me. I have not always seen clearly and I have not carried their burdens too well and I have stumbled around a lot, and on many days we have gone around in circles and fallen into ditches because the blind was leading the blind.

I do not know if they have discovered anything new, or if they are able to love God more, or if I have helped them in any way to find themselves, which is to say: to lose themselves. But I know what I have discovered: that the kind of work I once feared because I thought it would interfere with "solitude" is, in fact, the only true path to solitude. One must be in some sense a hermit before the care of souls can serve to lead one further into the desert. But once God has called you to solitude, everything you touch leads you further into solitude. Everything that affects you builds you into a hermit, as long as you do not insist on doing the work yourself and building your own kind of hermitage.

What is my new desert? The name of it is *compassion*. There is no wilderness so terrible, so beautiful, so arid and so fruitful as the wilderness of compassion. It is the only desert that shall truly flourish like the lily. It shall become a pool, it shall bud forth and blossom and rejoice with joy. It is in the desert of compassion that the thirsty land turns into springs of water, that the poor possess all things. There are no bounds to contain the inhabitants of this solitude in which I live alone, as isolated as the Host on the altar, the food of all men, belonging to all and belonging to none, for God is with me, and He sits in the ruins of my heart, preaching His Gospel to the poor.

Do you suppose I have a spiritual life? I have none, I am indigence, I am silence, I am poverty, I am solitude, for I have renounced spirituality to find God, and He it is Who preaches loud in the depths of my indigence, saying: "I will pour out my spirit upon thy children and they shall spring up among the herbs as willows beside the running waters" (Isaias, 44:3-4). "The children of thy barrenness shall say in thy ears: The place is too strait for me, make me room to dwell in" (Isaias, 49:20). I die of love for you, Compassion: I take you for my Lady, as Francis married poverty I marry you, the Queen of hermits and the Mother of the poor.

There came from France a tiny, ancient leaflet, printed somewhere in the Auvergne at least half a century ago. It is about Our Lady of the Olive Trees, at Murat. Had I heard of her? I must have. I stood in the shadow of her church. She knew me when I was under the fig tree. Or under her olives—in the mountain where no olives grow.

January 10 [1952]

The sun comes out, and so does the typewriter. All week I have been knocking myself out trying to prepare conferences and Scripture classes and give spiritual direction. Half my spiritual

children have colds and some of them are depressed and one
just changed over to the laybrothers, which was a good thing,
while two of them are trying to kill themselves with overwork, being cantors and directing the choir even during the
psalmody of the little hours. I understand their anguish which,
five years ago, was my own anguish. But I do not approve of
their exhaustion. The choir now is different beyond all belief
from what it was when I was a student and a sub-cantor.

All week I have been deacon, because last week I sang the
High Mass. So this week I sing the Epiphany Gospel, and as I
sing it the trees of the woods come before me, because when I
was working alone in the woods all week I sang over to myself
some of the phrases of the Gospel. The questions of the Magi
and the plot of Herod. *Ubi est qui natus est rex Judaeorum?* I
know where He is. He and I live in the trees. And yet I am more
of a family man than I ever was in my life—and for that precise
reason I have now become, as I think, a mature hermit. (Mature:
today as we marched back into the sacristy after the High Mass,
I thought to myself that in a few days I would be thirty-seven
and that a graceless middle age was descending upon me.)

Thanks to my job in the woods, the curve below my chest has
flattened out again. I had feared I was in for a corpulent middle
age like any other writer.

The job in the woods is this: since October I have been the
timber marker. I suddenly found out all about the trees. Next
spring I shall presumably be in charge of planting ten thousand
seedlings to replace what has been cut down. I started out with
my pot of paint in October. The work began on the northeast
flank of the lake knob, behind Donohue's place. After that we
worked north. I am generally a couple of days' work ahead of
the brothers who are after me with chain-saws and axes and that
orange army truck and the old jeep. The old jeep is distinguished
from the flashy red jeep which some brother postulant brought
from Kansas but this "new" jeep is reserved for the novices.

Right now we are in a deep valley I never knew about before.
It is between two knobs which do not have names, but one of
which has become for me Mount Carmel. I have marked the

trees in many different colors. Sometimes white, sometimes slate-blue. I began the year nineteen fifty-two with canary yellow. So all the west side of the smallest knob we see at the east end of our line of knobs, is splashed with canary yellow, and it was there, too, that I sang the Epiphany Gospel to the silent glens. *Videntes autem stellam gavisi sunt gaudio magno valde!*

On the whole, the best paint was that casein paint I used on the beech trees and the blighted elms and on the twisted tan oaks along that slope outside the valley, where Frater Caleb brought the novices a couple of times. Frater Caleb the undermaster is one of my scholastics. That was also the place where, just after a lot of timber had been cut down and stacked for loading, and a lot of brush was lying around, a forest fire broke out in November, on the feast of the Dedication of the Church. Brother Gelgan got the jeep in the afternoon and I went out with him and three other brothers and we put out the fire with Indian pumps strapped on our backs. These are very effective—much more so than flapping at the flames with a cedar branch, or scuffing them with pitchforks.

On the feast of the Holy Innocents I took four of the scholastics out on this knob which I secretly call Mount Carmel. It is the finest of all the knobs. It runs north and south behind the lake knob and from the top, which is fairly clear of trees, you can see all over this part of Kentucky—miles of woods over to the northwest, and in the direction of Hanekamp's house and New Haven. Out there somewhere, a few miles on, lies the place where Lincoln was born.

So we took a truck as far as Donohue's. After that we got out and walked to the last cornerstone of our property at the end of the valley, and then climbed the knob. There was a high wind blowing and it was cold but wonderful. And I looked down into the big wide bowl of woods which is McGinty's hollow because somebody called McGinty once had a log cabin there or something. But it is all woods now, and I got lost there exactly a year before, on the feast of the Holy Innocents in 1950.

The more I get to know my scholastics the more reverence I have for their individuality and the more I meet them in my own solitude. The best of them, and the ones to whom I feel closest, are also the most solitary and at the same time the most charitable. All this experience replaces my theories of solitude. I do not need a hermitage, because I have found one where I least expected it. It was when I knew my brothers less well that my thoughts were more involved in them. Now that I know them better, I can see something of the depths of solitude which are in every human person, but which most men do not know how to lay open either to themselves or to others or to God.

The young ones, I admit, do not have half the problems I used to have when I was a scholastic. Their calmness will finally silence all that remains of my own turbulence. They come to me with intelligent questions, or sometimes with an even more intelligent absence of questions. They refresh me with their simplicity. Very spontaneously, they come to share my love of anything I may have discovered, around here, that is simple. But they ignore my persistent interest in theological complications. This is to me both a confusion and an education—to see that they can mostly get along quite well without what I used to think I needed, even though, when I was sane, I realized I did not need it at all.

I say theological complications, not theology. For I constantly preach to them from the encyclicals that they must know theology. Myself, in the afternoons after dinner, I read and love Saint Thomas on a pile of logs beyond the horse-pasture where the neighbors come on Sunday afternoons to hunt with shotguns. And there I have discovered that after all what the monks most need is not conferences on mysticism but more light about the ordinary virtues, whether they be faith or prudence, charity or temperance, hope or justice or fortitude. And above all what they need and what they desire is to penetrate the Mystery of Christ and to know Him in His Gospels and in the whole Bible (some of them seem to read nothing else but the Bible).

Thus it is that I live in the trees. I mark them with paint, and the woods cultivate me with their silences, and all day long even in choir and at Mass I seem to be in the forest: but my children themselves are like trees, and they flourish all around me like the things that grow in the Bible.

February 26 SHROVE TUESDAY
The blue elm tree near at hand and the light blue hills in the distance: the red bare clay where I am supposed to plant some shade trees: these are before me as I sit in the sun for a free half hour between direction and work. Tomorrow is Ash Wednesday and today, as I sit in the sun, big blue and purple fish swim past me in the darkness of my empty mind, this sea which opens within me as soon as I close my eyes. Delightful darkness, delightful sun, shining on a world which, for all I care, has already ended.

It does not occur to me to wonder whether we will ever transplant the young maples from the wood, yonder, to this bare leveled patch—the place where the old horsebarn once stood. It does not occur to me to wonder how everything here came to be transformed. I sit on a cedar log half chewed by some novice's blunt axe, and do not reflect on the plans I have made for this place of prayer, because they do not matter. They will happen when they will happen. The hills are as pure as jade in the distance. God is in His transparent world, but He is too sacred to be mentioned, too holy to be observed. I sit in silence. The big deep fish are purple in my sea.

Different levels of depth.
First, there is the slightly troubled surface of the sea. Here there is action. I make plans. They toss in the wake of other men's traffic: passing liners. I speak to the scholastics. I make resolutions to speak less wildly, to say fewer of the things that surprise myself and them. Where do they spring from?
Second, there is the darkness that comes when I close my eyes. Here is where the big blue, purple, green, and gray fish swim by. Most beautiful and peaceful darkness: is it the cave of my own inner being? In this watercavern I easily live, whenever I wish. Dull rumors only of the world reach me. Sometimes a drowned barrel floats into the room. Big gray-green fish, with

silver under their purple scales. Are these the things the blind men see all day? I close my eyes to the sun, and live on the second level, a natural prayer, peace. When I am tired it is almost slumber. There is no sound. Soon even the fish are gone. Night, night. Nothing is happening. If you make a theory about it you end up in quietism. All I say about it is that it is comfortable. It is a rest. I half open my eyes to the sun, praising the Lord of glory. Lo, thus I have returned from the blank abyss, re-entering the shale cities of Genesis. Ferns and fish return. Lovely dark green things. In the depth of the waters, peace, peace, peace. Such is the second level of waters under the sun. We pray therein, slightly waving among the fish.

Words, as I think, do not spring from this second level. They are only meant to drown there.

The question of socialization does not concern these waters. They are nobody's property. Animality. Game preserve. Paradise. No questions whatever perturb their holy botany. Neutral territory. No man's sea.

I think God intended me to write about this second level, however, rather than the first. I abandon all problems to their own unsatisfactory solutions: including the problem of "monastic spirituality." I will not even answer, as I answer the scholastics, that the Desert Fathers talked not about monastic spirituality but about purity of heart and obedience and solitude, and about God. And the wiser of them talked very little about anything. But the divine life which is the life of the soul as the soul is the life of the body: this is a pure and concrete thing and not to be measured by somebody else's books. God in me is not measured by your ascetic theory and God in you is not to be weighed in the scales of my doctrine. Indeed He is not to be weighed at all.

Third level. Here there is positive life swimming in the rich darkness which is no longer thick like water but pure, like air. Starlight, and you do not know where it is coming from. Moonlight is in this prayer, stillness, waiting for the Redeemer. Walls watching horizons in the middle of the night. *In velamento diei et in luce stellarum nocte.* Everything is charged with intelligence, though all is night. There is no speculation here. There is vigilance; life itself has turned to purity in its own refined depths. Everything is spirit. Here God is adored, His coming is recognized, He is received as soon as He is expected and because He is expected He is received, but He has passed by sooner than He arrived, He was gone before He came. He returned forever. He never yet passed by and already He had disappeared for all eternity. He is and He is not. Everything and Nothing. Not light, not dark, not high not low, not this side not that side. Forever and forever. In the wind of His passing the angels cry "The Holy One is gone." Therefore I lie dead in the air of their wings. Life and night, day and darkness, between life and death. This is the holy cellar of my mortal existence, which opens into the sky.

It is a strange awakening to find the sky inside you and beneath you and above you and all around you so that your spirit is one with the sky, and all is positive night.

Here is where love burns with an innocent flame, the clean desire for death: death without sweetness, without sickness, without commentary, without reference and without shame. Clean death by the sword of the spirit in which is intelligence. And everything in order. Emergence and deliverance. I think this also is the meaning of Ash Wednesday: mourn man because you are not yet dust. Receive your ashes and rejoice.

Receive, O monk, the holy truth concerning this thing called death. Know that there is in each man a deep will, potentially committed to freedom or captivity, ready to consent to life, born consenting to death, turned inside out, swallowed by its own self, prisoner of itself like Jonas in the whale.

This is the truth of death which, printed in the heart of every man, leads him to look for the sign of Jonas the prophet. But many have gone into hell crying out that they had expected the resurrection of the dead. Others, in turn, were baptized and delivered: but their powers remained asleep in the dark and in the bosom of the depths.

Many of the men baptized in Christ have risen from the

depths without troubling to find out the difference between Jonas and the whale.

It is the whale we cherish. Jonas swims abandoned in the heart of the sea. But it is the whale that must die. Jonas is immortal. If we do not remember to distinguish between them, and if we prefer the whale and do not take Jonas out of the ocean, the inevitable will come to pass. The whale and the prophet will soon come around and meet again in their wanderings, and once again the whale will swallow the prophet. Life will be swallowed again in death and its last state will be worse than the first.

We must get Jonas out of the whale and the whale must die at a time when Jonas is in the clear, busy with his orisons, clothed and in his right mind, free, holy and walking on the shore. Such is the meaning of the desire for death that comes in the sane night, the peace that finds us for a moment in clarity, walking by the light of the stars, raised to God's connatural shore, dry-shod in the heavenly country, in a rare moment of intelligence.

But even if we are not always intelligent, we must inevitably die.

I pursue this thought no further. It came to me because Frater John of God got a lot of kids' pictures from a sister in a school somewhere in Milwaukee. The pictures were supposed to be by backward children. Backward nothing. Most of them were of Jonas in or near the whale. They are the only real works of art I have seen in ten years, since entering Gethsemani. But it occurred to me that these wise children were drawing pictures of their own lives. They knew what was in their own depths. They were putting it all down on paper before they had a chance to grow up and forget. They were proving better than any apologist that there is something in the very nature of man that expects a Redeemer and resurrection from the dead. The sign of Jonas is written in our being. No wonder that this should be so when all creation is a vestige of the Creator but also contains, written everywhere, in symbols, the economy of our Redemption.

The Communion antiphon sounded like bugles at the end of the Conventual Mass. That was because it is in the fifth tone and the fifth tone is full of melodies that echo, in the new Jerusalem, the silver trumpets that sounded in the temple of the old. The sun is bright, and the spring is upon us, though the winds are cold. There are daffodils coming out by the door of the secular kitchen and in the beds outside this window. The Traxcavator roars merrily where they are trying to haul beams that weigh three tons up to the top floor of the new brothers' novitiate. And for my own part, I came out of Mass thinking about the trench where Frater John of God and I made haste to heel in six thousand seedlings for the forest on Saturday afternoon. Today I hope to take about twenty novices out to the section of the woods behind Donohue's and start planting these seedlings in the places we logged most heavily last winter. The seedlings are yellow poplar, and short leaf pine, and loblolly pine. The latter have the most curious name and the most interesting smell and I like the red and purple tinge on the end of their needles. Yesterday when I was coming in for Vespers I saw a fire out there in the knobs in the section where we hope to start planting. The second fire in that spot since last November. I hope it will be the last for a long time, but I also hope the brothers will dig us a firebreak out there with one of their cats.

If the weather is nice maybe I can take some of the scholastics out to plant on the feasts of Saint Joseph and Saint Benedict. And now I think of last year's feast of Saint Benedict, when I was walking around out there in those same woods, praying that the Abbot General would give me permission to spend a day each month alone and praying in the woods. The permission to go out merely for the sake of prayer was denied: and now I find that instead of going out there once a month to pray, I have been out, day after day, to work: and the work I do does not interfere with prayer but even in some sense makes it better: because when you do something with an exceptional permission, you tend to be hampered by the latent consciousness that you are indulging in some unusual behavior of your own choosing and it makes the prayer less pure. On the other hand, when you are doing some work (and believe me nothing is more usual in a monastery than work) which is assigned by obedience, then you are paradoxically much more free to pray, providing the work is not the kind of work that takes up all your mind—or all your time!

So in the end I realize that Saint Benedict answered my prayer in a much wiser way than I myself had asked or hoped for it to be answered, and as is usual, in the Kingdom of Heaven, by giving up what I wanted I ended up by having more than I had thought of wanting.

When your tongue is silent, you can rest in the silence of the forest. When your imagination is silent, the forest speaks to you, tells you of its unreality and of the Reality of God. But when your mind is silent, then the forest suddenly becomes magnificently real and blazes transparently with the Reality of God: for now I know that the Creation which first seems to reveal Him, in concepts, then seems to hide Him, by the same concepts, finally *is revealed in Him,* in the Holy Spirit: and we who are in God find ourselves united, in Him, with all that springs from Him. This is prayer, and this is glory!

June OCTAVE OF CORPUS CHRISTI

It is June. On Pentecost Sunday it is my turn again to take my week as hebdomadary and sing the Conventual Mass. Then I am deacon the next week, when Corpus Christi comes. Once again, the cloister is paved with flowers, the sanctuary white hot under the floodlights concealed behind the pillars, high in the ceiling. You look up at the monstrance through a cloud of hot, sweet smoke from the censer, and the sweat runs down into your eyes! I feel as though I had never been anywhere in the world except Gethsemani—as if there were no other place in the world where I had ever really lived. I do not say I love Gethsemani in spite of the heat, or because of the heat. I love Gethsemani: that means burning days and nights in summer, with the sun beating down on the metal roof and the psalms pulsing exultantly through the airless choir, while, row upon row of us, a hundred and forty

singers, we sway forward and bow down. And the clouds of
smoke go up to God in the sanctuary, and the novices get thin
and go home forever.

On two sides of us the new buildings are complete. Half factory and half a Venetian palace, the new "garden house" with
the cheese factory in the cellar and the brothers' novitiate on
the roof, rises enormous over the cabbages in the garden. Then
on the other side half veiled behind the trees, the slick new yellow
guest house is full of priests from Evansville who have been coming here on retreat, in shifts, week by week all June. I looked at
their name-cards where they vested in the sacristy and wondered
who these Fathers were: old Fathers and young Fathers, Father
Hut, Father Mattingly, Father Pfau. And right at the place where
our Father Raymond is vesting for the Mass *pro defunctis*, this
week, they have a card for a Father Flanagan, of the Evansville
retreat. Now this is very funny, but of course you, reader, do
not understand why it is funny because you do not know that
Father Raymond's last name is also Flanagan.

Meanwhile there is supposed to be *another* new building. This
time it will have to be an infirmary. And when Dom Gabriel
Sortais (he is our new Abbot General) came back again last
month and made another Visitation, he told us to make rooms
opening on the infirmary chapel so that the partition can be
rolled back and the very sick monks, the dying monks, can
hear Mass from their beds. I do not stop to ask myself if I
shall die in such a bed, or in any bed at all. It means another
year of cement mixers and air compressors in the yard outside this window, where I no longer have time to write books
and where my spiritual children come to talk about God. But if
the cement mixers mean that someone who is dying can hear
Mass in bed it is all right with me.

This week I am the third hebdomadary, which means it is
my turn to say the brothers' Communion Mass, Our Lady's Mass.
It is always a votive Mass of the Blessed Virgin, always the same.
I like it that way. In the summer time, this Mass is said at three
o'clock in the morning. So I leave the choir after morning meditation to go and say it while the rest of the monks recite Matins

and Lauds. I generally finish the brothers' communions by the end of the second nocturn, and then go off into the back sacristy and kneel in the dark behind the relic case next to Saint Malachy's altar, while the sky grows pale outside over the forest, and a little cool air seeps in through the slats of the broken shutters. The birds sing, and the crickets sing, and one priest is silent with God.

As soon as the morning angelus rings, I go out into the new day, my own new private dawn, which belongs to me alone. The other priests are now saying their Masses. The novices and scholastics are getting ready for Communion and the brothers are peeling potatoes in the work room or slinging milk-cans around the tile floor of the new dairy.

I walk out and have the dawn to myself. I have almost two hours to pray or read or think by myself and make up the Night Office. I am all alone in the cool world of morning, with the birds and the blue hill and the herd that lows across the fields in our neighbor's pasture, and the rooster that sings *sol-do* in the coop behind the apple trees, and Aidan Nally growling at a team of mules on the side of his hill over yonder.

Already I am hoping that it will be somewhat the same one day next week, on the feast of Saint John the Baptist, when I will say Mass late, and consequently have this same long interval to myself, in the blue, wide-open, lonely morning. On that day Frater Caleb's family are coming from St. Louis and he wants me to say Mass for them, and thus I will give communion to his little sister Mary Ann who just made her first communion and who thinks she wants to be either a policewoman or a Carmelite when she grows up.

How lovely are thy tabernacles, O Lord of hosts! The sparrow hath found herself a house and the turtle dove a nest for herself where she may lay her little ones!

This is the land where you have given me roots in eternity, O God of heaven and earth. This is the burning promised land, the house of God, the gate of heaven, the place of peace, the place of silence, the place of wrestling with the angel. Each tomato patch is named after a saint. And the tomatoes called "*St. Bene-*

dict, ora pro nobis" are under the care of Rod Mudge who
came down with Dan Walsh to my ordination. A year later he
came back as a novice and soon expects to make profession.

   *Blessed are they who dwell in thy house, O Lord! They shall
praise thee for ever and ever.*

   The roof is peeling off the old garden house, which has become a rejected building. One of the pillars of the old wagon
shed has been knocked down by a tractor. There will be a new
metal hangar for all the machines. This corner of the farm, where
the old horsebarn used to be, is the desert that has been given to
me for the planting of shade trees, that it may some day be a
place of contemplation. *Altaria tua, Domine virtutum!*

   Down there, the young bulls still sleep behind the single
strand of their electric fence.

   It is four o'clock in the morning.

   The Lord God is present where the new day shines in the mois-
ture on the young grasses. The Lord God is present where the
small wildflowers are known to Him alone. The Lord God passes
suddenly, in the wind, at the moment when night ebbs into the
ground. He Who is infinitely great has given His children a
share in His own innocence. His alone is the gentlest of loves:
whose pure flame respects all things.

   God, Who owns all things, leaves them all to themselves. He
never takes them for His own, the way we take them for our
own and destroy them. He leaves them to themselves. He keeps
giving them all that they are, asking no thanks of them save that
they should receive from Him and be loved and nurtured by
Him, and that they should increase and multiply, and so praise
Him.

   He saw that all things were good, and He did not enjoy them.
He saw that all things were beautiful and He did not want them.
His love is not like ours. His love is unpossessive. His love is pure
because it needs nothing. *If I should be hungry I would not tell
thee.* But in Him there is no hunger. He is unknown to those
who need delight. Those who are thirsty have never heard of
Him Who thirsts for nothing.

All things belong to Him. They owe Him everything, and they can repay Him nothing. They exist in Him with an uncreated existence, holy and pure, infinitely above them.

We who are ruined by our own indigence to the point of thinking that we can possess something, think that God *needs* the things He makes—as if He used His own creation, or depended upon it!

God is pure, and because He is pure He does not need to keep the birds in cages. God is great, and because He is great He can let the grasses grow where they will, and the weeds go rambling over our fallen buildings (for the day will come when all our buildings will have fallen down, because they were somebody's possession).

God is His own law and the law of all things is in His freedom. Therefore the stars serve Him freely and the sun rises with a song of joy and the clean gentle speechless moon goes down to her bed without protest.

Every wave of the sea is free. Every river on earth proclaims its own liberty. The independent trees own nothing and are owned by no one and they lift up their leafy heads in peace and exultation. Never were two of them alike. Never were two leaves of the same tree identical. Never were two cells of the same leaf exactly the same. Because the trees grow the way they like: and all things do the things they do for the pleasure of God. Yet He does not need to find pleasure in His creation. But we use the word pleasure, and we say He is pleased, because in all these things His liberality and wisdom and mercy take their pleasure in His own infinite freedom.

God, without being touched by them, without being mixed in with His creatures, without descending Himself to the level of their joy, shares with them His secret, His innocence, His being, His mystery. That is what we mean by glory. That is what His creatures have to give Him: glory. But what is glory? God's glory is God in them without touching them. God in them without being touched by them. God giving them everything and retaining His own infinite separation. God being their Father without being related to them. They are related to

Him, but never come near Him Who is within them. God's glory and God's shyness are one. His glory is to give them everything and to be in the midst of them as unknown.

O children of men! Don't you know that God refuses to be seen? If you only could see how unlike our glory is His glory, you would die for love of Him. But how can we believe who seek glory one from another? If we only knew that God seeks glory by *giving glory*. He does not ask us to give Him any glory we have not received from Him. . . . And where can we find Him to give Him back what we have received from Him? The moment we have found Him, He is already gone!

Fire Watch, July 4, 1952

Watchman, what of the night?

The night, O My Lord, is a time of freedom. You have seen the morning and the night, and the night was better. In the night all things began, and in the night the end of all things has come before me.

Baptized in the rivers of night, Gethsemani has recovered her innocence. Darkness brings a semblance of order before all things disappear. With the clock slung over my shoulder, in the silence of the Fourth of July, it is my time to be the night watchman, in the house that will one day perish.

Here is the way it is when I go on the fire watch:

Before eight o'clock the monks are packed in the belly of the great heat, singing to the Mother of God like exiles sailing to their slavery, hoping for glory. The night angelus unlocks the church and sets them free. The holy monster which is The Community divides itself into segments and disperses through airless cloisters where yellow lamps do not attract the bugs.

The watchman's clock together with the watchman's sneakers are kept in a box, together with a flashlight and the keys to various places, at the foot of the infirmary stairs.

Rumors behind me and above me and around me signalize the fathers going severally to bed in different dormitories. Where there is cold water some stay to drink from celluloid cups. Thus we fight the heat. I take the heavy clock and sling it on its strap over my shoulder. I walk to the nearest window, on my silent feet. I recite the second nocturn of Saturday, sitting outside the window in the dark garden, and the house begins to be silent.

One late Father, with a change of dry clothes slung over his shoulder, stops to look out the window and pretends to be frightened when he sees me sitting around the corner in the dark, holding the breviary in the yellow light of the window, saying the Psalms of Saturday.

It is ten or fifteen minutes before there are no more feet echoing along the cloisters, shuffling up the stairs. (When you go late to the dormitories you have to take off your shoes and make your way to bed in socks, as if the others were already sleeping in such weather!)

At eight-fifteen I sit in darkness. I sit in human silence. Then I begin to hear the eloquent night, the night of wet trees, with moonlight sliding over the shoulder of the church in a haze of dampness and subsiding heat. The world of this night resounds from heaven to hell with animal eloquence, with the savage innocence of a million unknown creatures. While the earth eases and cools off like a huge wet living thing, the enormous vitality of their music pounds and rings and throbs and echoes until it gets into everything, and swamps the whole world in its neutral madness which never becomes an orgy because all things are innocent, all things are pure. Nor would I have mentioned the possibility of evil, except that I remember how the heat and the wild music of living things can drive people crazy, when they are not in monasteries, and make them do things which the world has forgotten how to lament. That is why some people act as if the night and the forest and the heat and the animals had in them something of contagion, whereas the heat is holy and the animals are the children of God and the night was never made to hide sin, but only to open infinite distances to charity and send our souls to play beyond the stars.

Eight-thirty. I begin my round, in the cellar of the south wing. The place is full of naked wires, stinks of the hides of slaughtered calves. My feet are walking on a floor of earth, down a long catacomb, at the end of which there is a brand-new locked door into the guest wing that was only finished the other day. So I punch the clock for the first time in the catacomb, I turn my back on the new wing, and the fire watch is on.

Around one corner is a hole in the wall with a vat where they stew fruit. Under this vat Dom Frederic told me to burn all the letters that were in the pigeonholes of the room where he had been Prior. Around another corner is an old furnace where I burned the rest of the papers from the same room. In this musty silence which no longer smells of wine (because the winery is now in another building) the flashlight creates a little alert tennis ball upon the walls and floor. Concrete now begins under the watchman's cat-feet and moonlight reaches through the windows into a dark place with jars of prunes and applesauce on all the shelves.

Then suddenly, after the old brooding catacomb, you hit something dizzy and new: the kitchen, painted by the brother novices, each wall in a different color. Some of the monks complained of the different colored walls, but a watchman has no opinions. There is tile under the shining vats and Scripture close to the ceiling: "Little children, love one another!"

There are blue benches in the scullery, and this one room is cool. Sometimes when you go up the stairs making no noise, a brother comes in late from the barns through the kitchen door and runs into you by surprise in the darkness, blinded by the flashlight, and (if a novice) he is probably scared to death.

For a few feet, the way is most familiar. I am in the little cloister which is the monastery's main stem. It goes from the places where the monks live to the places where they pray. But now it is empty, and like everything else it is a lot nicer when there is nobody there. The steps down to the tailor shop have a different sound. They drum under my rubber soles. I run into the smell of duck and cotton, mixed with the smell of bread. There is light in the bakery, and someone is working late, around the corner, behind the oven. I punch the clock by the bakery door: it is the second station.

The third station is the hottest one: the furnace room. This time the stairs don't drum, they ring: they are iron. I fight my way through a jungle of wet clothes, drying in the heat, and go down by the flanks of the boiler to the third station which is there up against the bricks, beneath an engraving of the Holy Face.

After that, I am in the choir novitiate. Here, too, it is hot. The place is swept and recently painted and there are notice boards at every turn in the little crooked passageways where each blue door is named after a saint. Long lists of appointments for the novices' confessions and direction. Sentences from the liturgy. Fragments of severe and necessary information. But the walls of the building have their own stuffy smell and I am suddenly haunted by my first days in religion, the freezing tough winter when I first received the habit and always had a cold, the smell of frozen straw in the dormitory under the chapel, and the deep unexpected ecstasy of Christmas—that first Christmas when you have nothing left in the world but God!

It is when you hit the novitiate that the fire watch begins in earnest. Alone, silent, wandering on your appointed rounds through the corridors of a huge, sleeping monastery, you come around the corner and find yourself face to face with your monastic past and with the mystery of your vocation.

The fire watch is an examination of conscience in which your task as watchman suddenly appears in its true light: a pretext devised by God to isolate you, and to search your soul with lamps and questions, in the heart of darkness.

God, my God, God Whom I meet in darkness, with You it is always the same thing! Always the same question that nobody knows how to answer!

I have prayed to You in the daytime with thoughts and reasons, and in the nighttime You have confronted me, scattering thought and reason. I have come to You in the morning with light and with desire, and You have descended upon me, with great gentleness, with most forbearing silence, in this inexplicable night, dispersing light, defeating all desire. I have explained to You a hundred times my motives for entering the monastery and You have listened and said nothing, and I have turned away and wept with shame.

Is it true that all my motives have meant nothing? Is it true that all my desires were an illusion?

While I am asking questions which You do not answer, You ask me a question which is so simple that I cannot answer. I do not even understand the question.

This night, and every night, it is the same question.

There is a special, living resonance in these steep hollow stairs to the novitiate chapel, where You are all alone, the windows closed tight upon You, shutting You up with the heat of the lost afternoon.

Here, when it was winter, I used to come after dinner when I was a novice, heavy with sleep and with potatoes, and kneel all the time because that was the only period in which we were allowed to do what we liked. Nothing ever happened: but that was what I liked.

Here, on Sunday mornings, a crowd of us would try to make the Way of the Cross, jostling one another among the benches, and on days of recollection in summer we would kneel here all afternoon with the sweat running down our ribs, while candles burned all around the tabernacle and the veiled ciborium stood shyly in the doorway, peeping out at us between the curtains.

And here, now, by night, with this huge clock ticking on my right hip and thè flashlight in my hand and sneakers on my feet, I feel as if everything had been unreal. It is as if the past had never existed. The things I thought were so important—because of the effort I put into them—have turned out to be of small value. And the things I never thought about, the things I was never able either to measure or to expect, were the things that mattered.

(There used to be a man who walked down the back road singing, on summer mornings, right in the middle of the novices' thanksgiving after Communion: singing his own private song, every day the same. It was the sort of song you would expect to hear out in the country, in the Knobs of Kentucky.)

But in this darkness I would not be able to say, for certain, what it was that mattered. That, perhaps, is part of Your un-answerable question! Only I remember the heat in the beanfield the first June I was here, and I get the same sense of a mysterious, unsuspected value that struck me after Father Alberic's funeral.

After the novitiate, I come back into the little cloister. Soon I stand at the coolest station: down in the brothers' washroom, at the door of the ceramic studio. Cool winds come in from the forest through the big, wide-open windows.

This is a different city, with a different set of associations. The ceramic studio is something relatively new. Behind the door (where they burnt out one kiln and bought a new one) little Father John of God suddenly made a good crucifix, just a week ago. He is one of my scholastics. And I think of the clay Christ that came out of his heart. I think of the beauty and the simplicity and the pathos that were sleeping there, waiting to be-come an image. I think of this simple and mysterious child, and of all my other scholastics. What is waiting to be born in all their hearts? Suffering? Deception? Heroism? Defeat? Peace? Be-trayal? Sanctity? Death? Glory?

On all sides I am confronted by questions that I cannot an-swer, because the time for answering them has not yet come. Be-tween the silence of God and the silence of my own soul, stands the silence of the souls entrusted to me. Immersed in these three silences, I realize that the questions I ask myself about them are perhaps no more than a surmise. And perhaps the most urgent and practical renunciation is the renunciation of all questions.

The most poignant thing about the fire watch is that you go through Gethsemani not only in length and height, but also in depth. You hit strange caverns in the monastery's history, layers set down by the years, geological strata: you feel like an archeol-ogist suddenly unearthing ancient civilizations. But the terrible thing is that you yourself have lived through those ancient civili-zations. The house has changed so much that ten years have as many different meanings as ten Egyptian dynasties. The mean-ings are hidden in the walls. They mumble in the floor under the watchman's rubber feet. The lowest layer is at once in the catacomb under the south wing and in the church tower. Every other level of history is found in between.

The church. In spite of the stillness, the huge place seems alive. Shadows move everywhere, around the small uncertain area of light which the sanctuary light casts on the Gospel side of the altar. There are faint sounds in the darkness, the empty choirstalls creak and hidden boards mysteriously sigh.

The silence of the sacristy has its own sound. I shoot the beam of light down to Saint Malachy's altar and the relic cases. Vestments are laid out for my Mass tomorrow, at Our Lady of Victories altar. Keys rattle again in the door and the rattle echoes all over the church. When I was first on for the fire watch I thought the church was full of people praying in the dark. But no. The night is filled with unutterable murmurs, the walls with traveling noises which seem to wake up and come back, hours after something has happened, to gibber at the places where it happened.

This nearness to You in the darkness is too simple and too close for excitement. It is commonplace for all things to live an unexpected life in the nighttime: but their life is illusory and unreal. The illusion of sound only intensifies the infinite substance of Your silence.

Here, in this place where I made my vows, where I had my hands anointed for the Holy Sacrifice, where I have had Your priesthood seal the depth and intimate summit of my being, a word, a thought, would defile the quiet of Your inexplicable love.

Your Reality, O God, speaks to my life as to an intimate, in the midst of a crowd of fictions: I mean these walls, this roof, these arches, this (overhead) ridiculously large and unsubstantial tower.

Lord, God, the whole world tonight seems to be made out of paper. The most substantial things are ready to crumble or tear apart and blow away.

How much more so this monastery which everybody believes in and which has perhaps already ceased to exist!

O God, my God, the night has values that day has never

dreamed of. All things stir by night, waking or sleeping, conscious of the nearness of their ruin. Only man makes himself illuminations he conceives to be solid and eternal. But while we ask our questions and come to our decisions, God blows our decisions out, the roofs of our houses cave in upon us, the tall towers are undermined by ants, the walls crack and cave in, and the holiest buildings burn to ashes while the watchman is composing a theory of duration.

Now is the time to get up and go to the tower. Now is the time to meet You, God, where the night is wonderful, where the roof is almost without substance under my feet, where all the mysterious junk in the belfry considers the proximate coming of three new bells, where the forest opens out under the moon and the living things sing terribly that only the present is eternal and that all things having a past and a future are doomed to pass away!

This, then, is the way from the floor of the Church to the platform on the tower.

First I must make a full round of the house on the second floor. Then I must go to the third-floor dormitories. After that, the tower.

Cloister. Soft feet, total darkness. The brothers have torn up the tent in the cloister garden, where the novices were sleeping two winters ago, and where some of them got pneumonia.

Just yesterday they put a new door on Father Abbot's room, while he was away with Dom Gabriel, visiting the foundations.

I am in the corridor under the old guest house. In the middle of the hallway a long table is set with knives and forks and spoons and bowls for the breakfast of the postulants and family brothers. Three times a day they eat in the corridor. For two years there has been no other place to put them.

The high, light door into the old guest wing swings back and I am on the stairs.

I had forgotten that the upper floors were empty. The silence astonishes me. The last time I was on the fire watch there was a

retreat party of fifty lined up on the second floor, signing their
names in the guest register in the middle of the night. They had
just arrived in a bus from Notre Dame. Now the place is absolutely empty. All the notices are off the walls. The bookshelf
has vanished from the hall. The population of holy statues has
been diminished. All the windows are wide open. Moonlight falls
on the cool linoleum floor. The doors of some of the rooms are
open and I see that they are empty. I can feel the emptiness
of all the rest.

I would like to stop and stand here for an hour, just to feel the
difference. The house is like a sick person who has recovered.
This is the Gethsemani that I entered, and whose existence I had
almost forgotten. It was this silence, this darkness, this emptiness
that I walked into with Brother Matthew eleven years ago this
spring. This is the house that seemed to have been built to be remote from everything, to have forgotten all cities, to be absorbed
in the eternal years. But this recovered innocence has nothing
reassuring about it. The very silence is a reproach. The emptiness
itself is my most terrible question.

If I have broken this silence, and if I have been to blame for
talking so much about this emptiness that it came to be filled
with people, who am I to praise the silence any more? Who am I
to publicize this emptiness? Who am I to remark on the presence
of so many visitors, so many retreatants, so many postulants, so
many tourists? Or have the men of our age acquired a Midas
touch of their own, so that as soon as they succeed, everything
they touch becomes crowded with people?

In this age of crowds in which I have determined to be solitary, perhaps the greatest sin would be to lament the presence of
people on the threshold of my solitude. Can I be so blind as to
ignore that solitude is itself their greatest need? And yet if they
rush in upon the desert in thousands, how shall they be alone?
What went they out into the desert to see? Whom did I myself
come here to find but You, O Christ, Who have compassion on
the multitudes?

Nevertheless, Your compassion singles out and separates the
one on whom Your mercy falls, and sets him apart from the mul-

titudes even though You leave him in the midst of the multitudes. . . .

With my feet on the floor I waxed when I was a postulant, I ask these useless questions. With my hand on the key by the door to the tribune, where I first heard the monks chanting the psalms, I do not wait for an answer, because I have begun to realize You never answer when I expect.

The third room of the library is called hell. It is divided up by wallboard partitions into four small sections full of condemned books. The partitions are hung with American flags and pictures of Dom Edmond Obrecht. I thread my way through this unbelievable maze to the second room of the library, where the retreatants used to sit and mop their brows and listen to sermons. I do not have to look at the corner where the books about the Carthusians once sang to me their siren song as I sail past with clock ticking and light swinging and keys in my hand to unlock the door into the first room of the library. Here the scholastics have their desks. This is the upper Scriptorium. The theology books are all around the walls. Yonder is the broken cuckoo clock which Father Willibrod winds up each morning with a gesture of defiance, just before he flings open the windows.

Perhaps the dormitory of the choir monks is the longest room in Kentucky. Long lines of cubicles, with thin partitions a little over six feet high, shirts and robes and scapulars hang over the partitions trying to dry in the night air. Extra cells have been jammed along the walls between the windows. In each one lies a monk on a straw mattress. One pale bulb burns in the middle of the room. The ends are shrouded in shadows. I make my way softly past cell after cell. I know which cells have snorers in them. But no one seems to be asleep in this extraordinary tenement. I walk as softly as I can down to the far west end, where Frater Caleb sleeps in the bell-ringer's corner. I find my station inside the door of the organ loft, and punch the clock, and start off again on soft feet along the other side of the dormitory.

There is a door hidden between two cells. It leads into the infirmary annex, where the snoring is already in full swing. Beyond that, steep stairs to the third floor.

One more assignment before I can climb them. The infirmary, with its hot square little chapel, the room that contains the retreats I made before all the dates in my monastic life: clothing, professions, ordinations. I cannot pass it without something unutterable coming up out of the depths of my being. It is the silence which will lift me on to the tower.

Meanwhile I punch the clock at the next station, at the dentist's office, where next week I am to lose another molar.

Now the business is done. Now I shall ascend to the top of this religious city, leaving its modern history behind. These stairs climb back beyond the civil war. I make no account of the long laybrothers' dormitory where a blue light burns. I hasten to the corridor by the wardrobe. I look out the low windows and know that I am already higher than the trees. Down at the end is the doorway to the attic and the tower.

The padlock always makes a great noise. The door swings back on swearing hinges and the night wind, hot and gusty, comes swirling down out of the loft with a smell of ancient rafters and old, hidden, dusty things. You have to watch the third step or your feet go through the boards. From here on the building has no substance left, but you have to mind your head and bow beneath the beams on which you can see the marks of the axes which our French Fathers used to hew them out a hundred years ago. . . .

And now the hollowness that rings under my feet measures some sixty feet to the floor of the church. I am over the transept crossing. If I climb around the corner of the dome I can find a hole once opened by the photographers and peer down into the abyss, and flash the light far down upon my stall in choir.

I climb the trembling, twisted stair into the belfry. The darkness stirs with a flurry of wings high above me in the gloomy engineering that holds the steeple together. Nearer at hand the old clock ticks in the tower. I flash the light into the mystery which keeps it going, and gaze upon the ancient bells.

I have seen the fuse box. I have looked in the corners where I think there is some wiring. I am satisfied that there is no fire in this tower which would flare like a great torch and take the whole abbey up with it in twenty minutes. . . .

And now my whole being breathes the wind which blows through the belfry, and my hand is on the door through which I see the heavens. The door swings out upon a vast sea of darkness and of prayer. Will it come like this, the moment of my death? Will You open a door upon the great forest and set my feet upon a ladder under the moon, and take me out among the stars?

The roof glistens under my feet, this long metal roof facing the forest and the hills, where I stand higher than the treetops and walk upon shining air.

Mists of damp heat rise up out of the fields around the sleeping abbey. The whole valley is flooded with moonlight and I can count the southern hills beyond the watertank, and almost number the trees of the forest to the north. Now the huge chorus of living beings rises up out of the world beneath my feet: life singing in the watercourses, throbbing in the creeks and the fields and the trees, choirs of millions and millions of jumping and flying and creeping things. And far above me the cool sky opens upon the frozen distance of the stars.

I lay the clock upon the belfry ledge and pray cross-legged with my back against the tower, and face the same unanswered question.

Lord God of this great night: do You see the woods? Do You hear the rumor of their loneliness? Do You behold their secrecy? Do You remember their solitudes? Do You see that my soul is beginning to dissolve like wax within me?

Clamabo per diem et non exaudies, et nocte et non ad insipientiam mihi!

Do You remember the place by the stream? Do You remember the top of the Vineyard Knob that time in autumn, when the train was in the valley? Do You remember McGinty's hollow? Do You remember the thinly wooded hillside behind Hanekamp's place? Do You remember the time of the forest fire? Do You know what has become of the little poplars we planted in the spring? Do You observe the valley where I marked the trees?

There is no leaf that is not in Your care. There is no cry that was not heard by You before it was uttered. There is no water in the shales that was not hidden there by Your wisdom. There is no concealed spring that was not concealed by You. There is no glen for a lone house that was not planned by You for a lone house. There is no man for that acre of woods that was not made by You for that acre of woods.

But there is greater comfort in the substance of silence than in the answer to a question. Eternity is in the present. Eternity is in the palm of the hand. Eternity is a seed of fire, whose sudden roots break barriers that keep my heart from being an abyss.

The things of Time are in connivance with eternity. The shadows serve You. The beasts sing to You before they pass away. The solid hills shall vanish like a worn-out garment. All things change, and die and disappear. Questions arrive, assume their actuality, and also disappear. In this hour I shall cease to ask them, and silence shall be my answer. The world that Your love created, that the heat has distorted, and that my mind is always misinterpreting, shall cease to interfere with our voices.

Minds which are separated pretend to blend in one another's language. The marriage of souls in concepts is mostly an illusion. Thoughts which travel outward bring back reports of You from outward things: but a dialogue with You, uttered through the world, always ends by being a dialogue with my own reflection in the stream of time. With You there is no dialogue unless You choose a mountain and circle it with cloud and print Your words in fire upon the mind of Moses. What was delivered to Moses on tables of stone, as the fruit of lightning and thunder, is now more thoroughly born in our own souls as quietly as the breath of our own being.

The hand lies open. The heart is dumb. The soul that held my substance together, like a hard gem in the hollow of my own power, will one day totally give in.

Although I see the stars, I no longer pretend to know them. Although I have walked in those woods, how can I claim to love them? One by one I shall forget the names of individual things.

You, Who sleep in my breast, are not met with words, but in

the emergence of life within life and of wisdom within wisdom. You are found in communion: Thou in me and I in Thee and Thou in them and they in me: dispossession within dispossession, dispassion within dispassion, emptiness within emptiness, freedom within freedom. I am alone. Thou art alone. The Father and I are One.

The Voice of God is heard in Paradise:

"*What was vile has become precious. What is now precious was never vile. I have always known the vile as precious: for what is vile I know not at all.*

"*What was cruel has become merciful. What is now merciful was never cruel. I have always overshadowed Jonas with My mercy, and cruelty I know not at all. Have you had sight of Me, Jonas My child? Mercy within mercy within mercy. I have forgiven the universe without end, because I have never known sin.*

"*What was poor has become infinite. What is infinite was never poor. I have always known poverty as infinite: riches I love not at all. Prisons within prisons within prisons. Do not lay up for yourselves ecstasies upon earth, where time and space corrupt, where the minutes break in and steal. No more lay hold on time, Jonas, My son, lest the rivers bear you away.*

"*What was fragile has become powerful. I loved what was most frail. I looked upon what was nothing. I touched what was without substance, and within what was not, I am.*"

There are drops of dew that show like sapphires in the grass as soon as the great sun appears, and leaves stir behind the hushed flight of an escaping dove.

BOOKS BY THOMAS MERTON
AVAILABLE IN PAPERBACK EDITIONS
FROM HARCOURT BRACE JOVANOVICH, INC.

No Man Is an Island

The Seven Storey Mountain

The Sign of Jonas

The Waters of Siloe